All This Stuff
Archiving
the Artist

All This Stuff
Archiving the Artist

edited by Judy Vaknin | Karyn Stuckey | Victoria Lane

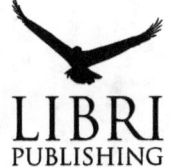

LIBRI
PUBLISHING

First published in 2013 by Libri Publishing

Copyright © Libri Publishing

Authors retain copyright of individual chapters.

The right of Judy Vaknin, Karyn Stuckey and Victoria Lane to be identified as
the editors of this work has been asserted in accordance with the Copyright,
Designs and Patents Act, 1988.

ISBN 978 1 907471 76 6

A CIP catalogue record for this book is available from The British Library

Cover design by Helen Taylor

Design by Helen Taylor

Libri Publishing
Brunel House
Volunteer Way
Faringdon
Oxfordshire
SN7 7YR

Tel: +44 (0)845 873 3837

www.libripublishing.co.uk

ACKNOWLEDGEMENTS

The editors would like to thank all those who supported and helped with the publication of this book. It would not have been possible without the enthusiasm, knowledge, imagination, professionalism and hard-work of the ARLIS Art Archives Committee. The members have changed over the years, but the commitment and energy have not: Sue Breakell, Catherine Moriarty, Neil Parkinson, Adam Waterton, Clive Phillpot, Jessica Collins, Anna McNally, Alexia Kirk, Charlotte Brunskill, Wendy Russell and Bryony Millan. Thanks also to the Education and Events team at Tate Britain, especially Dr Victoria Walsh who supported our proposals for the study days that formed the basis of this book. We also express our gratitude to the contributors at the two events who challenged and inspired us to continue exploring the relationship between artists and archives.

As archivists, we tend to exist outside the mainstream and so we are eternally grateful to ARLIS for putting up with our maverick ways and supporting our projects over the years. Particular thanks go to Lorraine Blackman, Chris Fowler, Penny Dade and Stephanie Sylvester.

Special appreciation goes to Paul Jervis at Libri for his support and his patience.

Above all, we would like to thank all the contributors to this book. We hope you regard the final product as worthy of your input.

Judy Vaknin
Karyn Stuckey
Victoria Lane

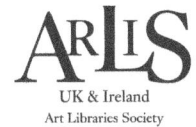

ARLIS
UK & Ireland
Art Libraries Society

CONTENTS

INTRODUCTION:
SHAKING UP THE ARCHIVE
Clive Phillpot

The Art Libraries Society, otherwise known as ARLIS, was established in Britain in 1969 in response to the rapid development of art libraries in art schools, universities and museums. In the 1960s, partly due to a restructuring of art education and partly as the result of a publishing boom, art libraries were growing and consolidating and art librarians were emerging as a distinct branch of the wider profession. By the end of the decade, there was a band of mostly quite young professionals who had been appointed specifically as art librarians; natural networkers, they began to affiliate for reasons of self-help and in 1969 formalised their situation by founding ARLIS.

National groupings of art librarians had begun in France and Canada in 1967; but after the invention of the odd but memorable acronym ARLIS (chosen for obvious reasons over the more logical ARTLIS), the next such organisation to form, in the USA in 1972, simply introduced a suffix to denote North America, becoming ARLIS/NA. ARLIS was thus required to transform itself into ARLIS/UK (and later ARLIS/UK&Ireland). More groups were founded: in Australia and New Zealand in 1975 (ARLIS/ANZ), the Netherlands in 1982, Norway in 1983 (ARLIS/Norge), the five Nordic Countries in 1986 (ARLIS/Norden) and subsequently in Italy and Japan, among other nations.

In contrast to this international proliferation, the original ARLIS (and some of its siblings) developed to the point where it began to sub-divide into sub-specialisms such as cataloguing and classifying, slide curating and, eventually, archiving. Thus in 1995 an Art Archives Committee (known initially as the Visual Archives Committee) was established. The emergence of art archivists parallels the original emergence of art librarians as a specialist group within a larger field; and again, the reasons for this are to do with recent institutional growth in this area and the feeling that people with similar concerns needed an opportunity to talk to each other and shape a collective voice.

As the Art Archives Committee's activities grew, so did its ambition. Thus in 2007, under the leadership of Judy Vaknin, it was decided to organise a substantial day conference under the title: 'The Archival Impulse: Artists and Archives'. With the help of the then Tate Archivist, Sue Breakell, Tate Britain was secured as the venue and funding was obtained not only from ARLIS/UK&I but also from the Arts Council of England. The conference took place on 16th November 2007.

The title of the conference was derived from that of an essay by Hal Foster in *October* magazine, 'An Archival Impulse'. Here Foster says that the examples of Thomas Hirschhorn, Sam Durant and Tacita Dean, among contemporary artists, "point to an archival impulse at work internationally in contemporary art... an archival impulse with a distinctive character of its own", pervasive enough "to be considered a tendency in its own right".[1]

There are, however, several ways of regarding this phenomenon. Foster is mainly concerned with artists working in pre-existing archives, their involvement often leading to new hybrid art works. This kind of involvement with archives is, indeed, a hot potato in current art practice. But, to other artists as well as to archivists, equally deserving of attention is the proliferation of artists' own archives, especially given the variety of media that now constitute contemporary archives. With regard to this latter territory, Sue Breakell, in her introduction to the conference, identified three aspects to archives: "creation, curation and consumption", as well as three constituencies: "archivist, artist and researcher".[2]

The underlying theme of 'The Archival Impulse: Artists and Archives' at Tate Britain was to explore artists' use of archival themes, as well as the interpretation of archives in their work. In the event, the successful programme and particularly the audience's response to this programme tended inevitably to fall into the two main areas of specialisation: artists and their concerns over their own practice or their own archives; and archivists and their concerns over the archives in their care. Since 'The Archival Impulse' was substantially over-subscribed, the Art Archives Committee, in appraising the success of the conference, quickly decided that the need for a follow-up day conference had been amply demonstrated. Consequently a sequel, 'Archiving the Artist', was organised eighteen months later and held again at Tate Britain on 12th June 2009. On this occasion, the main emphasis of the conference was on artists' own archives, but speakers were included from the three constituencies identified earlier – not only artists and archivists, but also researchers in artists' archives.

Following the two conferences, Tate agreed to publish some of the papers on its website under the rubric *Tate Papers*. Since only a few papers given at the conferences were included in *Tate Papers* (though others were made available on the website as 'Online

1 Foster, Hal, 'An Archival Impulse', *October*, no.110, Fall 2004 (3)

2 Breakell, Sue, 'Perspectives: Negotiating the Archive', *Tate Papers*, Spring 2008 (6), http:www.tate.org.uk/download/file/fid/7288 (accessed 16/7/2012)

Research Publications'), the Art Archives Committee began to examine the possibility of assembling a book on the subject of artists and archives which would include papers from the conferences supplemented by newly invited essays that would give the book more substance and balance. The book has been divided into three sections: Artists; Archivists; and Art Historians and Theorists.

The diligent and sensitive appreciation of the contents of the archive by the archivist is set out here in exemplary fashion in the chapter by Anna McNally. She reminds us that "few researchers are aware of the archivist's hand in the process" of using an archive and, quoting Ernst van Alphen, that the act of archiving introduces "meaning, order, boundaries, coherence and reason into what is disparate or confused". She also cautions us not "to blur the documentation of the archive with the archive itself." When the researcher in the archive is similarly diligent and sensitive, as is Jane Stevenson, writing here about her work with archival material from the artist Edward Burra, one can expect many useful discoveries. For example, Stevenson's alertness contributes directly to the re-dating of artworks but also to a much better understanding of her subject. She explains that "what biographers want most is maximum preservation and minimum censorship" especially since a "subject's sex life and income… explain so much about anyone's life, famous or otherwise."

We are grateful to Penelope Curtis, Director of Tate Britain, who, with substantial experience of administering and supporting archives, has contributed an overview of artists' archives drawing upon her experiences when Curator of the Henry Moore Institute in Leeds. In her essay, which focuses on the imaginative use of a pre-existing archive by artists to "foster the creation of new work", she remarks that "traditionally the artist's archive told the art historian more about the art", whereas "now we see increasingly how an artist can use it to tell us more about the nature of the archive." Thus contemporary artists, in addition to being more conscious of their role in creating an archive of their own history, very often also make primary work out of an engagement with another archive. In the process they frequently shake up traditional notions of archival practice.

However, it is perhaps also possible to suggest that "creative archiving" as defined here by Athanasios Velios, when practised on the archive of a deceased artist, specifically the John Latham Archive, can shake up not only archival practice but also the received archive. Of course, this is only practical and morally acceptable when the archive is replicated digitally, thereby offering the possibility that its surrogate can be manipulated separately while leaving the original as received. The potential blending of minds of the artist and the archivist strays into the subjectivity highlighted by Foster when he says that archives "call out for human interpretation, not machinic reprocessing."[3]

Barry Flanagan laid down the future framework of his own archive while he was still alive. He decided that it would be independent of institutions but also would include "exhibition display". As Jo Melvin says, his enlightened and professional intention was "to develop a database and website that combines the exhibition of artworks as a catalogue raisonné with archive", giving "a fluid interaction of components between archive catalogue and artwork catalogue" thereby "bringing the archive into the open… into the domain of an art exhibition." This way of proceeding could be a model for other artists.

Yet another variation on shaking up the archive occurs when artists are still around to shake up their own archive and here we have the example of Bruce McLean, who has engaged creatively with his own comprehensive archive and produced new work as a result of this. Although this revisiting and even reworking of older material is perhaps only a variation on what artists have always done with their previous work, whether they re-interpret earlier examples or simply utilise the agency of memory, it is a new twist in a climate where archiving has been given much greater prominence. Memory, of course, operates in every one of us as an organic filter, processor and synthesiser of the past.

But we can go further in shaking up the archive: what if the artist *is* the archive? Now in one sense every artist, indeed every individual, is the embodiment of their own archive. Memory again! But in the case of Barbara Steveni, the artist has embarked upon a series of what one might call documentary performances under the rubric "I AM AN ARCHIVE". She often triggers these events by utilising archival documents relating to her own life and re-engages with her past life by engineering re-encounters with people from those times in the very location where significant events happened. These re-visitings are in turn recorded, often in image and sound, thus laying down a compounded version of past and present. In a way, this is a kind of *son et lumière* oral history – with all the temporal distortions involved in a post-factual recording of the past.

It is not often that the negative side of archival accumulation is aired. In the case of one very archive-conscious artist, Gustav

3 Foster, op. cit. (5)

Metzger, it is clear that sometimes this accumulation becomes a burden. And while this is evident in the interview included here, in fact many artists express regrets about the quantity of stuff that they have accumulated and the inhibiting effect of a documented past. But overriding this personal burden there is also what Sas Mays calls "archival antipathy", which he characterises as "the issue of the non-archival, the anti-archival and the extra-archival." This might be thought to contradict the statement of Jacques Derrida in *Archive Fever*, quoted by Sue Breakell, that we "have a compulsive, repetitive and nostalgic desire for the archive", that we are "in need of archives."[4] These different positions draw attention to the contemporary richness of the topic of archives as a site of intellectual conflict.

It is only a few steps from this situation to a consideration of the 1965 multiple *Total Art Match-Box* by the sometime Fluxus artist, Ben Vautier, following in the footsteps of Marinetti and the Italian Futurists who railed against the instruments of the oppression of the past. Ben exhorts us to "use these matches to destroy all art – museums – art libraries" etc. I am sure that he would be open to the inclusion of art archives in this list.

Both Uriel Orlow and Ruth Maclennan cite the example of *Breakdown* by the artist Michael Landy in their correspondence. In 2001, Landy notoriously destroyed all his possessions, from his passport to his car; but Orlow points out that while engaged in destruction he diligently created "an inventory of destruction". Thus his new beginning paradoxically included a record of what used to be. Ruth Maclennan observes further that "artists have destroyed their work only to be reborn as a different kind of artist altogether". As it happens, the principal impulse of both Orlow and Maclennan is the preservation of histories that might be lost, were it not for archives.

The vulnerability of archives is brought out in a different way by Victoria Lane in her vivid description of the potential threat to the archive if an uncredited person were to be given access to its inner sanctum, the strong room. In the event, the actual granting of permission for a photographer to enter this space, and the resulting photographs, leads her to muse on the utopic nature of what the archivist does in establishing intellectual control over documents, through description and arrangement, in contrast to the physical, heterotopic space of the archive revealed by the photographs.

Finally, the essay by Neal White takes us to a new place, the shaking up of social and cultural hegemony by means of the

4 Breakell, op. cit. (4)

autonomous archival practices of groups of artists and other individuals. While it is tempting to ally these practices with the "aesthetics of resistance" attributed by Hal Foster to "archival artists" such as Thomas Hirschhorn, with his "counter-hegemonic archive"[5], Neal White actually declares a different stance. He suggests that it would be incorrect to characterise these highly articulated structures within the political economy as "resistant through counter-institutional, marginal or avant-garde forms", for they "are not necessarily even opposed to the institution, but instead represent emerging networks that are establishing a set of new practices and sharing resources".

The art archivists and art librarians who came together to offer the public thoughtful discussions of the interactions between artists and archives at Tate Britain in 2007 and 2009 hope that this collection of essays will not only bring some of the papers into print but assist in propelling these discussions further and contributing to the diversity of practice.

5 Foster, op. cit. (10, 5, 9)

FROM OUT OF THE SHADOWS[1]

Penelope Curtis

1

The Archive inside the Archive

Artists may well keep their own stuff in the belief that, in due course, ideas expressed in different ways on bits of paper or in other media will once again become useful. This is perhaps not so very different to anyone's reason for keeping notes from the past; but in the artist's case there is the additional task of developing and then maintaining a reputation, so that, towards the end of a career, the retained stuff may acquire more value than it had at the beginning. Rather than being a question of financial gain (though that can be involved), this is about how much the work of a whole career can make the early stuff count.

Archives tend to be seen as two dimensional, which is a great problem for artists who try out their ideas in the round. Rather few places keep much in the way of three-dimensional artistic archive, though architectural archives are an obvious exception.[2] The Henry Moore Institute in Leeds[3] can be seen as unusual in its collecting activity, which ranged across period and practice, as well as media, taking it well beyond the monographic archive where, as in the case of the Musée Rodin or of Moore himself,[4] diversity of medium is offset by the purely monocular lens.

The recent display at Tate Britain, which revealed a good deal of Naum Gabo's archive for the first time in public, also implicitly revealed why this material was in the archive and, indeed, why it had ever been archived at all: it was flat, or could be made flat. Gabo's bank of ideas for sculpture was expressed in a form that lay exactly on the threshold between the two- and the three-dimensional. These proto-sculptures were expressed in 'archival' form from the very outset; the idea of the archive was, indeed, integral to their meaning. In this sense, they signal that which is particular to the archive and which I want to signal here: its often peculiar position between past and future tense.

The Henry Moore Institute not only housed the archives of sculptors but also asked artists to come and use those archives. This meant, obviously enough, relating the archive of one artist to another. Sometimes this was straightforward and the artist acted primarily like an art historian, seeking to understand a given research area more thoroughly. On occasion we specifically invited one artist to work on the archive of another, but just as often artists

1 An earlier version of this paper was given at the ARLIS annual conference in Leeds, 13th July 2011.

2 For example, the Royal Institute of British Architects, London (with its link to the Heinz Archive now held at the V&A Museum); the Canadian Centre for Architecture in Montreal; the University of Parma archive for architecture. Museums with sections devoted to architecture, such as MoMA, will invariably hold architectural models but rarely sculptural ones.

3 I was Curator of the Henry Moore Centre for the Study of Sculpture (1994–9) and then of the Institute which grew out of it (1999–2010).

4 Kept at the Henry Moore Foundation headquarters in Perry Green, Hertfordshire.

would find their way by instinct and empathy towards the archive which spoke to their work.[5]

Beside the Archive

This happened with projects which were primarily premised on the archives of individual artists. It happened with Jaki Irvine's recuperation of Betty Rea and Neal White's of Jacob Epstein. One was gracefully romantic, the other more confrontational, but both were nostalgic for what might have been. What links these projects, as different as they were, is the fact that their subjects had been side-lined by a dominant artistic establishment. A less personalised but nonetheless effective reanimation was in play with Mark Wilsher's use of reproductions of 1960s sculpture, as with that of Falke Pisano's collaged recreations. They use the archives of other artists; and whilst artists have always more or less furtively used other artists, they were able to do so explicitly, now that the archive is seen to occupy its own space rather than furnish that of others.

Some artists keep their archives carefully, secure in the knowledge of their importance. This was something inculcated in students at the Academy in Dusseldorf and its fruits were seen, for example, in the exhibition we made with Thomas Schütte, which was extensively drawn from that early material. Other artists seem almost to live in their own archive, as with Imi Knoebel and, more acutely, Ettore Spalletti. This rigorous record keeping can lead to the oeuvre becoming a world of its own, endlessly self-referencing.

It is a truism that most artists have essentially one idea; and the archive replays its variations and its continual refinding. Whether this is done in the work, or on paper before the work, varies. Whether we track that gradual evolution in the oeuvre, as we might do through a catalogue raisonné or through the archive, depends on the status of the artist, their facility and their opportunity. Whether we see it in the form of art or of archives is circumstantial.

Traditionally the artist's archive told the art historian more about the art. Now increasingly we see how an artist can use it to tell us more about the nature of the archive. Occupying a place that is both before and after the archive has become very current, or very actual. It embodies a kind of continual present which denies the past and exalts it too. Between the unmade and the made, artists use the stuff which they leave behind to reclaim authority for their peers.

5   See my essay in Victoria Worsley, *A Guide to the Henry Moore Institute Archive*, Leeds, 2005.

The Archive beyond the Archive

The project on which I wish to focus here involved something of the same impetus – using the archive to foster the creation of new work – but had at its core the idea of an archive conceived more widely. Having worked for a number of years with artists using our own archives, I was interested in thinking of how the archive as a platform could be extended beyond our strongroom. This made particular sense at a time when artists themselves were increasingly turning to the archive and to their own recent past for the subject and the material of their work.

This project, which concluded as an exhibition entitled 'The New Monumentality', involved three artists: Dominique Gonzalez Foerster, Gerard Byrne and Dorit Margreiter. I had visited all three to talk about an exhibition which might be themed around their common use of modernist architecture from the 1960s.[6] Gonzalez Foerster asked me what reason I might give her to come to Leeds, given that she had subject matter aplenty in Brazil (where she had a home) or in the Far East. She was interested in these locations because of the local inflections they offered on an international theme, as were Margreiter and Byrne.

My answer took their cue and seemed always to have been the topos at the core of my enquiry, if only implicitly, identified not by me but by the artists. The subject was to be the University of Leeds and the campus designed by Chamberlin, Powell and Bon in the 1960s. This was a setting in which the staff of the Institute all lived, through which many of us walked every day, where many had studied or were indeed still studying, but which remained strangely uninterrogated. We returned to the local, to its particular inflection, and in so doing not only learnt more about the nature of the campus, but also about a potential re-siting of the archive within its own expanded field.

Since the 1970s, the art world has become habituated to site-specific work; but more recently, the meaning of 'site-specific' has moved to encompass a wider definition. The site was a geography and a history, an archive in itself. The sensitivity of rapport by which we had judged earlier more architectural inventions was now applied to the sense of the place or, to use the phrase which was well established in France in the '80s but took another generation to become similarly common in the UK, the "*lieux de mémoire*".[7]

The use of the Leeds campus as our site meant understanding the archive in a number of ways, the most obvious of which was architectural; but the social and cultural became as, if not more, important. The term 'archivist', too, was widely defined and

6 Notably in Rio de Janeiro and Sao Paolo (in the case of Gonzalez Foerster), in Maastricht and Dublin (in the case of Byrne) and in Leipzig and Los Angeles (in the case of Margreiter).

7 Pierre Nora's seminal seven-volume opus (1984–92) was only completely translated in 2012.

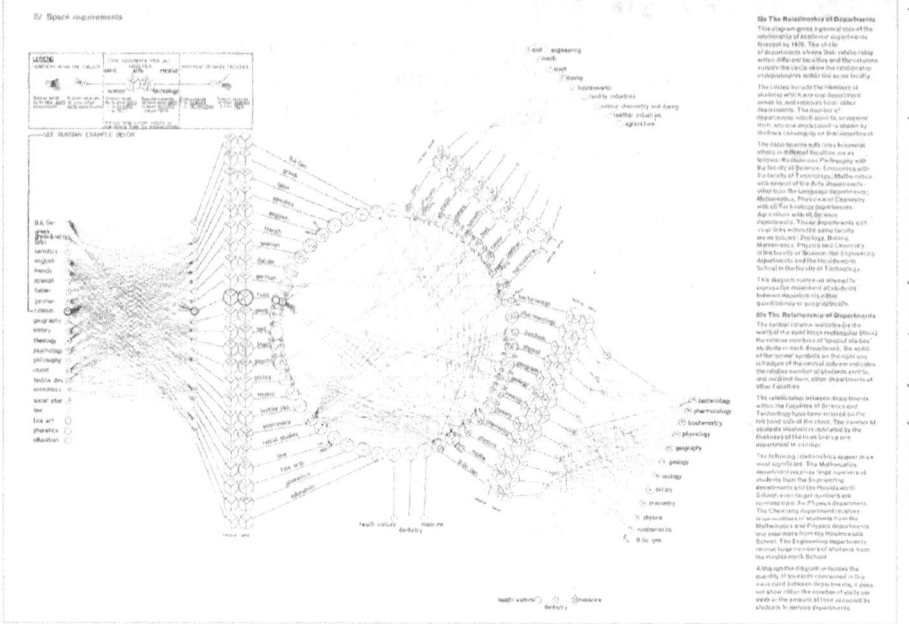

included the artist, the curator, interns and actors, as well as the archivists of archives proper, which included the University's own archive, and of Special Collections, as well as those of the RIBA, of New Hall, Cambridge and the City of London Metropolitan Archives.[8] To a degree, I acted as the onsite research assistant to artists based elsewhere and this led to an interesting and evolving dialogue of give-and-take, of directed and undirected discoveries.

My own archival research focused my understanding of the Leeds University project as both extraordinarily ambitious, in the sense that it was premised on major demolition and transformative urbanistic projects to make it even possible, but also extremely traditional in its continual referencing of an earlier vocabulary, in the form of the late-medieval monastic or educational establishment. When Chancellor's Court, the principal focus of the new scheme, was opened, several series of impressive photographs were taken by different professional photographers. Many of these appeared in the largely enthusiastic press coverage and survive today in the RIBA and Leeds archives.

The match, or mis-match, between empty photographs of new architectural projects and the people behind them is difficult to mine; but in the case of Leeds, the task was more acute. Firstly, the audience research which the architects themselves undertook was impressive and had been instrumental in getting them the job.

Space Requirements: The Relationship of Departments, Chamberlin, Powell and Bon, University of Leeds Development Plan, 1960

8 To research similar buildings by the same practice: the Cambridge college and the Barbican centre.

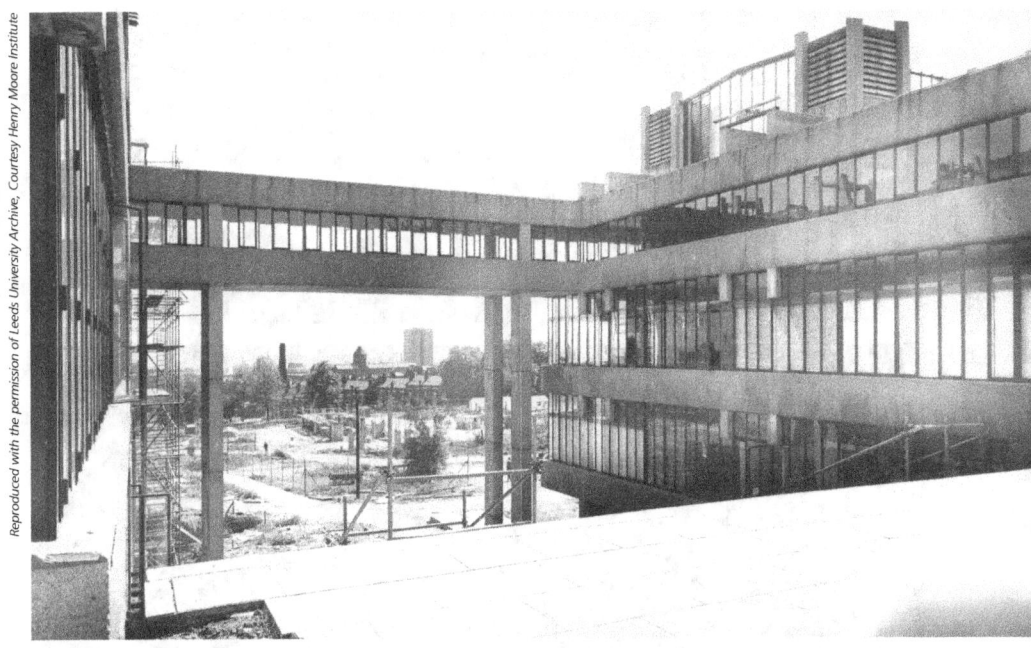

University of Leeds development, site clearance and construction c.1964–74

Secondly, the scale of their scheme demanded exceptional commitment on the part of the clients. Thirdly, the project was already up and running; its future inhabitants were, in significant measure, already there.

Byrne was interested by these clients and wanted to know more about them. Where possible, I found senior academic staff and asked them about this moment, a long moment perhaps, but one when the University of Leeds was at the forefront of European university planning. Byrne wanted also to find out more about what these buildings produced; thinking of them as a generative space. We looked in the registers for the faculty members of those years. I put forward for his consideration the names and texts of, primarily, a generation of left-wing historians and, in particular, E.P. Thompson, who wrote much of *The Making of the English Working Class* (1963) while teaching there.[9] I also scanned the Special Collections for the archives left by academics or artists who had been there at this time and the poet Jon Silkin, who enrolled in Leeds in 1959, came to my attention.

Both Byrne and Margreiter paid especial attention to the television studio which was part of strategic planning for both the university teaching programme and for the architectural response to its needs. The concept of the site responding to cultural activities was key for both artists in the way they went about thinking of

9   Other avenues taken might have included Perry Anderson, Raphael Samuel and the *New Left Review*.

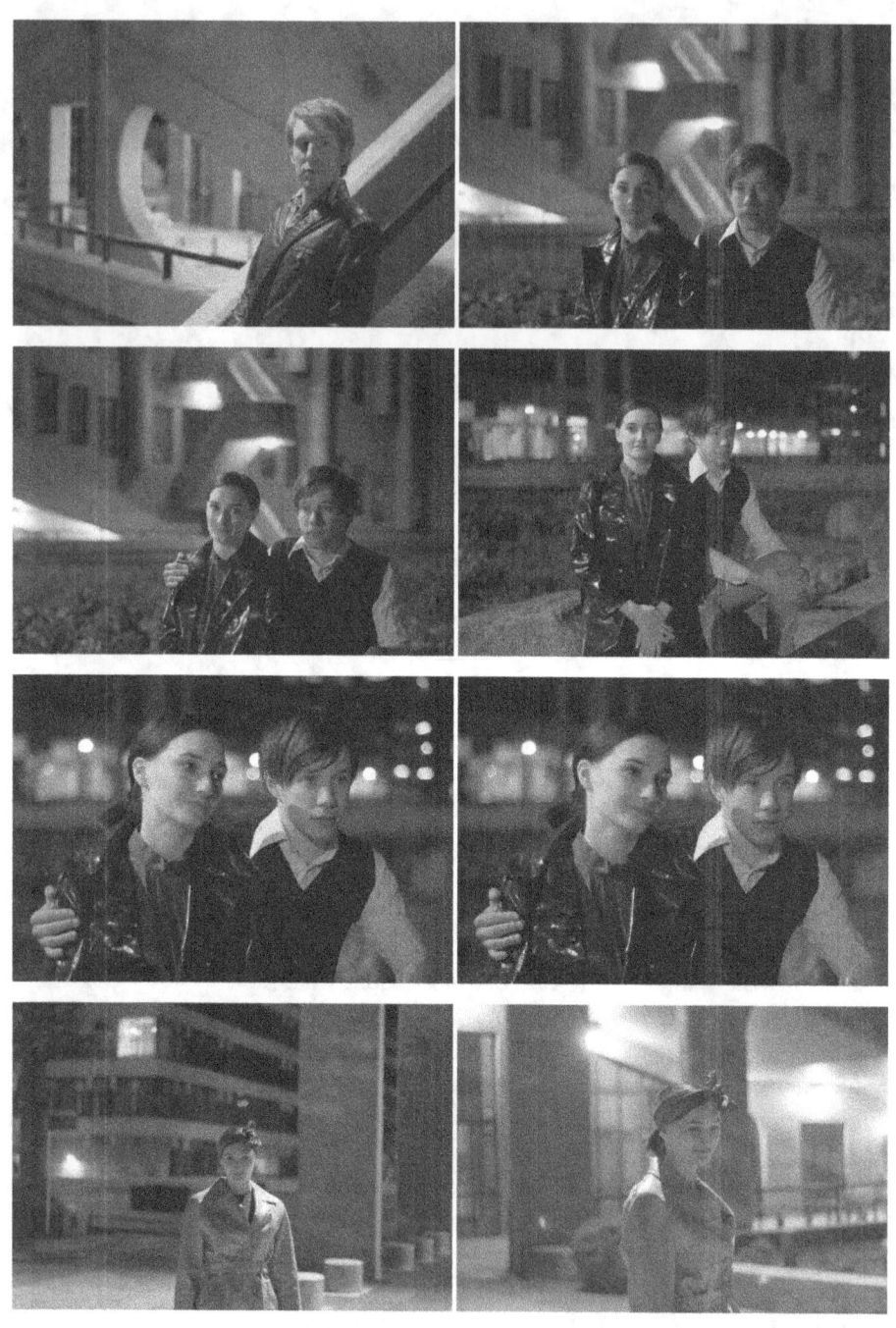

Gerard Byrne, *Subject*, 2009, a
historical dramatisation with actors,
filmed on high-definition video, c.30
minutes; commissioned by the Henry
Moore Institute, 2007

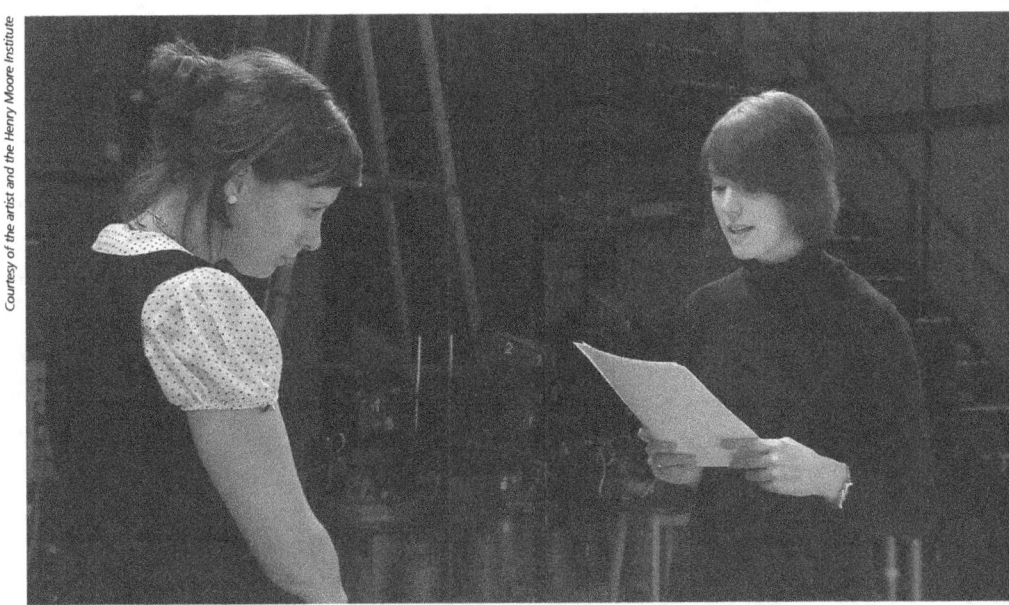

this project. Margreiter also used the diagram drawn up by the practice as a result of Chamberlin's seemingly exhaustive audience research about the accommodation needs of different subject areas. Its infamous illegibility, at apparent cross-purposes with all it purports to reveal, was highlighted by Margreiter in her text-less version.

Both the artists visited the TV centre and both used the studio in their subsequent work. The fact that the man who proudly showed us round had been there himself for over thirty years made a difference, as did the fact that the studio was now under threat.[10] Within the campus as a whole, and within our project in particular, this interior space in which so much had been invested, and still equipped with equipment that was state of the art circa 1970, was remarkable. This was the empty stage designed to disseminate the institution's teaching, broadcasting tutorials to the ever-increasing student body which was to be suitably accommodated within the multi-purpose rooms designed by the architects. This was, one might say, the University's voice, one which sat underneath the monumental set of teaching rooms which represented that function.[11] Both Byrne and Margreiter sought ways in which to re-find that voice.

Unlike Byrne, Margreiter chose to use real students rather than actors. She made no attempt to return them to the 1960s, instead leaving them to wear their usual clothes. She shot in colour, rather

Dorit Margreiter, Aporia, 2009, 35mm film installation, c.12 minutes, with framed photograph; commissioned by the Henry Moore Institute, 2007

10 Indeed, the whole campus was under threat. One concrete result of the project was to help to get it listed.

11 The Roger Stephens Building, which acted too as a prototype for the architects in their planning of the Barbican's theatre.

than in black and white, and used the words of a writer who had never been to Leeds, who indeed had written a text about other places, any place, any place other than Leeds. This script, by Norman Klein, was about the replicated city, the Venice of Las Vegas or California, the utopian no-place which is always and never itself in its manifold recreations. Margreiter's film of unactorly actors, reading a doubtful script, on an unset set, both accentuated the impossibility and undermined the possibility of the archival task.

We had architecture, we had poetry, we had political history. We had a place and ideas for or from that place. Whose voice was to be heard? Byrne asked us to send him copies of student magazines and focused on those which responded to key questions of the time about sex and drugs in relation to youth culture. To bring this text alive, he sourced and dressed young local actors who revoiced the students' words in period settings almost unchanged for fifty years. De-peopled, these environs still speak of the future, of a place that Britain never dared to build, but occasionally approached. Restored to life, so to speak, with the vernacular of their time, the settings seem to avoid being pinned down with their actual dating.

I have dwelt upon this project because it points up the emptiness of the archive, the depopulation which the work of the artist can recuperate. It is perhaps a commonplace that architectural photographs are empty of inhabitants but this project brought that home, showing that it is not just the architectural past which is empty but the artistic past as well – and that the magical reanimation which an artist can bring to documentation is something almost unarchival, or a-archival. And yet their activity reveals so much about the archive in its fuller sense: about its locality, its physicality, its occupation, its range of voices. They set up their topos as an archive, with its own known and neglected components, a stage with its cast of actors and audience, revealing of cause and effect. Of the relation of part to whole, of fact to fiction. A place for reconstitution.

In quite different ways, the work of Margreiter and Byrne points to this truth. Byrne's still photographs echoed exactly the photographs of the late 1960s. Nothing had changed; the beautiful spaces were still empty. Byrne used time and place in a reproductive or representative manner, to speak of another place again, a past (or a future) which never happened. The archive is full of such false dawns, such impossibilities, and its promise of something and nothing is endlessly appealing. Margreiter was well furnished with documentation about Leeds but ultimately went elsewhere for something that might speak of this place and this time.[12] For that place, and that time, were unknown, or known only vaguely, existing in the spaces of the memory, or of the archive.

The activity of historians such as Dorothy and E. P. Thompson is not so far removed. The words of the students were spoken in local voices, aloud. The words of E. P. Thompson, written silently on the wall, were nonetheless eloquent of the archival impulse:

> The question, of course, is how the individual got to be in this 'social role', and how the particular social organisation (with its property-rights and structure of authority) got to be there. And these are historical questions. If we stop history at a given point, there are no classes but simply a multitude of individuals with individual experiences. But if we watch these men over an adequate period of social change, we observe patterns in their relationships, their ideas, and their institutions. Class is defined by men as they live their own history, and in the end, this is its only definition.[13]

12 Gonzalez Foerster too was represented by a film (*Marquise*, set in Sao Paolo) which showed a 1960s building as it lives today, animated by those who passed through it and also by the voice of a young boy who thought he had seen the architecture move.

13 E.P. Thompson, *The Making of the English Working Class*, Harmondsworth: Penguin, 1968, p.12

SECTION ONE
Artists

AN INTERVIEW WITH GUSTAV METZGER
Talking to Victoria Lane and Clive Phillpot
about Archives
London 25 October 2011

2

Gustav Metzger was born in Nuremberg in 1926. He came to England as a refugee in 1939 with his brother after most of his family were killed. After early work in cabinet and furniture making, and later gardening, he turned to carving and eventually became an art student. At one time he worked closely with the painter David Bomberg, at the Borough Bottega in London, but moved to Norfolk in 1953. While living there he became involved with the Anti-Nuclear movement and was later a founder of the more radical Committee of 100. Upon settling back in London in 1959 he published Auto Destructive Art, *the first of five manifestos. He followed this by making a model for an auto-destructive sculpture, as well as developing the radical destructive technique of painting with acid on nylon sheet – sometimes performing in public spaces. In the same year, 1960, he began presenting daily newspapers in exhibitions. In 1966 Metzger initiated DIAS, the Destruction in Art Symposium, in London, which attracted such artists as Günter Brus, Hermann Nitsch, Jean Toche, Rafael Ortiz, Yoko Ono and Wolf Vostell, amongst others. Subsequently Metzger was involved with radical art events, as well as research involving science, society and art history; he also initiated 'Years without Art' (the Art Strike) in 1974. Several other innovations, such as his Liquid Crystal Projections and his series of installations,* Historic Photographs, *continue today.*[1]

Clive Phillpot: Can we turn the discussion round to your views about archives, Gustav? I was very intrigued to ask you – with your interest in destruction, in the past – [that] you seem to have a complimentary interest in preserving things. You, yourself, have several archives it would seem, in different places, different locations. Is that a deliberate strategy for you: to separate them and put them in different places?

Gustav Metzger: No. No it's not. It's just humpty dumpty. It's how it happened, bit by bit. And there are not that many anyway. And I can assure you, if you put it all together, it wouldn't be in the least comparable to the archive [of Richard Deacon, that Victoria was working on].[2]

1   The most comprehensive source of information on Gustav Metzger's life and work is: Sabine Breitwieser (ed.) *Gustav Metzger: History, History,* Vienna: Generali Foundation, 2005. There are also, however, several useful recent exhibition catalogues, including: *Gustav Metzger* (Oxford: Museum of Modern Art, 1998) and *Gustav Metzger: Decades 1959–2009* (London: Serpentine Gallery/Koenig Books, 2009).

2   This interview was preceded by a short discussion about the large size and comprehensive nature of Deacon's archive.

The Metzger archive stored in an attic in North London, photographed by Clive Phillpot in 2010

CP: I was just thinking [about] what we found in your cousin's attic, not only the artwork, but also this enormous box full of material of various kinds, with publications and so on inside. Were you archiving that material when you put it up there? Was that an archival position, to say: I'm putting all this stuff away safely for the future?

GM: Well, certainly that is how that developed, out of necessity. I had to put the works, the artworks, somewhere safe or they would have disintegrated. Before they came to that [final resting] place they were outside and beginning to be in danger...

CP: What, in a shed or something?

GM: Yes, in the open outside the house. So I suddenly realised that

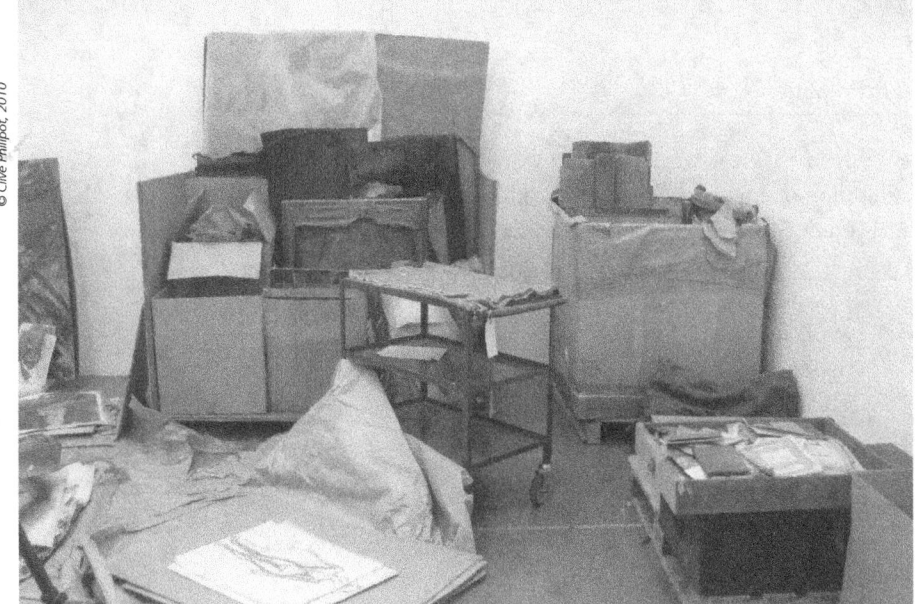

something drastic [had to happen] and I got permission to use that place. So there's a mortality in all that, and that was the dominant feature. But I was very lucky. We were all lucky, I think, that it's happened. And that everything was in good order, there [had been] no mice, or dampness…

CP: A little dust on top, and that was it.

GM: It was only a tiny bit. Then of course, I am quite different to Richard [Deacon] – he started from childhood and whatever was of my childhood, if there's something left, it would be minute. A few photographs – there could be some somewhere, everything is possible in time.

CP: So you're very supportive of the idea of archiving material?

GM: I am, yes, totally. And when you include libraries, which I'm sure we do, then without good libraries, I would have got nowhere in the years until 1960, when it was essentially the physical activity.[3] And, after that, I was totally involved with the ideas, and stimulated by ideas, and many of these ideas come from the printed material, from the solid material aspects of culture, and that was crucial, and I'd like you to check the latest development of this, it is taking place in Freiburg. I don't know if I've mentioned Freiburg? We were approached about a year ago by two young art historians; they aim to have an entire academic year on my work.[4]

The archive, after moving to a south London warehouse, November 2010

3   In 1960 Gustav Metzger effectively abandoned painting, developing instead his technique for painting with acid on nylon; then in 1963 he moved on to experiments with light projections using liquid crystals.

4   Samuel Dangel and Sören Schmelling, of the Albert-Ludwigs-University (exhibition at the Morat-Institut Freiburg). See: http://www.kunstges chichte.uni-freiburg.de/lehrveran staltungen/kgi-freiburg-ws-201112.pdf/at_down load/file (p.16)

CP: [Whistles.]

GM: And they've started that, and then they want to have an exhibition on my work. They are the kind of people I was, ja, years ago, young, they're energetic – extraordinary quality. And yesterday I was shown images on the screen, of their latest development, which is in fact to combine their text and my text with book covers which I had collected.

CP: Where did they get those from? An archive?

GM: Actually – from me. And so, to come back to your question, this printed material and manuscript material has been of very great significance for me. And I enjoy working with archives. Yes! So I'm on your side!

[Laughter]

Victoria Lane: I just wanted to ask about how you felt about the documentation around your own practice? Your early work? Because you said not much of it exists. There's not much left compared to Richard [Deacon]. You also seem like a great collector as well – of various things?

GM: I have collected. Yes, that's a fact. And, also, when you said Richard kept everything, well I've tried to do that. But I had to repeatedly move and leave things behind and that's a crucial, major difference between our experiences.

CP: So you weren't always able to put stuff in a safe place like you did with your cousin's attic.

GM: No, not at all.

VL: What did it feel like to give – well, to let go of – your work in that way? All the documentation in that way? When you said sometimes you couldn't keep that material. What did it feel like to have to let it go?

GM: It's good.

CP: Really?

GM: It's a good feeling. Yes, as I said, I enjoy collecting everything that came my way. And, of course, I bought books, I bought quite [a lot] in the course of my life. Some of them are still in my possession.

CP: But you didn't have regrets about abandoning stuff? When you had to move on and leave things?

GM: Yes, yes.

[…]

Abandoning painting was a tremendous risk. Nobody had heard of this idea. I hadn't heard of this idea, but I was impelled to move along this historical track. Having studied art and art history I had a pretty good idea of what was needed, so I abandoned painting – it's like exposing yourself to the elements. Anything can happen! I could have been completely outcast from the art world; especially living in this country which isn't – or it wasn't, especially then – particularly interested in avant-garde. It was a foreign thing: Paris or New York or other [places], for that period, in which I was, in fact, having to change over. It was other countries that were leading the way, and that's one reason I have done what I have done.

I have had an immense feeling and need to balance myself in relation to England – and Britain – saving my life. And so, as I grew older I think I had, deep down, the need to give back. The rescue, which it was, ja, of me and thousands of other young Jewish people. And so, taking risks and moving forward could be seen – I want to be careful I'm not – I can't analyse my lifework, and I shouldn't attempt to.

CP: Other people will do that. Does the phrase 'tabula rasa' resonate with you? It seemed like at some point you would just go whoosh and everything accumulated was gone and you could start afresh. Could you feel you could start afresh?

GM: I think it was more of a continuation. The erasing – I accept what you have just said about the erasure – took place – had to take place.

CP: But it was putting you *back* on track in some way.

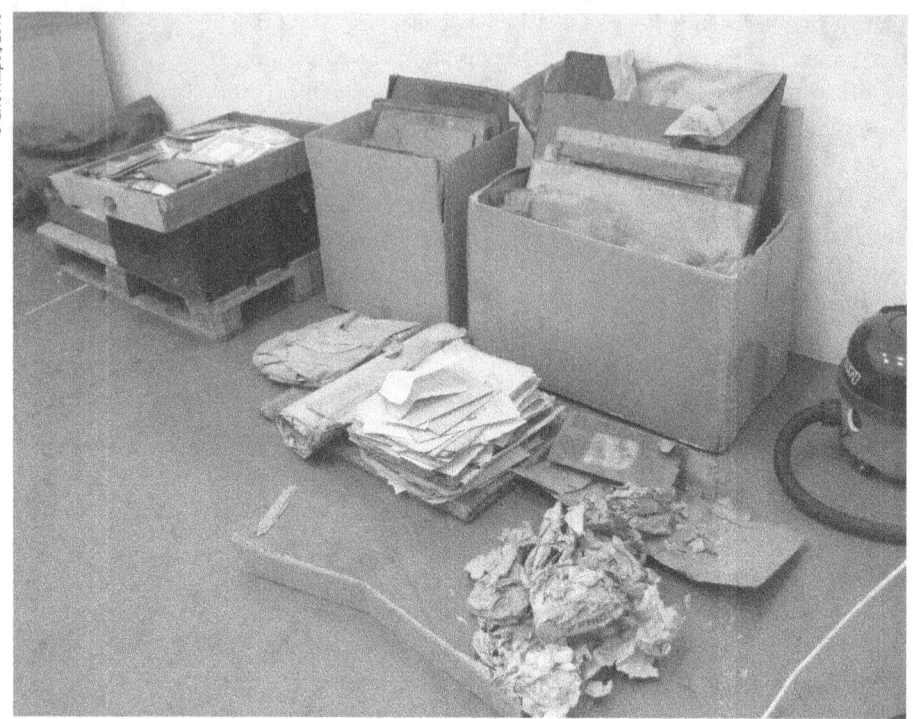

GM: Oh yes, I was re-integrating with avant-garde. I was re-integrating, I was aware of reintegrating with Futurism, with Vorticism, and with the early work of my teacher.

CP: [David] Bomberg.

GM: Ja. And that was a necessary part of my exhibiting then. It's to do all that, and do all that at once. So simultaneously that's how I was operating. I was aware that everything I was doing had to be rushed through, as quickly as possible, and it was. If you look at the development from the first manifesto [in nineteen fifty-nine] to sixty-[four].[5]

CP: Is this because of the threat of nuclear annihilation, or more personal things?

GM: That would be involved. That's exactly my point, it would be this, that, and the other, and having, kind of, sorted out something in my mind, often – not in the middle of the night – but going to sleep – I have seen: go that way, check on that, reflect on that, do that. But it was essentially an intellectual activity. As you know, the

5 First manifesto, November 1959: *Auto Destructive Art* Second manifesto, March 1960: *Manifesto Auto-Destructive Art* Third manifesto, June 1961: *Auto-Destructive Art, Machine Art, Auto Creative Art* Fourth manifesto, October 1962: *Manifesto World* Fifth manifesto, July 1964: *On Random Activity in Material/Transforming Works of Art* (For full texts, see: Gustav Metzger, *Damaged Nature, Auto-Destructive Art*, London: Coracle/ workfortheeyetodo, 1996.)

period between the first manifesto and the lecture at the A.A. [the Architectural Association, in 1965] to me sums up everything, and still does – it's still the best text I've written on the subject of auto-[destructive] and auto-creative art. And I believe I've mentioned when you look at the second edition – in the first edition there's one page of notes, the second edition has two pages of notes – when you look at these notes, for example, it hits you that I'm spending more time mentioning auto-creative art then, because at that point auto-creative art was still less certain, and still a creative challenge to me.[6]

CP: But you see there was a duality. You see them as a duality. One is not replacing the other?

GM: Oh yeah. Exactly. As a duality, and [it] was seen in every action, like in my own actions: all the liquid crystal activity, all the light projections. It's making and losing, building and chopping off. And then I think that is the strength of my work, that it has faced all these major difficulties both intellectual and art-historical, and come through – and now being fully recognised. I just saw two or three books that Tate have published, where it says clearly "inventor

6 Gustav Metzger, *Auto-Destructive Art: Metzger at AA*, first published London: ACC, June 1965; expanded edition, London: Destruction/Creation, October 1965 (This book reprints the five manifestos.)

of auto-destructive art". Now in the early days I had to fight for even a mentioning of any of this work. Now it's just, you know, run of the mill acceptance.

VL: Why do you think that shift has happened – to acceptance?

GM: I think through long exertions on my part…

[Laughter]

GM: …and the part of friends who kept pushing and saying: look this is important, do take it seriously. And that is a large part – and the work itself began to convince people year by year that it has to be taken seriously.

CP: Do you think the fact that you have been in one place now [London] for – I don't know how long it would be – fifteen or more years – helps? Because before that you were very elusive, and I was [living] a long way away, and I was [often] wondering where you were. Last I heard you were in this city, then another city, but I wonder if now that you're staying in the same place, involving yourself in this particular society, that also helps to build up knowledge of what you can do, and what you've done. It's another factor in this; as well as people gradually becoming aware through publishing and exhibitions of what you have actually achieved?

I'm just trying to think; is there more to say about archives?

VL: I suppose maybe about how you use archives in your work? How do you see the value of archives, when you use it in your work?

GM: Yes, there again, to return to Richard [Deacon], I'm not in a position to go somewhere and say: oh, this is my archive, for example, even at the moment I couldn't do that. Whenever I am relatively stable, I *am* in London. I'm glad I came to London and it was the right decision to do that. But my things are still scattered, yes. I'm not in a position to use my archive, except occasionally here and there.

CP: Would you like to see the elements brought together somewhere, or are you happy that they're scattered?

GM: That's a very difficult question. As I said, the future of all that is still very, very insecure, and I just have to go on living with that. The idea of everything together doesn't necessarily appeal to me. Because, when you are depriving, for example, other countries of something that they could have, and perhaps should have – So I'm not a unilateralist in the sense that I want everything definitely together. And also if you reflect on what's happening, the future of everything that I've built up, that I've collected, is uncertain. There is more of it now than ever before in security, in really super conditions, but what happens to that material is open to question.

CP: With current technology, one can make a record, a duplication, of every different segment of your oeuvre. And they could be brought together digitally, or whatever, and still remain in different places, so…

GM: That's right.

VL: That's a good point. You could do that.

GM: That's what should happen. I'd be in favour of that happening. That's right. And that should be so easy, and that is actually – would – satisfy my inner problems better, because it wouldn't just be depending on the physical.

[…]

And so, when [my assistant] Ula [Urszula Dajerling] showed me some of the work which is being done in Freiburg, I felt so relieved. You will see how – with what feeling – these two young men are working, such delicacy and intelligence. Now, if you follow up what you've just said, that this could be the future, then that could be the future, and would be especially applicable to my situation, past, present and future. I could say everybody can [follow] both paths, we can use both paths, the paths of immediate access through technology, and the long-term, daily research of researchers in Tate, or wherever, Sohm, ja – I'd rather not have everything in one place.

CP: If it was, it would be vulnerable in certain ways.

GM: Well, that's right, it's more vulnerable if it's all in one place.

VL: Exactly. How many different places have you put your archive in – bits of your archive in?

GM: Well, with, of course, Tate [in] London, Sohm Archive [in Stuttgart], [I have given] consciously over the years, or put things on loan. And actually it's regrettable, but I think MoMA in New York has not a collection, and Pompidou. And so the not-having all my things in one place would also obviate this repeated necessity to 'get rid of'. 'Getting rid of' had to do with getting rid of security – cutting things off. It's – you see – I'm in a sense perhaps putting myself at risk? I'm just speculating.

CP: Sure, sure.

[...]

Do you use, have you used, institutional archives for any reason yourself? I was thinking in your Serpentine show you had all these Nazi promulgations on the wall – copies of them.[7] Did you find that kind of material in archives or did you use archives to research that kind of thing? I'm just trying to see what you – beyond your own archive – might have used for whatever purpose…

GM: Yes.

CP: – for research or work or…

GM: Again, this answer [lies in] contacting the Freiburg – they were showing parts of a collection I made – obviously in Germany – in the eighties, in through the eighties, when I spent quite a lot of time there.

CP: So this is another justification for scattering your records. Things can grow up in different places. They can foster new growth in other places.

GM: Well, this is being discussed. And again, it's open now to decisions which I will have to take in conjunction with other people. But anyhow, these are safe. This material is in perfect condition; they're putting it on shelves. One day you might go and visit.

VL: Brilliant. Yes, it's necessary sometimes because – as an archivist

7   *Gustav Metzger, Decades: 1959–2009*, London: Serpentine Gallery/Koenig Books, 2009

– I come across different types of peoples: some are squirrels that keep things. I call them squirrels – and they keep *everything* – and other people have to get rid of [material, to allow them to forget] – because it is part of, you know – carrying on, as you said. So I don't think it's irrational at all, I think it's, it's a coping mechanism, because you can actually be imprisoned by all this material and stuff…

GM: Well, I'm not surprised [by] what you've just said, and – it's fundamental. Well, I'm glad to hear this from you.

CP: There's nothing casual about [your] attitude. It's very hard in a way, very clear that you preserve – or you don't preserve – it's like auto-creation, auto-destruction, it's, in a sense, creating an archive, destroying an archive. It would seem to run through. So if you're saying there's a consistency, I think I would see that. Does that make sense to you, Gustav? Am I taking too big a step there?

GM: Could you simplify that?

CP: Well, I was just thinking: auto-creation, auto-destruction, is a leitmotif going through most of your work, but it would also seem to be going through your attitude to your records: that sometimes you will *actively* create them and conserve them, other times you will *actively* destroy them.

GM: Or letting go.

CP: Or letting go, perhaps, yeah. So it's another polarity, another dichotomy.

GM: I accept that.

CP: So it is consistent, I think. It's what you were saying.

VL: Yes.

GM: I think this is a very good summing up of key aspects of our discussion.

CP: Can I ask you just one [more] thing? Again it seems to add up in a way. It seems like a lot of the things you have at Tate Britain are on loan. It's like pending a decision: will they stay there, will they go somewhere else, or do you not want actually to have to make that decision? I wonder what your thinking is behind that?

GM: Yes, because I can't make up my mind where it should go to. And also there is the question of ownership: I'm now owning this and I'm not sure I want to abandon my ownership. It's a very, very complex situation. But since they are quite happy to go on in the present space, and also they don't have that much material, you are only talking of a small amount of space. So let it just rest for now. It's resting and it's not lots and lots of material, it is resting, waiting.[8]

[...]

[FIN]

8   The full recording of this interview has been deposited at the National Sound Archive in the British Library. Two other interviews with Gustav Metzger by Clive Phillpot are also in the collection, but none of the interviews can presently be accessed by the public.

THE IMPOSSIBILITY OF ARCHIVING IN THE MIND OF AN ARTIST STILL LIVING

A Text by Donald Smith, annotated by Bruce McLean (BM)

3

Artists including the late Terry Frost and John Hoyland had said that they hated the idea of the 'Retrospective' because they saw it as a curatorial form of burying an artist alive, foregrounding past achievements and summarily dismissing the value of any current or future works, thus signalling that the art world need not bother with the artist again during their lifetime.

Bruce McLean decided that he would get his retrospective out of the way at the beginning, so that his art 'career' (a word he loathes) would effectively be over before it had really begun and so he could then pursue an unfettered creativity. 'King for a Day: A One Day Retrospective' took place at Tate Gallery (now Tate Britain) on 11th March 1972. The show consisted of a gallery floor covered in a grid of books containing a list of 1,000 fictitious and real projects – McLean's premature 'retrospective' catalogue or his archive of ideas. In this conceptual comment on the nature of the

Bruce McLean, 'King for a Day: A One Day Retrospective', 11 March 1972, Tate Gallery, London

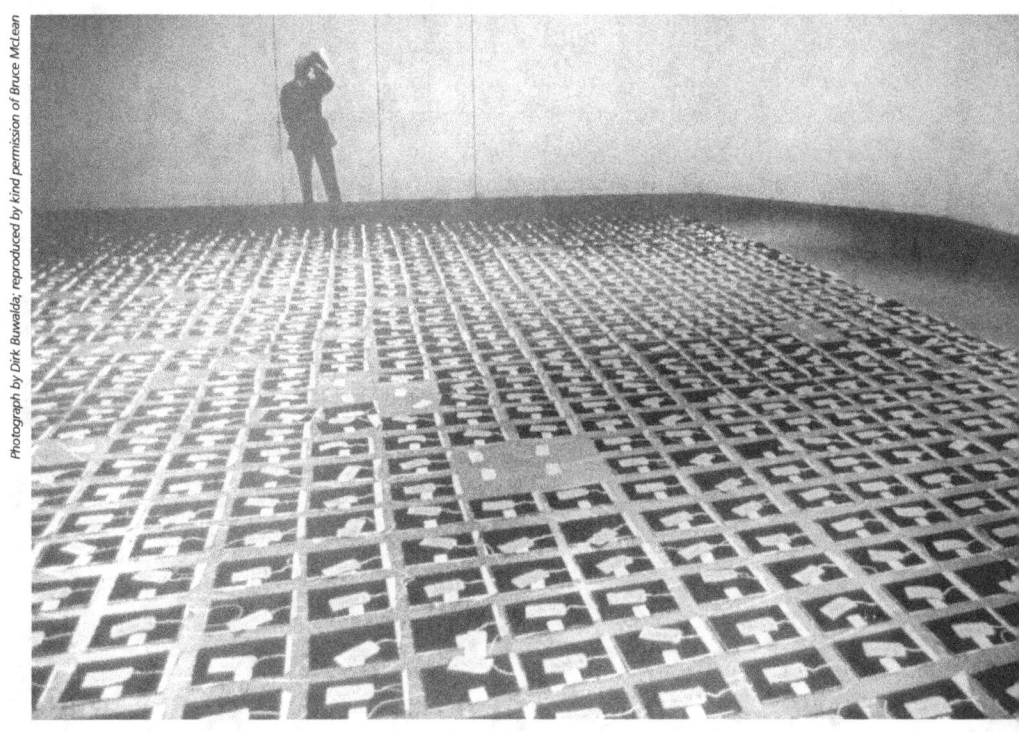

Photograph by Dirk Buwalda; reproduced by kind permission of Bruce McLean

retrospective and art-world hierarchies it was also tacitly understood that the 'King' of 'King for a Day' had another meaning, making a precocious and somewhat irreverent reference to Phillip King, one of McLean's teachers and a more established artist than McLean at that time.

This reference is incorrect and was, I think, an assumption made by Phillip King. The title 'King for a Day' was taken from a late '20s record 'King for a Day' by the singer and band leader Ted Lewis. (BM)

The exhibition 'Bruce McLean: Process Progress Project Archive' held at CHELSEA space between 28th January and 11th March 2006 was intended as an open experiment in the re-presentation of forty years of McLean's archives and past artworks as relevant, active elements in a new live performance/installation – constantly changing, updated, renewable and re-useable. The phrase 'process-spective' was coined and the ensuing string of events was conceived simultaneously as a one-person show and a collaborative dialogue between Bruce McLean (the artist), myself (the director–curator), Liz Lawes (the librarian) and Eddie Farrell (the documentary film maker and sound recordist), with interventions from the visiting audience and invited guests.

Far from being the end of the matter, the CHELSEA space 'process-spective' has led to a series of new collaborations and further uses of McLean's archive to trigger new works. My intention here is to outline some of the projects made between 2006 and 2011 that have occurred as a direct result of CHELSEA space's initial exploration into the archive of an artist; to show how the use of the archive material and responses to his archive by others has inspired and defined some of McLean's recent practice; and to note the artist's recidivist activities, returning to earlier work and art historical references. In order to discuss these projects I am forced to make references throughout to CHELSEA space and my involvement, for which I apologise in advance. Beyond the projects mentioned, McLean has also been engaged in a wide range of other projects internationally during this period. I asked Bruce McLean to annotate my text where he felt I needed correcting or where he wanted to add a comment. He adds some important historical detail and interesting insights. The title of this text is a bastardisation of the title of Damien Hirst's shark suspended in a tank of form-aldehyde – *The Impossibility of Death in The Mind of Someone Still Living*, 1991. The shark – a creature that needs to move continually in order to stay alive – is perhaps a worthy analogy for creativity.

Bruce McLean,
Throwaway Archive
Piece, 2006

My particular interest in CHELSEA Space is because of the energy, enthusiasm and intelligence of its director Donald Smith, and his clear-sighted vision of how things could be. Situations in Horse Shoe Yard in the late '60s, early '70s functioned in a similar way, enabling the artist/s to make new works. (BM)

Throwaway Archive Piece, 2006

Bruce McLean started the CHELSEA space show as he meant to go on: at the private view, tables were set up and the artist sat flanked by Liz Lawes and myself whilst the private viewers stood in front of the table expectantly. McLean was handed a rare black-and-white photograph of one of his *Floataway* pieces from the late 1960s. When asked what the precious archive was he promptly threw it across the table and into the audience announcing "It's *Throwaway Archive Piece*, 2006". It was shocking. Here was a document that librarians and archivists of modern and contemporary art would covet, being violently thrown into a crowd of people with no care for conservation, damage or theft. In the very moment the document was handled by the artist it was transformed into raw material for a new art work – after all, as the artist owned the photograph, he was free to do what he liked. At the Archival Impulse symposium he described this reckless creative act as "showing off" but the audience were privileged to witness a lively creative mind in action and a hint of more to come.

It WAS showing off, an activity I am not keen on. (BM)

King for the 11th of March

The end date for the CHELSEA space show was a historic reference to the date of McLean's 'King for a Day: A One Day Retrospective', 11th March 1972. One part of the closing event on 11th March 2006 was an en-masse walk through Tate Britain led by McLean. This 'flash mob' phenomenon has its roots in the political activities of Situationist International and the Tate security staff certainly looked anxious that havoc would ensue; however, Tate staff member Adrian Shaw was amongst the group and his presence pacified his concerned colleagues. When the group reached the octagon space in the Duveen Galleries, McLean threw down a copy of his CHELSEA space publication in a gesture referencing his 1972 display of books on the Tate Gallery floor and theatrically playing out the defiance of an artist against the conventions of the art institution. The reference to this auspicious date was repeated again for the opening of CHELSEA space's fifth anniversary on 11th March 2010.

Bruce McLean leads a crowd into Tate Britain on the last day of the show at CHELSEA space

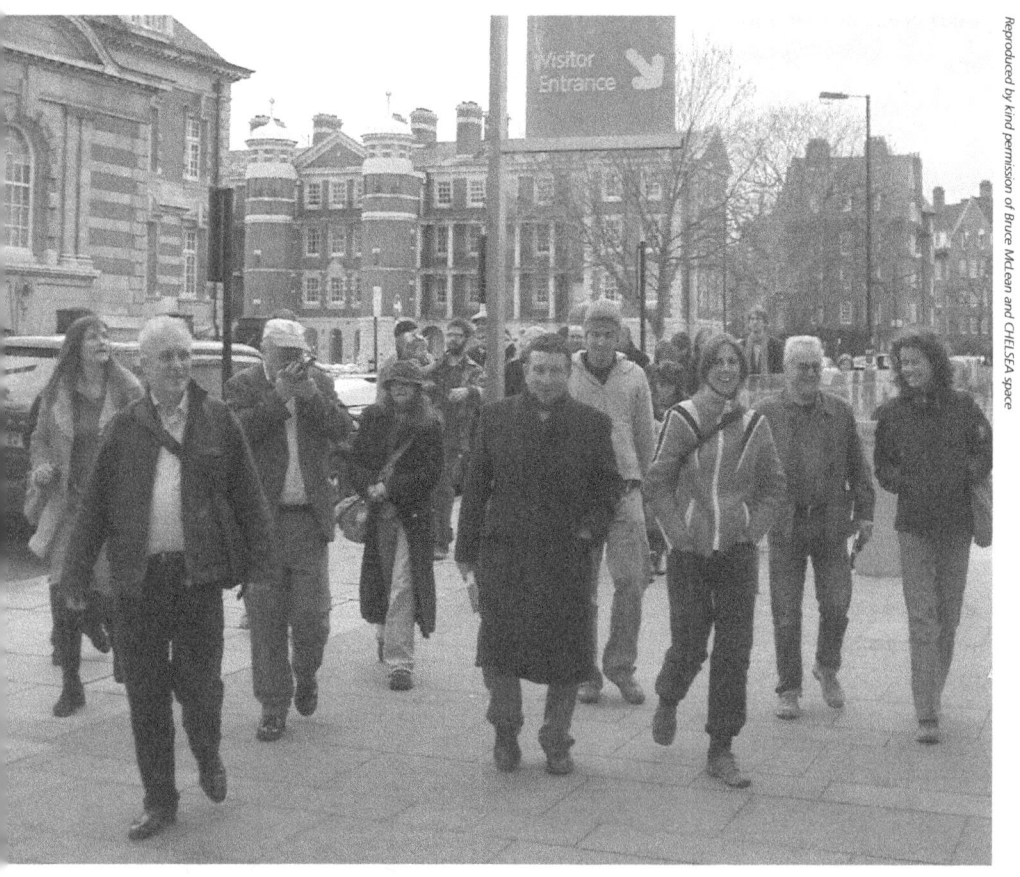

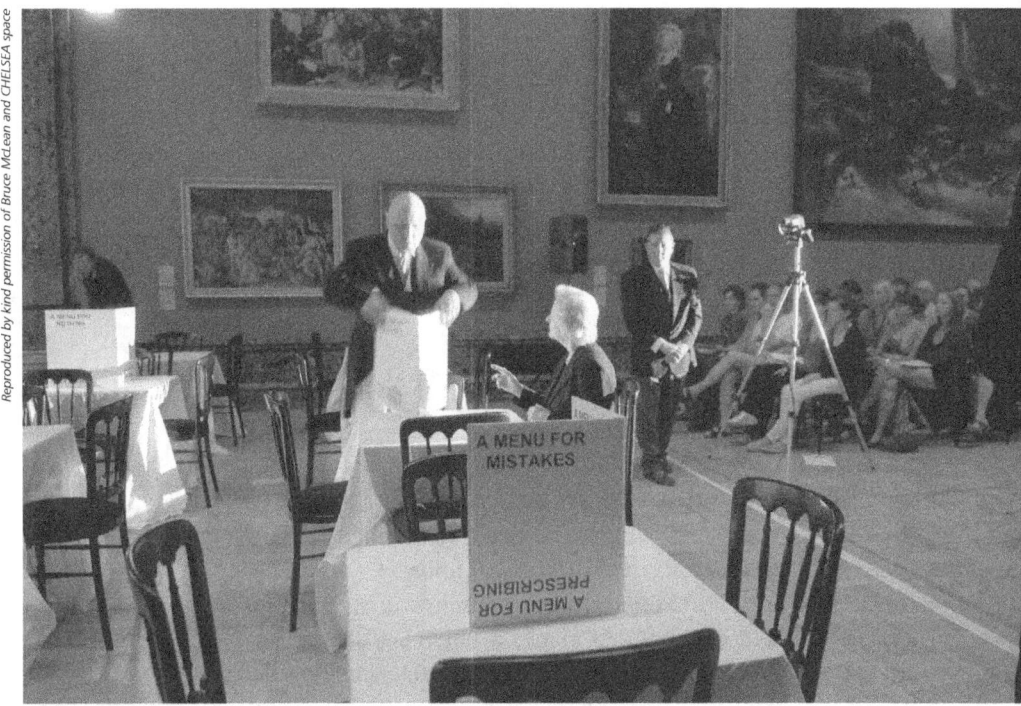

Maitre D

A minimal, one-part, carefully placed and balanced menu sculpture in two sittings (collaborative, sustainable) for an Art Gallery – Late at Tate Britain, August 2007

Bruce McLean, 'Maitre D Minimal One Part', Tate Britain, 2007

In 2007 I was invited by Adrian Shaw to co-curate the August 'Late at Tate Britain' evening of events. The programme included a live photographic portrait project by Faisal Abdul Allah, music from the Trojan Sound System, talks from, amongst others, Peter Tatchell, a painting on a London Cab by Stephen Farthing and a performance by comedian Frank Sidebottom – plus Bruce McLean's first large performance work for some years and his first at Tate since his major performance work *Good Manners and Physical Violence* in 1985. *Maitre D* was made in collaboration with artist Eddie Farrell who had documented the CHELSEA space show and was inspired by observations of the behaviour of staff in an empty restaurant, culminating in a lone customer (Mary Rose Beaumont) being presented with a plate containing a small cut-out of a Henry Moore sculpture, in response to which she exclaims "Waiter! There's a sculpture in my soup." This line is a reference to a photographic and video work that McLean originally showed at Situations, London in 1971 entitled *There's a Sculpture in My Soup* in which he examines and rejects the influence of an earlier generation of artists.

> *It should be noted that the sculpture in the soup was a photograph of a sculpture by Henry Moore. Also it should be noted that it was used simply as a symbol for sculpture. It might have been a Calder or a Picasso. The first installation at Situations was 'Objects No Concepts', a series of photographs of objects on plinths. This idea of the sculpture as a photograph is still with me and I am presently working on the photograph as a starting point for the sculpture, and working backwards. (BM)*

The Archival Impulse
Tate Britain, November 2007

Invited to talk about McLean's 2006 CHELSEA space show for this conference at Tate Britain, the four original collaborators on 'Process Progress Project Archive' conceived of a scenario. This involved McLean being interviewed in front of a projected backdrop of the CHELSEA space website archive of his show and a specially edited version of the films documenting the activities around 'Process Progress Project Archive', 2006, made by Eddie Farrell. The intention was to be both entertaining and informative.

Gymposium: Drawing and Posing, 13.11.09.
The Life Room, curated by Donald Smith and Stephen Farthing, CHELSEA space, November–December 2009

The Life Room was an interactive gym-cum-drawing studio. Throughout the show, artists, actors and designers were invited to interact with *The Life Room* facilities, among them Biba store designer Steve Thomas, printmaker and racing cyclist David Ferry, actor Dudley Sutton, artist Bruce McLean and digital scenographer David Barnett. McLean's involvement was in two parts – a series of poses using *The Life Room*'s gym equipment referring to his 1970s Nice Style pose band works and a series of 23 portraits drawn using a digital Wacom graphics tablet for the first time. McLean's drawings exist as a work in themselves but David Barnett also filmed the making of the portraits resulting in a new work using a combination of the original footage and motion-capture animation. The introduction of Bruce McLean to David Barnett has resulted in several major new collaborations.

> *The intelligence and imagination of Donald Smith in putting me together with David Barnett has created a whole range of new working possibilities for me and David and others including Sam Belinfante. (BM)*

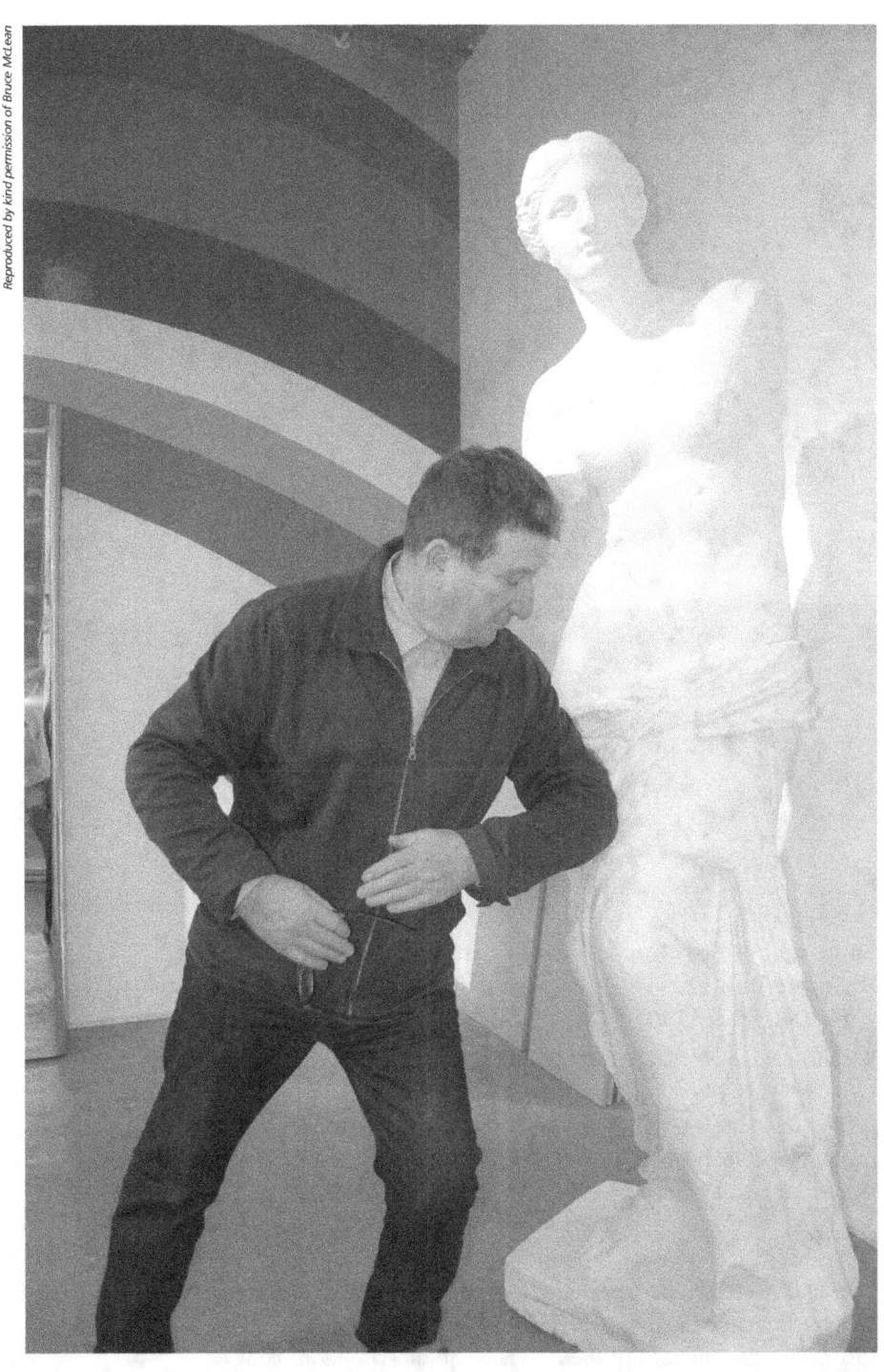

Bruce McLean, *The Life Room GymPosium*,
13 November 2009, CHELSEA space

Bruce McLean, 'Should I Stay or Should I Go – Still High Up on a Baroque Palazzo', CHELSEA space

Should I Stay or Should I Go – Still High Up on a Baroque Palazzo

CHELSEA space, 2010

For the fifth anniversary of CHELSEA space, the directors of RUN Gallery, Hana Noorali, Lynton Talbot and Elena Crippa, were invited to curate a series of exhibitions and events. 'Should I Stay or Should I Go' opened on 11th March 2010, the anniversary of Bruce McLean's 'King for a Day: A One Day Retrospective' in 1972 and the closing date of his exhibition at CHELSEA space in 2006. The curators divided the show, like a play, into a series of 'acts' and Act One was hosted by Bruce McLean and the artistic director David Gothard, who in the late 1970s had invited McLean to work in the environs of the Riverside Studios, London, along with others including the architect Will Alsop, the dancer Michael Clark and the composer Michael Nyman.

McLean chose to make a photographic and sculptural reconstruction of the Nice Style pose band's seminal work 'High Up on a Baroque Palazzo', which was originally performed on Tuesdays, Thursdays and Saturdays for four weeks between October and November 1974 at The Garage in Earlham Street, London WC2 for a ticket price of 80p. The CHELSEA space installation included a life-size image of Nice Style performing the piece wearing dinner suits and bow ties, integrated with real objects projecting into the space including plinths suspended on ropes, a hanging jacket, a 'pose pole', a lemon on a shelf and a potato on a plinth – motifs which have re-occurred throughout McLean's work and feature again in collaborative works after 'Should I Stay or Should I Go'. In homage to the formal dress of Nice Style's 1974 performances, Bruce McLean, Will Alsop, curator Lynton Talbot and myself wore dinner suits and bow ties standing against the backdrop of the 2010 'High Up on a Baroque Palazzo' installation whilst serving drinks to the private view visitors.

A Political Hot Potato on a Dark Background
Testbed 1, London, 25th March 2010

and

CHELSEA cab
in and around London, March–December 2010

As a result of introducing Bruce McLean to David Barnett during *The Life Room*, it was proposed that the two work together on a large-scale project. 'A Political Hot Potato on a Dark Background' was the resulting multi-media performance including film, projections, live performers with props, and contemporary

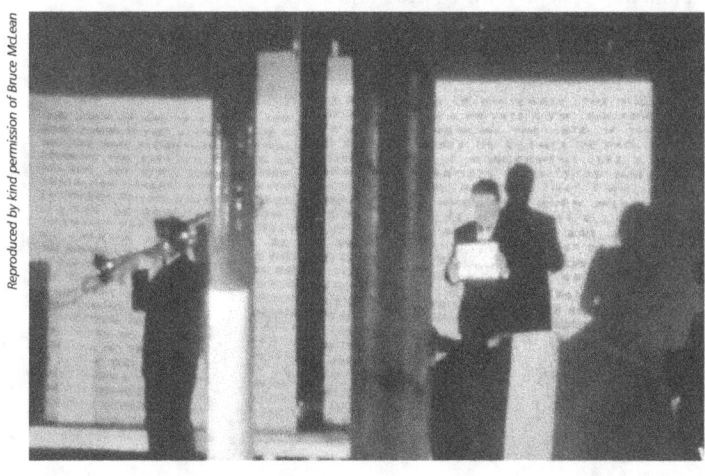

Bruce McLean, 'A Political Hot Potato on a Dark Background', 25 March 2010, CHELSEA space and Testbed 1

musicians and singers conducted by Sam Belinfante. A related photographic work was displayed on the side of Jason Brown's CHELSEA cab, a licensed London black taxi working in the capital.

The performances took place on 25th March 2010 as a part of CHELSEA space's fifth anniversary celebrations. At the close of the private view of Teresa Gleadowe and Richard Wentworth's *Act*, visitors were ushered onto a coach and transported from CHELSEA space to Testbed 1, a raw warehouse space in Battersea, south London used for the first time as a cultural venue. The performers included three Korean artists and curators, Daeun Jeung, Su Jin Lee and Gyeyeon Park, who had all been CHELSEA space assistants. Another element of the piece was a filmed performance of McLean and myself acting out a meeting between opposing political leaders. This cameo was performed in exaggerated gestures that I had learned from McLean as an audience member watching his performance *Good Manners and Physical Violence* at the Tate Gallery in 1985. The original reference to a potato on a dark background had come from McLean's childhood memory of the 1950s when, every Sunday, his grandfather would give him the choice of drawing a potato on a black background or a scone off a plate.

A Book, A Print, A Poster, A Sculpture, A Photo Work, A Film, A Model, A Vase, A School, A Failed Project, A Pose, A Masterwork, A Painting, A Text Piece and An Interview

Parfitt Gallery Croydon, October–November 2010, Director–curator: Michael Hall

In late 2009, Michael Hall, the new director of the Parfitt Gallery Croydon, contacted CHELSEA space with regard to his future programme. The legacy of the art school at Croydon, the punk designs of Malcolm McLaren and Jamie Reid, and the teaching of Bruce McLean were discussed and a meeting between Hall and McLean was brokered. The resulting show followed on from the last installation of the 2006 CHELSEA space process-spective and a subsequent exhibition at Galerie Fortlaan 17, Belgium, bringing together a diverse range of work and ideas from the 1960s to the present – an archive re-presented in a new configuration for a contemporary audience. New exhibits which extended the Croydon installation beyond the artefacts of the CHELSEA space show were some striking new large paintings made in 2008–9 and some recent ceramic "sculptures of jugs", as McLean defined them,

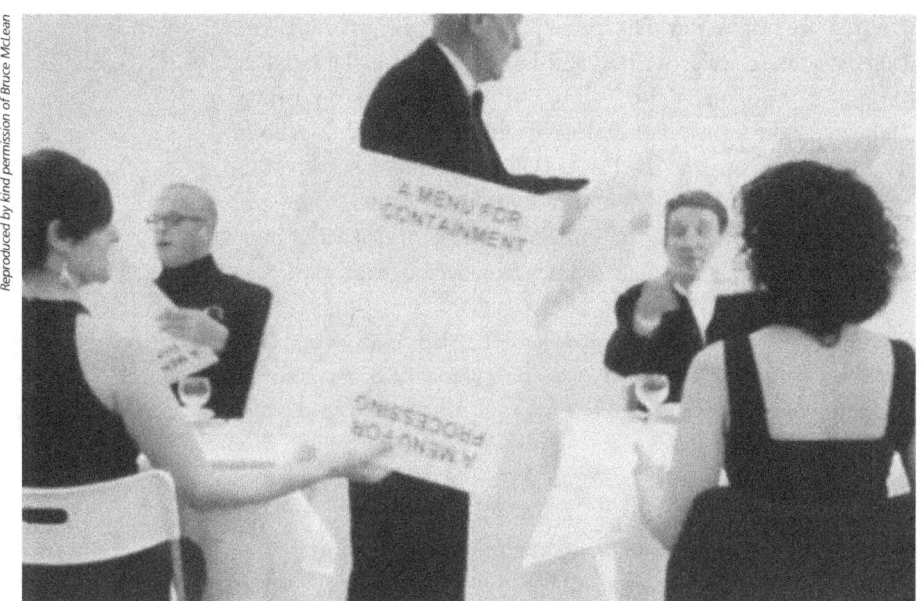

on a bespoke birch ply shelf by long-time collaborator, the artist Gary Woodley.

Bruce McLean, still from the short film, *Post-modern Minestrone*, 2011

A Modern Minestrone II and Post-modern Minestrone, 2011

My filmed cameo with McLean in 'A Political Hot Potato on a Dark Background' led him to invite me to perform in a new film he was making at his studio in Perrivale. There are two versions – *A Modern Minestrone II* and *Post-modern Minestrone* – and, as with his film *Conceptual Consommé* screened at Bernard Jacobson Gallery, London in November 2010 and the Late at Tate performance *Maitre D* in 2007, the new films are once again set in a restaurant and have titles that refer to soup. Amongst the props for the new film were cut-outs of sculptures by Barry Flanagan, Brancusi, Giacometti and Henry Moore, returning to the themes of *There's a Sculpture on My Shoulder*, 1971 and *Maitre D*, 2007, plus the large menus originally made for *Maitre D* with a series of headings such as "a Menu For Posing", "a Menu for Containment" etc. A further prop was a bright-yellow lemon dangling from a string on a pole. McLean is unsure whether the lemon motif first appeared in 'High Up on a Baroque Palazzo' in 1974, where a tomato added the colour red to the scenario, but he certainly recalls using a suspended lemon in a late 1980s edition of the TV culture programme *The South Bank Show*, presented by Melvyn Bragg, in a scenario narrated by the radio DJ Alan 'Fluff' Freeman. *Post-modern Minestrone* has a script written and narrated by Paul Tickell, the filmmaker who made the 1980s TV documentary on Bruce McLean for the series *South of Watford* which was later shown both at CHELSEA space and the Parfitt Gallery. Tickell opens with the exclamation "Waiter! There's a curator in my soup", a contemporary reworking of the *Sculpture on My Shoulder* and *There's a Sculpture in My Soup* themes employed by McLean.

> *The energy created by Donald Smith at CHELSEA Space attracts many different artists who pop in on a regular basis, generating an atmosphere of many working possibilities. Paul Tickell, a regular visitor, and I are presently working on a musical work based on the life and music of Johnnie Ray, collaborating with, amongst others, David Barnett. (BM)*

Nine Sculptures of Jugs on a Shelf Piece
Ideal Home, CHELSEA space, 2011

In 2011 I curated a show at CHELSEA space examining optimistic and dysfunctional relationships between art and daily life, showing over fifty artists including Gerrit Rietveld, Roy Lichtenstein, Gavin Turk and Rachel Whiteread, amongst others. I included Bruce

Bruce McLean, *Sculptures of Jugs on a Shelf Piece*, Ideal Home, CHELSEA space, 2011

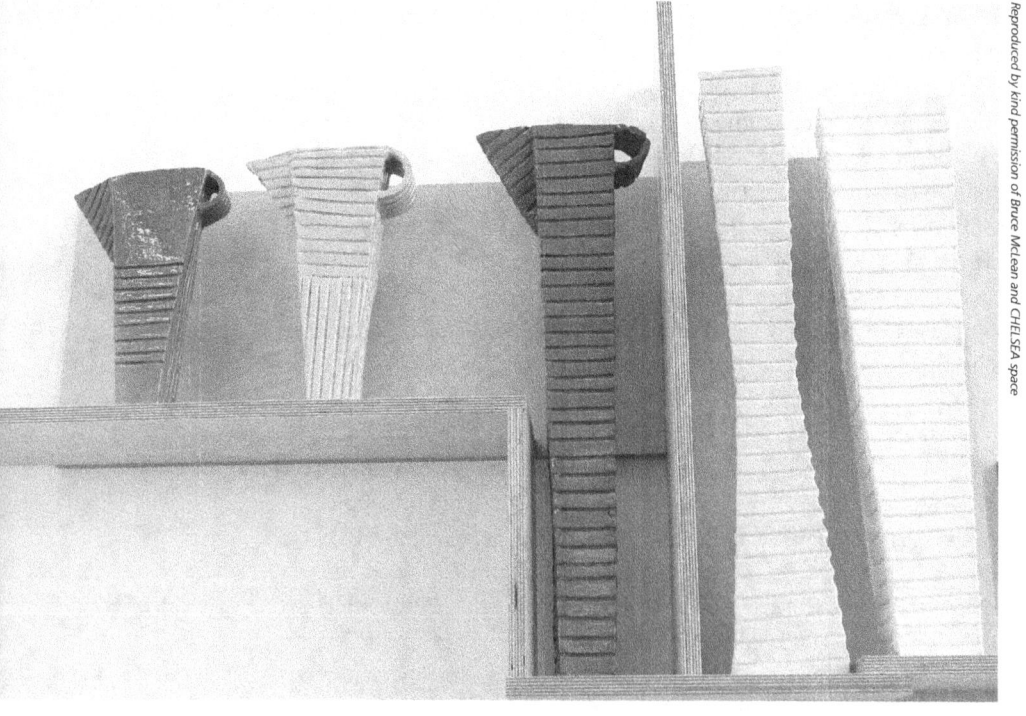

McLean in this exhibition, inspired by seeing the ceramic 'sculptures of jugs' at Parfitt Gallery, one of the contemporary elements that distinguished the Croydon show from the final installation at CHELSEA space in 2006.

Re-make/Re-model
Chelsea Futurespace, October 2011–January 2012

In May 2011 Bruce McLean brought a photograph from his archive that he had recently rediscovered. The black-and-white image showed the artist apparently suspended horizontally, jammed between two walls and was a part of the work *There's a Sculpture on My Shoulder* made at Situations, London in 1971 as one part of the 'Objects No Concepts Show'. McLean showed me this archive photograph at the same time that an article on his performance work written by Andrew Wilson appeared in *Tate etc.* magazine. A blog was added to the CHELSEA space website discussing the Tate interest in McLean's performance work, the 2006 and 2010 CHELSEA space Nice Style installations and the newly discovered archive image.

Around the same time, CHELSEA space assistant and artist Mike Iveson was organising a group exhibition for our sister gallery, Chelsea Futurespace. Iveson's theme was contemporary uses of ideas and processes relating to printmaking and collage. Having seen the blog, he asked Bruce McLean if he could use the 1971 photograph in the exhibition publication and requested some recent screenprints for the show itself. Bruce McLean, energised by the renewed interest in this work, decided to make a new piece for the exhibition revisiting the theme. The new work is a larger-than-life photographic cut-out of McLean which is propped between an architectural window column and a wall, giving the same impression of a feat of levitation as the original photograph.

This most recent reworking of the archive seems to sum up the predicament of the artist unable to neatly compartmentalise and finalise ideas whilst still engaged in a productive working life. In the case of Bruce McLean, his creativity in relation to his previous work is both stimulated by his own on-going enquiries and also triggered in response to the interest of others. The open dialogue between Bruce McLean and myself and those connected with CHELSEA space has spawned a number of new projects and ideas, and numerous other new relationships have been forged which may yet bear creative fruit. Even at the time of writing, Bruce McLean has just completed a new multi-media work – *A Cut A Scratch A Score* – at the Cooper Gallery, City Square and Botanical

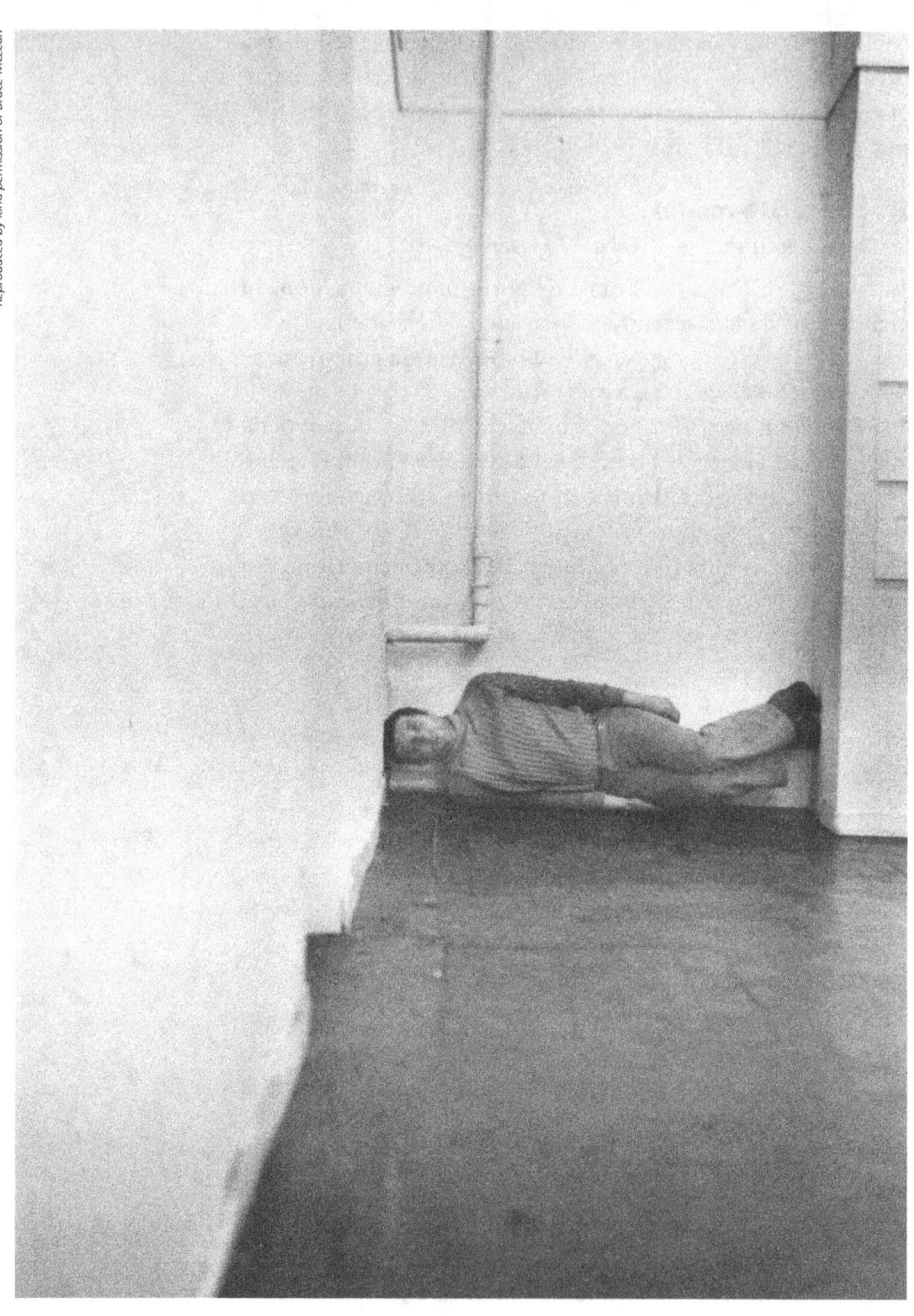

Gardens in Dundee, working again with David Barnett and Sam Belinfante, which was reviewed in *The Times* (1st November 2011). Stephen Farthing and myself are currently working on a proposal for a new version of *The Life Room* for a major venue during the

Bruce McLean, *A Sculpture On My Shoulder*, part of 'Objects No Concepts' exhibition, Situations, London 1971

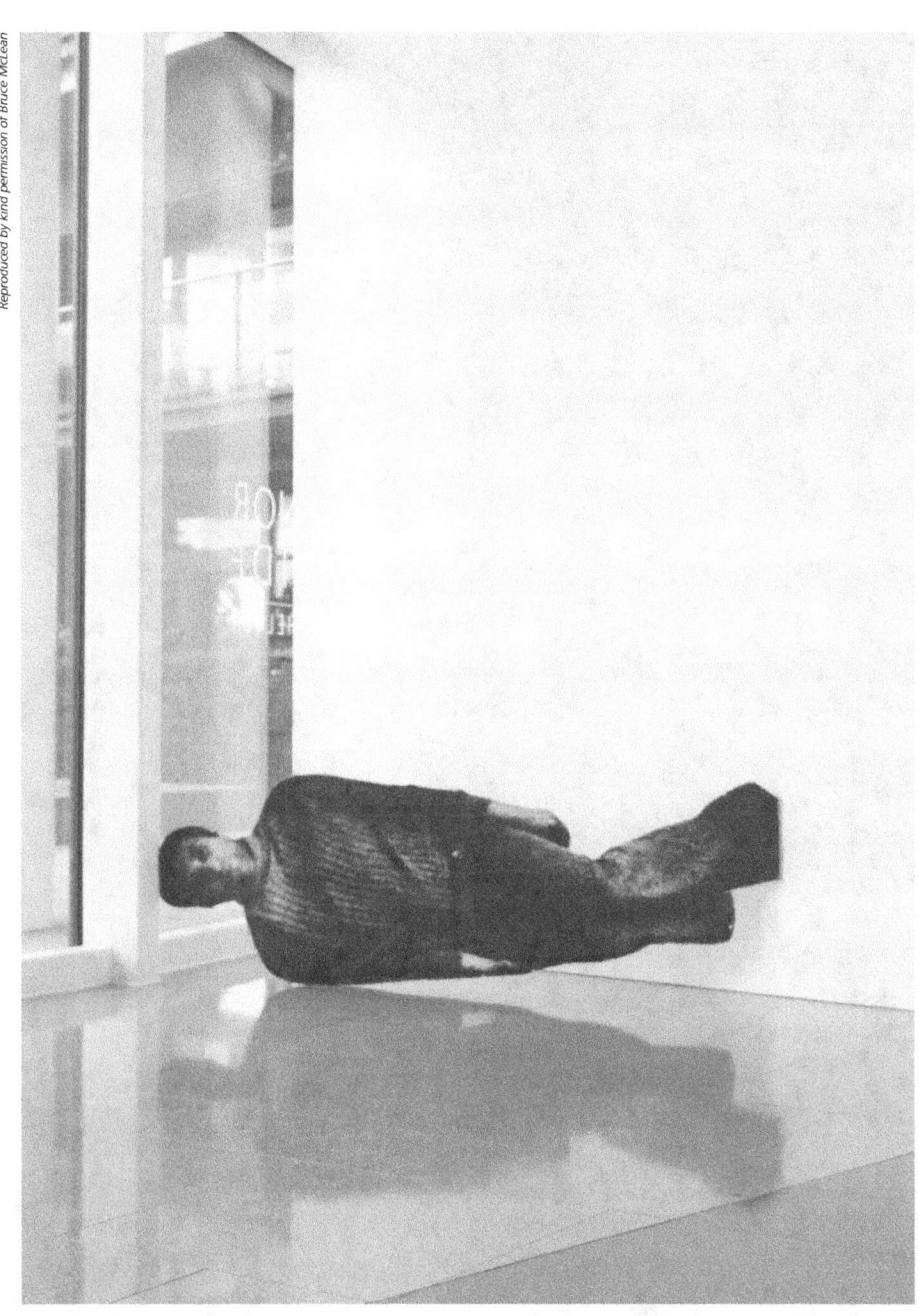

Olympics in 2012 and we are in discussions with David Barnett and Bruce McLean regarding a screening and reworking of some footage of Nice Style faux training and athletic posing – the archive will run and run.

Bruce McLean, *A Sculpture On My Shoulder*, Chelsea Futurespace 2011

EXPERIMENTS AND ARCHIVES IN THE EXPANDED FIELD
Neal White

4

The contexts in which artists work in relation to archives have changed enormously over recent years. At one end of the scale is the independent artist working on their own collection or archives, using the context of lost and found materials; at the other, there are artists working in well-known institutional archives, reshaping the taxonomies, classifications and scales of organisation. The former group includes a number of artists who have developed from the materials of the archive, both fictional and real, significant artistic practices, such as Walid Raad's largely fictional archives presented with the Atlas Group. Within an institutional context, there are those who have created their own visions, for example, Susan Hiller and her project 'After the Freud Museum'.[1] The impact that these artists have had on the definition of the archive, and its reading of documents and traces, has been explored in great depth in recent publications, including this one. Indeed, we are perhaps witnessing critical mass in what Hal Foster calls "the archival impulse", in which artists construct new realities for archives, even utopian visions, based on the logic of excavation of such sites.[2] However, the way in which artistic practice as research is currently engaging with the archive evokes other, deeper forms of knowledge production by the artist. There has been a shift in which the archival system (rather than a movement or impulse) is challenged and new emerging forms of archival practice are operating without the need to rely on major cultural institutions for valorisation.

The independent practice of artists such as Walid Raad is becoming more common as a form of engagement with the archive, but we are also witnessing a shift to new emerging knowledge-based organisations, collectives and initiatives which are seeking to establish themselves. Noticeably, they build on an historical tendency that moves from the singularity of the artist towards one of collective endeavour. These activities deliberately circumnavigate established territories occupied by the major institutional players such as large-scale museums, universities and their respective collections whose conception of the archive is as a source and font of wisdom. In respect of such changes, it is worthwhile considering in what way these tendencies are new, as undoubtedly they have emerged at a point where not only the

1   Susan Hiller, *After the Freud Museum*, The Freud Museum, London, 8 March 1994 – 24 April 1994; acquired by Tate 1998, http://www.tate.org. uk/susan-hiller-introduction/susan-hiller-freud-museum

2   Foster, H., 'An Archival Impulse', *October*, 110, Fall 2004, pp.3–22

means of production for the artist have become available to all via computer-based technologies, but also the means of production for entire institutions.

The Expanded Field of the Archive

I would like to give two examples that are useful in exploring some of the issues that are raised by an expanded field of the archive, in which the dimensions and form can start to be addressed in terms of their topology and architectonics.

For a number of years I have worked with artists attached to the Center for Land Use Interpretation (CLUI), as well as being a resident at their Desert Research Station in Utah from 2008 to 2010. The organisation, actually based in Los Angeles, has since 1994 established a physically and materially distributed model, with exhibition or interpretive sites in many key regions and a vast photographic collection catalogued as an archive, known as the 'ludb' or 'land use database'. The database itself supports their project, the 'American Land Museum'.[3] Set up by a group of like-minded artists, researchers and geographers, CLUI is a self-declared 'non-disciplinary'[4] organisation that, through projects such as the American Land Museum, records the use of land and the landscape of the United States. In examining the scale, breadth and uses of this space, from the military complex to environmental and energy-based consumption of resources, they have further extended the idea of what Krauss referred to in 1979 as the "expanded field of sculpture"[5], which was exemplified by land artists such as Robert Smithson, Mary Miss and Michael Heizer. The concept of the expanded field is critical in that it took sculpture not only beyond the physical site of the gallery, but also blurred the separation between landscape architecture, sculpture and the monumental.

CLUI draws heavily on this legacy and makes the assertion that in its land use the American landscape bears a cultural inscription. Even whilst there exists an interpretive layer, in terms of interpretive signage, themed towns and historic sites, CLUI has identified its own role as adding different and multiple voices to this public resource. Pursuing a goal that moves beyond standard interpretations or research methods, CLUI has also become internationally renowned in the art world. However, this profile does not simply emerge from an immersion in the art world by working to commission for international museums or other high-cultural events, or even selling work through private galleries; rather CLUI will use any appropriate venue to display the works that are part of its own archive and collection. So, whilst as an archivist or

3   http://www.clui.org/page/american-land-museum

4   Coolidge, M. and Simons, S., *Overlook, Exploring the Internal Fringes of America with the Center for Land Use Interpretation*, Metropolis Books, distributed by DAP/Distributed Art Publishers, 2006

5   The assertions are complex, but use a topological framework: "That is, the not-architecture is, according to the logic of a certain kind of expansion, just another way of expressing the term landscape, and the not-landscape is, simply, architecture. The expansion to which I am referring is called a Klein group when employed mathematically and has various other designations, among them the Piaget group, when used by structuralists involved in mapping operations within the human sciences." (Rosalind Krauss, 'Sculpture in the Expanded Field', *October*, Vol. 8, Spring 1979, pp.30–44)

artist you are likely to encounter them within the Whitney Biennale or Artforum, their activities are much broader and the exhibits are shaped by the sites in which they work, as Matt Coolidge, General Manager states:

> It doesn't require any physical relationship with the sites. It's just about context. Maybe its physical form will bubble up as an interpretive trailer parked between the Hirshhorn and the Smithsonian [Castle] on the Mall in Washington. Or as a giant IMAX theatre in Cheyenne Mountain. Or it will just remain on the Internet. But the physical form is just one potential mechanism for viewing the artefacts of the museum, which is a collection of places scattered across the landscape.[6]

The model developed by CLUI points to multiple cases of new forms and types of knowledge being embodied and transmitted, from the sites themselves to the way in which they organise their funding and their exhibits, interpret their own work and influence the work of others, particularly in America.[7] For example, they have for many years worked with emerging artists who have gone on to adopt some of these instituent modes of practice. One is the 'Center for Post-Natural History', a very recent initiative led by Rich Pell. This is a museum that is dedicated to the life and death of man-made organisms, from laboratory-based cells to mice and food crops. It encompasses many functions that large-scale institutions would look to develop – an education programme, a public interface, an interpretive framework – but is in fact based in an aesthetically rendered shop independently funded in Chicago. Pell created significant early works at CLUI Desert Research station and later, with Steve Rowell and Trevor Paglen, developed projects with the Institute of Applied Autonomy involving cartographic and surveillance-based systems for tracking flights.

Further to these two American examples, I would like to include one other archive of which I have intimate knowledge, that of Flat Time House, the former home of John Latham in Peckham, south London. (Latham's archive is explored further elsewhere in this book.[8]) Towards the end of his life, John Latham engaged with a number of younger artists with whom he felt an affinity. He asked us to help, along with his family, to continue his work and develop his compelling conceptual approach. After his death in 2006, a successful plan was put in place that would lead conceptual artists to explore his house both as a physical site and as a theoretical model. His house not only contained his archive but embodied

6 'Out There with the Centre for Land Use Interpretation: an Interview with Matthew Coolidge', in Taylor, C. and Gilbert, B., *Land Arts of the American West*, Austin, TX: University of Texas Press, 2009, p.206

7 Whilst influential, CLUI is perhaps an example that differs from groups engaged in tactical media. Activists such as Critical Art Ensemble, RTMark and the Yes Men have remained wed to a technological or political logic of media arts, art and science, instead highlighting a united logic in terms of sharing new artist-led knowledge and understanding. More relevant examples are included later.

8 See Chapter 9

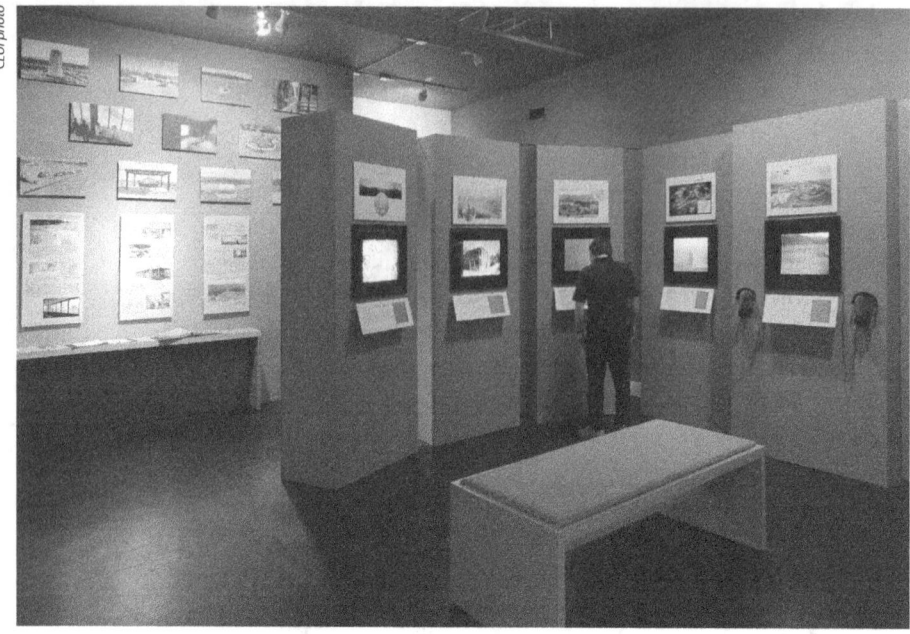

Latham's ideas around temporalities and 'event structures'. Following an initial process of archiving led by Simon Gould with the support of my own organisation, the Office of Experiments, a formal 'creative archive' process based on these ideas was funded by the Arts and Humanities Research Council. A new archive based on challenging concepts of the temporal nature of material things was developed with Antony Hudek. Rather than being set up by an independent group of like-minded thinkers, the archive is a centre for discourse. It is a product of foresight, grounded in a sense of the temporal nature of the archive, a legacy that Latham made apparent. It is clear that Latham understood intuitively the legacy of the physical site of the house, as an artwork, and how his own work could be contained within it even beyond his own lifetime; immobile but temporal.

The Center for Land Use Interpretation (CLUI) base in Los Angeles is home to various exhibits displayed in their visitor's centre gallery, adjacent to the Museum of Jurassic Technology.

These examples demonstrate how artists and independent researchers expand the field and the forms of archival practice. The evidence here is that they do not necessarily need to rely on collections housed in the cryogenic spaces and architectures associated with such collections or art works existing within other museums of cultural centres. The governing logic of these entities in form and structure is topologically different in that they not only occupy new space but question the logic of those spaces; and in their consequent temporalities or sense of permanence, which lie

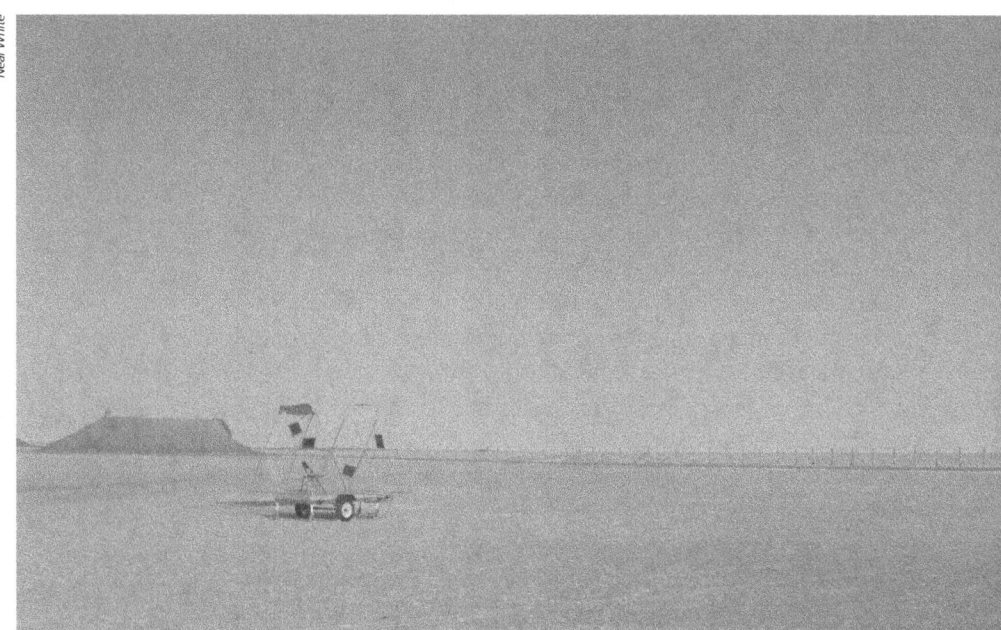

Neal White

at the heart of any historical associations, they are transformative across planes of engagement.

In starting to draw out some of the spatial and temporal dimensions of the archive that are of interest to the artist, I am trying to understand how these new experiments with archives and collections relate to shared and 'experimental' forms of knowledge production that will require the archivist to consider their own modes of engagement. If the highly articulated structure of the museum archive is only to be understood on its own limited terms, does it not risk becoming out of touch with the context of the archive today? These new practices represent ways of working which are resistant through counter-institutional, marginal or avant-garde forms; but are these less relevant than the opportunities they afford in terms of new technologies and audience access? It does appear that the examples I have given so far are not necessarily even opposed to the institution, but instead represent emerging networks that are establishing a set of new practices and sharing resources.

Exploring what Robert Smithson referred to as "The Museum of the Void", Office of Experiments F-Utility Unit at CLUI Wendover Research Station, Utah, 2008–10.

Experiments in the Archive

In terms of the analysis of the potential struggle that lies ahead, I will turn to the recent history of the experiment as a model for the historical analysis of science, which is currently being usefully applied to research in the arts, in books such as *Intellectual Birdhouse*.[9] In this approach, new 'epistemic things' and even 'technical objects', produced in the development of experimental systems, become methods of examining the nature and materiality of the archive and what knowledge is being produced in the development of experimental archives.

Since 2004, when I founded the Office of Experiments, an experimental art institution, I have been describing our work[10] in relation to Hans Jorg Rheinberger's influential work, *Epistemic Things*[11]. Although engaged in an historical project, his work indicates a shift from the singular laboratory space to multiple spaces of enquiry – and from one experiment to multiple experiments – the experimental system. This definition of the experimental system has, I would argue, affinities with the definition of an archive in the expanded field:

> the modern kind of experimentation has been contrasted with post-modern forms of experiment. The former, it is argued, relied on clear-cut separations between laboratory and society, facts and values, nature and culture. In contrast, the latter manifests itself as a socio-technological experiment (Latour) with no boundaries, carried out in real time and in the scale of 1:1, thus retrospectively changing our perspective on the seemingly modern form of experiment.[12]

Rheinberger's analysis of the history of biological science breaks down laboratory-based scientific experiments into the material aspects of the experiment, its 'technical objects' and quite separately its 'epistemic things'. To clarify, 'technical objects' consist of the materials, the technical objects, graphs, machines or experimental sites. The processes of the experiment, such as a technique used in biology for batch processing DNA as vectors used in genetics research, are its 'epistemic things'. This distinction is important in establishing an experimental system, as it separates the individual nature of a tested idea or theorem in the lab from the conditions through which knowledge about how to conduct experiments is learned, disseminated and reconfigured.

If, however, we apply this argument to the experimental system of the archive, can we separate the material conditions of a collection, its storage and preservation, from what might be learned about archival practice, that is, from its epistemic things? As an artist, I would argue that epistemic things are critical as they transgress any simple material–immaterial division of knowledge. They are bound to but are not dependent on these materials. Knowledge of, for

9   F. Dombois, *Intellectual birdhouse: artistic practice as research*, London: Koenig Books, 2012

10 Of particular relevance is 'Archives and Events', a talk that I gave at The Archival Impulse, ARLIS conference Tate Britain, 2007.

11 H. Rheinberger, *Toward a History of Epistemic Things: Synthesizing Proteins in the Test Tube*, Stanford University Press, 1997

12 'The Shape of Experiment', introduction to *PREPRINT 318*, Conference: The Shape of Experiment, Berlin, 2–5 June 2005, p.4

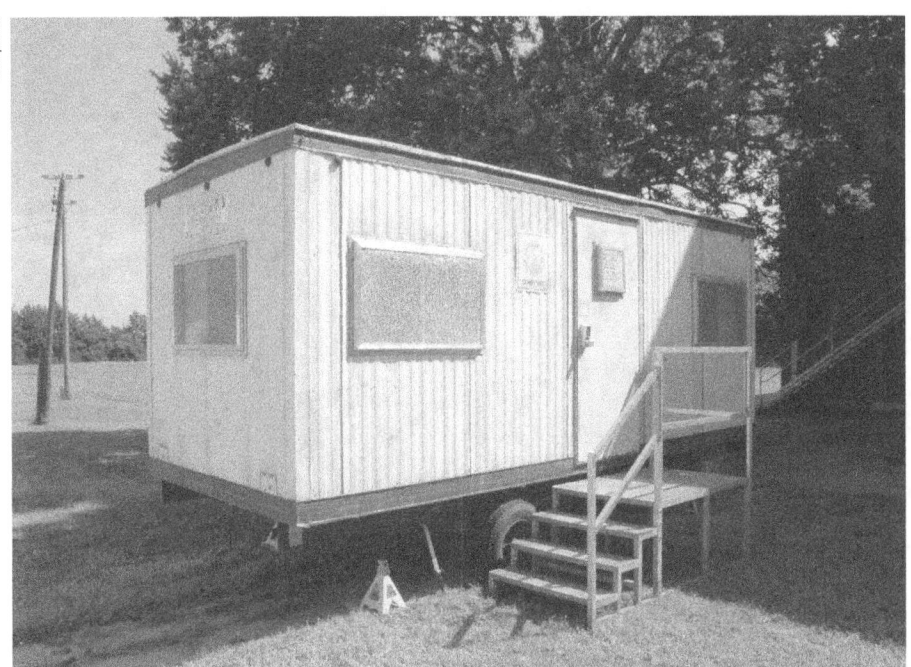

example, scale (CLUI) or temporalities (John Latham) and their conceptual positioning is as critical to the development of the technical objects' shaping of the expanded field of the archive as they are to the standard archive in how to store, preserve, capture or catalogue.

The CLUI trailer at the centre of the continental USA.

Further to this, it can be argued that, in part, the paradigmatic shift of such knowledge has been brought about by technology and its impact on concepts ranging from the near–far to inside–outside. However, there is nothing to separate such knowledge from what institutional archives might learn. What then remains the issue for the artist engaged in the new form of archival practice, and why not simply apply this knowledge within the institution?

In closing his paper 'An Archival Impulse', Hal Foster points to a need to recoup a failed vision by and on behalf of the artist, writer and philosopher:

> Perhaps the paranoid dimension of archival art is the other side of its utopian ambition – its desire to turn belatedness into becomingness, to recoup failed visions in art, literature, philosophy, and everyday life into possible scenarios of alternative kinds of social relations, to transform the no-place of the archive into the no-place of a utopia…[13]

13 Foster, op. cit., p.22

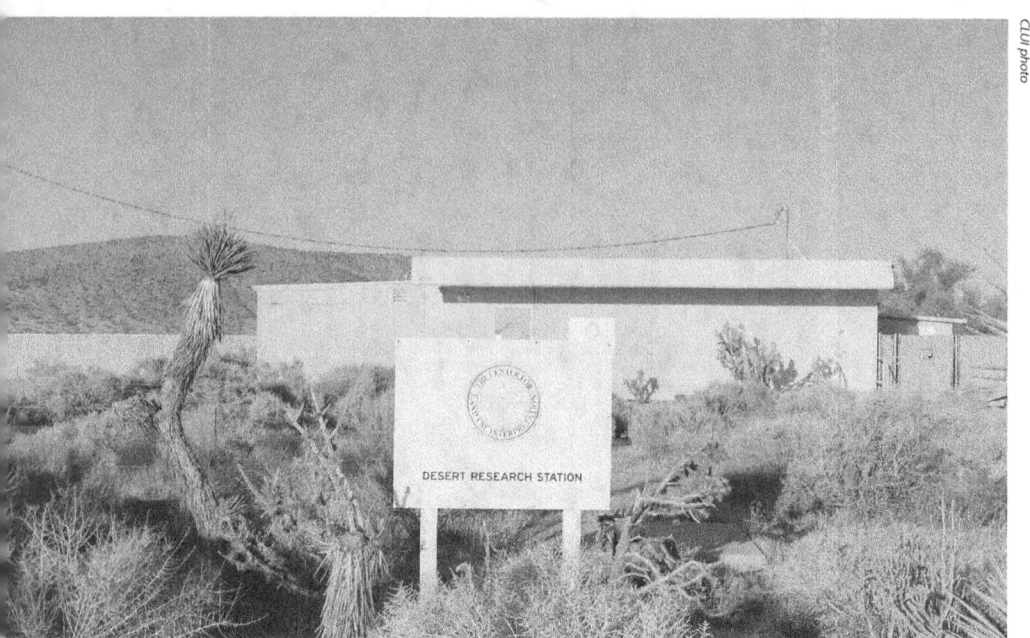

It would seem apparent, in examining the emerging archival practices, that Foster's reference to the 'failed visions' in art, literature and philosophy do not belong to the artist, writer or philosopher but instead are the failed visions of institutions. This crisis of the institution is nothing new but for artists it leads to the need for experiments with new archival practices, with a specific focus on what is of value to artists themselves – the epistemic things. Why as artists would we care?

In the aforementioned *Intellectual Birdhouse*, which focuses on artistic practice as research, Michael Schwab examines the role of the artists' artist and, in doing so, extends Foster's reflections when discussing 'love value' over exchange value. Drawing on the work of Bourdieu among others, Schwab describes what values the new archival context suggests for institutions that are looking to recoup their losses:[14]

> the 'artists' artist' is too epistemologically demanding on the market, which fails to capitalize (often during the lifetime of the artist) on the symbolic value that is produced while he or she delivers epistemological gain to his or her peers, who appear to be the only ones who are able to perceive such value in advance of the market.[15]

CLUI Desert Research Outpost, Mojave Desert

14 Many private collectors are currently engaged in collecting artists' archives, from Alex Sainsbury at Raven Row in London to an anonymous American-based private collector who bid against Tate to acquire the Artist Placement Group Archive.

15 Schwab in Dombois, op. cit., p.235

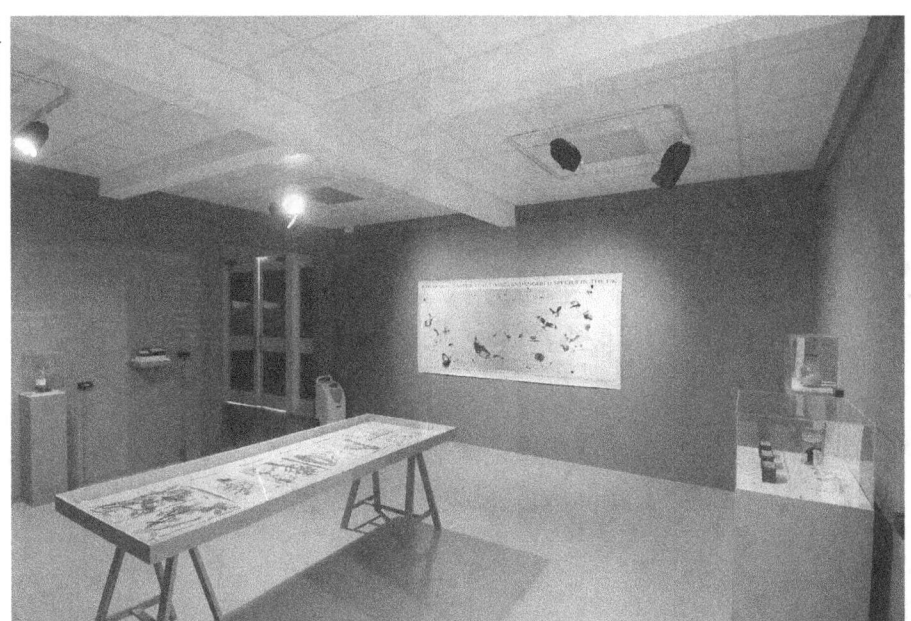

Schwab is arguing that the role of the artist in the production of knowledge through artistic research extends and can be differentiated from symbolic value. It is not the market that distinguishes the value of an artist to the artist, it is their epistemic value. In other words, it is what we can learn from that artist, not just their artworks. This produces a dilemma for the established institution that struggles to identify the cultural significance and value of the 'artists' artist' until late, sometimes too late, in the lifetime of the subject. It is not necessarily just a lack of vision on the part of museum staff, archivists and curators, but the values these institutions are increasingly forced to place on spectacular exhibitions in order to survive through corporate and media-driven sponsored relations. Archivists themselves acknowledge this limitation of working within institutions that have little room to speculate on cultural value except through established forms, such as the emerging contemporary markets. Many seek out and must work in new emerging archives, such as Flat Time House.[16] However, I would also argue that it is the artist's understanding of the potential value of 'becomingness' through cultural capital that applies to the present moment too. As has been stated by Derrida, the 'vision' to see what needs to be archived is now the work of the artist/s: to anticipate the archive itself.[17]

In 2006, the curator Maria Lind[18] proposed that 'institutional

Image from Beatriz da Costa showing part of the exhibition Dark Places, curated by Neal White, 2009

16 J. Latham et al., *The portable John Latham: occasional papers*, [London]: Occasional Papers, 2010

17 J. Derrida, *Archive Fever: A Freudian Impression*, translated by Eric Prenowitz, Chicago: University of Chicago Press, 1998, pp.8–12

18 M. Lind, B.K. Wood and B. von Bismarck, *Selected Maria Lind Writing*, Berlin, New York: Sternberg Press, 2010

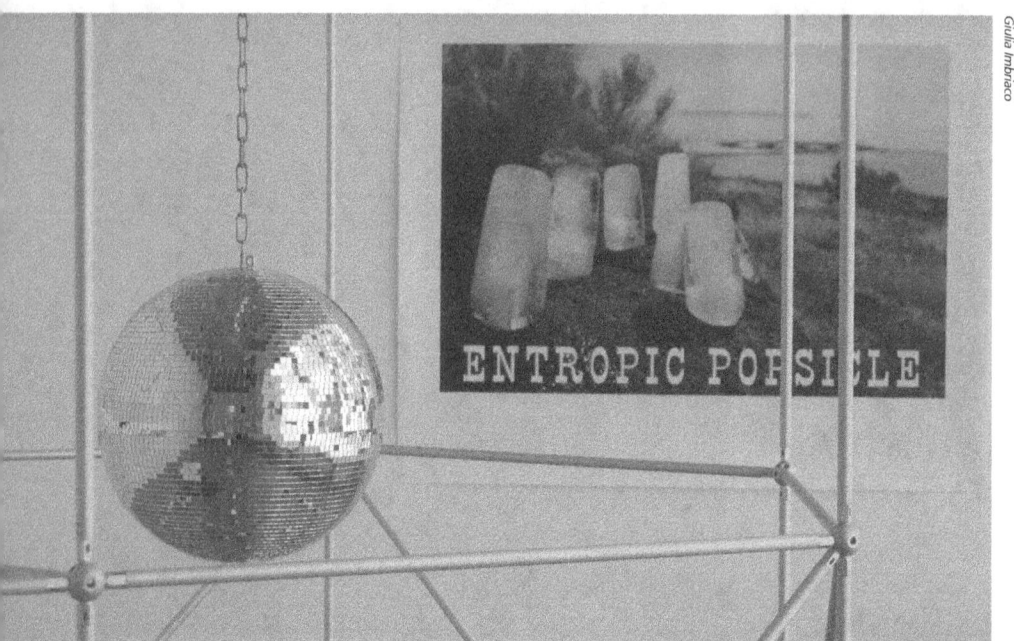

Giulia Imbriaco

critique' was happening in a new wave – a wave in which artist-led institutions, so called 'pseudo institutions', started to emerge driven by behaviours that seek to open out a critique not in opposition to existing cultural institutions but by imitating them within new models of organisation, knowledge and function. Further to this, Gerald Raunig[19] identified a group of practitioners and artists who were coming together and were already, or were becoming, instituted:

Detail of 'Fieldworks from the Museum of the Void', a series of projects made at the CLUI Wendover Residency Program; Chelsea Space, University of the Arts, London, 2010

> What is needed, therefore, are practices that conduct radical social criticism, yet which do not fancy themselves in an imagined distance to institutions; at the same time, practices that are self-critical and yet do not cling to their own involvement, their complicity, their imprisoned existence in the art field, their fixation on institutions and the institution, their own being-institution. Instituent practices that conjoin the advantages of both "generations" of institutional critique, thus exercising both forms of parrhesia, will impel a linking of social criticism, institutional critique and self-criticism.

19 Gerald Raunig, 'Instituent Practices. Fleeing, Instituting, Transforming', 2006, see: http://eipcp.net/trans versal/0106/raunig/en

Along with a legacy of institutional criticism implied in the work and experimental practices of conceptually engaged artists such as

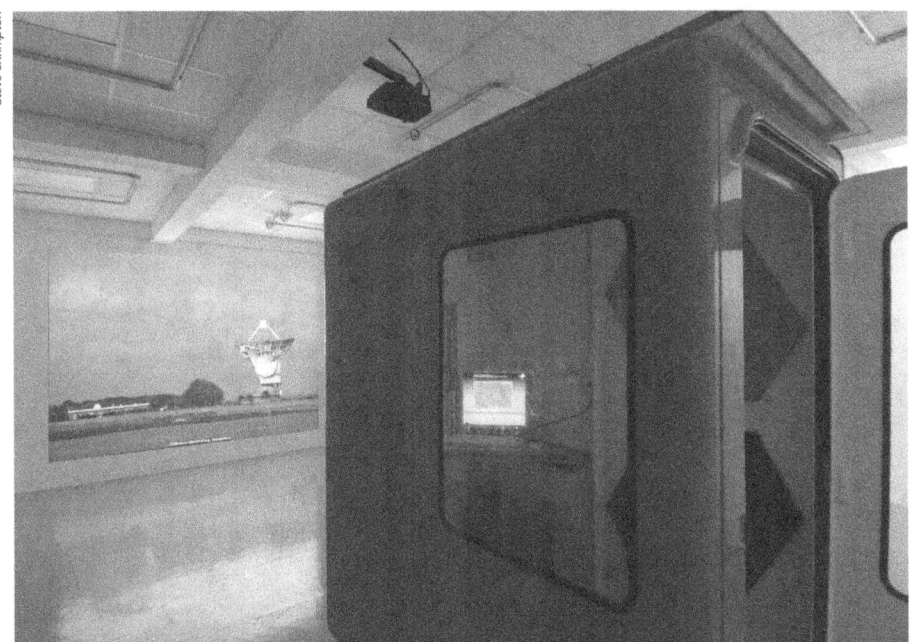

Stephen Willets, Gustav Metzger, John Latham and the Artist Placement Group [APG], a new wave of artists have now embodied a long history in which the artist operates outside of the institution, providing materials and cultural capital for artists and, I would also argue, creating solutions to the problems for institutions in describing the values of these artists.

Within this instituent tendency, however, is a range of more refined impulses, from the *pedagogic impulse* of Henrietta Heise and Jakob Jakobsen and the Copenhagen Free University; to the *interpretive impulse* of the Center for Land Use Interpretation; or to the *utopian impulse*, as with the architectural and social agenda of Danish architects N55.[20] Within each of these, 'experimental systems' are established, not precisely defined within a discipline, that share and utilise the epistemic things and the crafting of technical objects required to engage further within their network to produce additional artists' knowledge.

Within the new organisations dealing with these impulses, enthusiasm, love or politics are only part of a new vision that seeks to generate and extend the values first described by Foster. We could say that 'experimental' institutions are looking at what is missing, what has or cannot be described or what is overlooked in terms of the archive. So they are not just moving into an archive

Installation detail of the Overt Research Project by Office of Experiments from the exhibition Dark Places, John Hansard Gallery, UK, 2009

20 Other relevant examples with a range of impulses that are also epistemic might include: The Institute for Figuring, The Museum of Jurassic Technology, Temporary Services, The Institute for Applied Autonomy, The Museum of Accompaniment Animals, SpurseCenter for Urban Pedagogy.

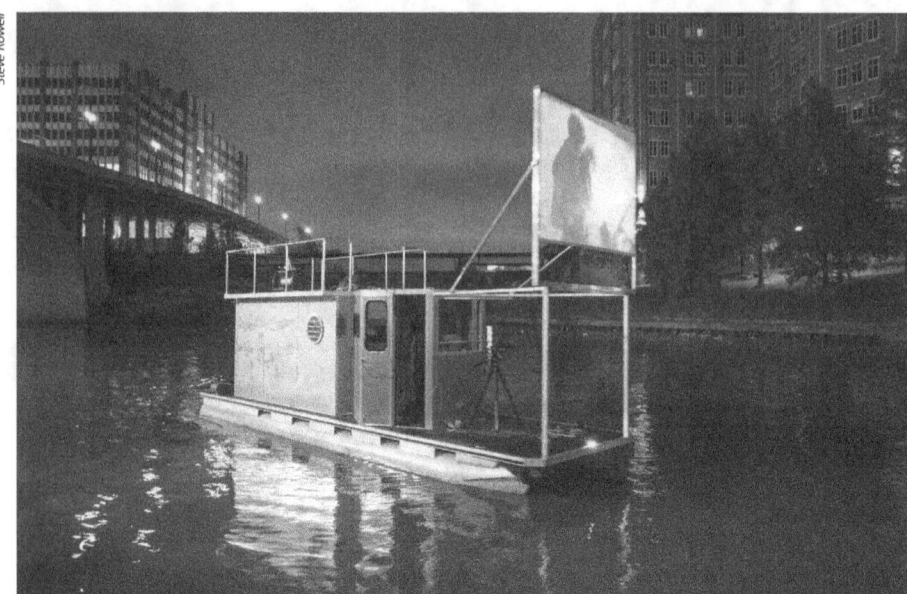

to consider what is missing or absent, they are interested in what is missing from the institutional perspective on archives per se and, in doing so, they produce new knowledge, first for the artist and then within culture and society more broadly.

TexHex floating field office and video barge built by Simparch in Houston Texas. Part of CLUI Inland Waterway Initiative.

Materiality

In considering the materiality of the archive, many institutions are bound and confronted by contradictory needs in terms of access to materials and the need for preservation. This is a topological problem, of the kind described by Krauss, in which there is an inverse logic in giving access as the desire to preserve the materials of the archive in a perceptually suspended state is almost absolute, even whilst it is in decay/entropic. Materiality is a problem for all archives as death visits the once-living materiality of life (thanks Latham and Derrida). However, it appears that in some new contexts of the archive this attitude to materiality is an inconvenient truth that can be circumnavigated. Just think of the quote from CLUI. Not only do they separate their online database, the 'land use database', from its geographic site but they keep all of their archive within a digital format. It does not exist materially except as locative data, digitally stored files or on a scale of 1:1. This catalogue is therefore not a tracing of the material of the archive; the archive is a map.

For users of the archive, this means they can have both access to primary materials and access to the means of interpretation, as well as to the processes being developed – key 'epistemic things'. The 'ludb' and many other online projects have for a long time used the applied knowledge of media artists (from whom many practices originate), who are able to utilise dynamic content management systems [Drupal etc.] even if they struggle to preserve the contexts of their work (digital archives of digital artworks using now-defunct operating systems and equipment). In the 'ludb', for example, unusual non-standard classifications become visible to the user, the interpretive layer of existing objects is opened out and can even be amended. The terms used for classification by CLUI, often in the interpretive materials that frame their displays and exhibits, also form part of a lexicon, an 'epistemic thing' of great interest to many artists working in these areas. The lexicon presupposes the taxonomy which is not only spatial but has a temporal range – from the Jurassic to the contemporary.

However, digitisation and the creation of new lexicons do not solve all of the problems of archival content. Within the United States, for example, many sites such as Smithson's Spiral Jetty are owned in all forms, even as images. Archives in digitised form are also contested spaces,[21] a yielding landscape across which multiple narratives unfold and whose commons, privacy and ownership are points of contention. This, however, is a two-sided issue, for outside the official spaces of art, culture and research, activity involving the sharing of content and exchange of files is happening. Access to files is both an issue of moral and intellectual property rights and of moral contention, sometimes legitimately targeted. It is here where the role of non-institutional organisations can be of value.

As part of the fieldwork for the online database Dark Places,[22] developed by Office of Experiments, I stumbled across an independent, autonomous researcher, Mike Kenner, based in Weymouth, England. His singularly focused work unearthed the true nature of events behind one institution that had been of interest to our project, which was examining sites of research not normally accessible to the public – in this case, Porton Down.[23] Working for over thirty years, Mike Kenner had amassed a huge wealth of information including public experiments, or experiments on the public, with alleged live pathogens. Not only is the archive a valuable asset in uncovering a story for public evaluation, built through thousands of Freedom of Information requests and countless correspondences with the government and Porton Down, it represents a body of research, an archive that was,

21 "The problem with most existing public archives, is that all creative work is born into copyright; every image, text, film or sound is automatically designated as the property of its apparent author – until death plus seventy years." (Cummings and Lewandowska, Enthusiasts, and the Enthusiasts Archive, p.11, released under a Creative Commons: Attribution ShareAlike v2.5 Licence)

22 www.dark-places.org.uk – developed with Office of Experiments' International Director, Steve Rowell, and Technical Director, Lisa Haskell

23 Porton Down has long been the home of bio-warfare research in the UK. Currently, its activities are organised under the DSTL and private partnerships including Ploughshare Limited.

until recently, inaccessible. If you approach Porton Down with an enquiry on the subject of Kenner's interest, they will give you his number. He has been co-opted and his autonomy threatened. However, through a donation of a digital facsimile of his entire archive, Office of Experiments was able not only to catalogue it in its entirety but to display elements of this to help establish the autonomy Kenner had lost.

Here the role of technology in the archive does not account for a new means of distribution, but in its duplicating logic provides new possibilities. So, the files themselves are not available online, because unlike the open-source database of Dark Places, they contain information that was explicitly secret and is in some cases controlled by the State. The operation of the archive is not to generate news, such as is generated by Wikileaks operations, but to make available the unknowable in a context that our institutions could not support due to ethical, moral or political positioning. For Office of Experiments, it provides a resource for the making of new interpretive and artistic works, as well as being the work itself.

Sustaining the Archive in an Expanded Field

I have shown how the new context of archives for artists has produced antagonism to existing institutions and points to the reconsideration of the nature of the archives' architectonics – that is the shape, spaces and forms which archives have until now relied on for sustainable futures. This is not to escape the problems that those archives that are embedded within our cultural institutions face, and their own serious challenges of sustainability that are sometimes made more difficult following the development of a more open agenda. Whilst free-to-access cultural forms are shaping the future of closed or restricted cultural forms, simply opening access to what you already own may not be enough.

In considering the artist and the archive, and in particular what can be learned through an expanded field for the archive, it is useful to consider how to identify the differences between the things, objects and systems which lead to knowledge. In a recent discussion with Hans-Jorg Rheinberger, I asked how he would characterise what science and art held in common, in terms of the production of knowledge, its epistemic things. His response was revealing of the limits and the productivity of limits. He stated that in either discipline it was critical that the person seeking knowledge should be attentive to the resistance within the materials themselves, and to then understand how that makes a difference.[24] I would argue

24 Dialogue recorded by the artist at Rheinberger Study Day, 11th and 12th July 2012 at the Orpheus Institute, Ghent, Belgium

that in remaining attentive to the material resistances of the archive, the artist, through collective endeavours, has more fundamental value to the archive than as a symbolic, aesthetically resistant, engaged individual. Just as artists are no longer the lone agent of the avant garde, the archivist is also no longer a gate-keeper of the institutional order; each are guides whose knowledge of the topology of domains can steer us through unchartered yet contested territories of the expanded field of the archive.

AN INTERVIEW WITH BARBARA STEVENI

5

Barbara Steveni (BS) is a conceptual artist who initiated the original concept of Artist Placement which was established as the Artist Placement Group (APG) in 1966. The papers, ephemera and audio-visual material of the APG were deposited at Tate in 2004. This interview with archivist Victoria Lane (VL) conducted in 2011–12 considers how her views on archives have changed over time and impacted her more recent work.

Victoria Lane: When did you become aware of the concept of the archive?

Barbara Steveni: My first experience of any archives at all was the APG archive, my own archive, and the whole business of negotiating its transfer to Tate. This brought me into actual and personal contact with repositories, where before I'd never actually researched in archives. So I was completely unaware of archives until I was tangling with my own, so to speak.

Barbara selecting images in the APG archive at Tate Britain.

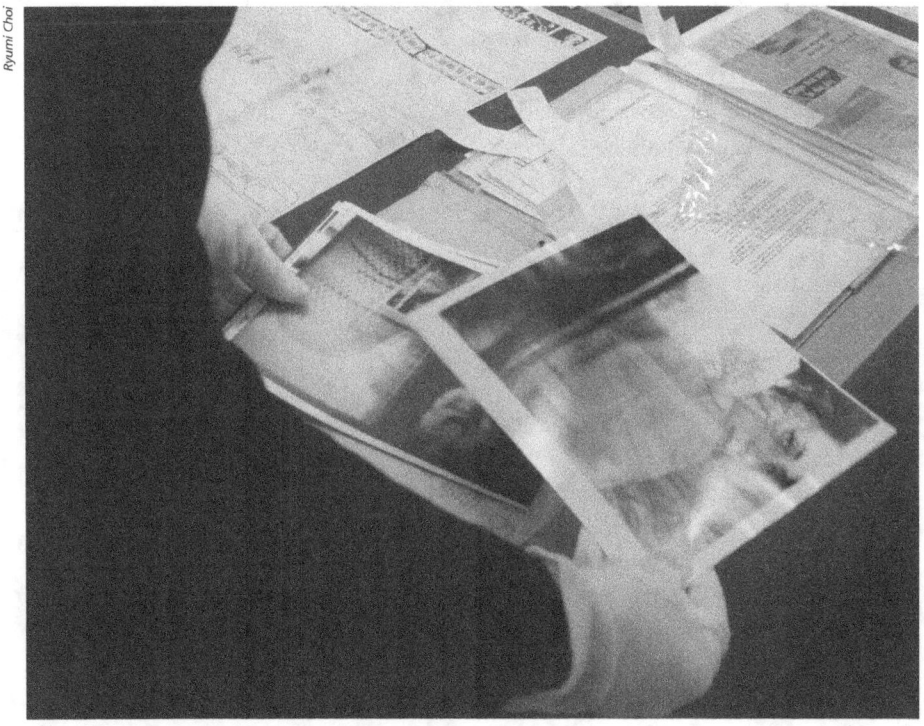

Ryumi Choi

VL: Could you explain what the APG was?

BS: The idea of the APG originally came to me when two of the Fluxus group, Robert Filliou and Daniel Spourri, came to stay in our house, for their London show at Gallery One I think it was. John [Latham] was in the States, and I said I would collect some material. They were thinking of things like industrial waste and sheets of plastic.

So I went to the Outer Circular road, to the large complex of industrial estates, but got lost in the factories. It was night time but the factories were well lit and humming with activity. I just got this idea saying to myself, "why aren't we in here not just to pick up scraps and buckets of plastic, this is a whole other context. We/people/artists talk about industry; we don't know anything about this world of industry". At that time, artists' association with industries was very much on the applied side, as designers and engineers. So called 'Fine Artists' were limited to, for example, Olivetti desk diaries, Pirelli posters, or to painting the chairman. When John came back from America, I told him about the idea of being inside these industries, and discussions began with John and other artists working on the parameters so to speak, about what such a role might be.

So, I am the originator and transmitter of the concept of the APG. The name was changed in 1986 to Organisation and Imagination (O + I) to distinguish it from the Arts Council's artists' placements, which copied the idea of the APG placement without the APG concept or context.[1] I developed the APG with artists working in the emergent fields of Multimedia and Conceptual Art in the late 1960s and early 1970s. This included John Latham – who contributed most of the written material to APG – Ian Breakwell, Barry Flanagan, David Hall, Ian McDonald Munro, Anna Ridley and Jeffrey Shaw.

The main premise of APG has been described as putting art into a new context of industrial and government concerns. I managed to do most of the initial negotiations of the placements; the idea being that the artist would be involved at all levels of the organisation. The key to the placement was an open brief where there was first a feasibility period. The artist was in the organisation with no requirement to produce a work or an idea until the context and artist within had arrived at a relevant direction which both the organisation and the artist agreed could be developed. This critical feasibility phase was paid and could then be followed by a longer development period where a new role and function for

1   See: http://www2.
    tate.org.uk/artistplace
    mentgroup/

art would be put on a par with any other specialist profession. (Described excellently by Ian Breakwell in *Art Monthly*, Issue 40, April 1980.) I have since come to think of this as my (and the others of APG of course) greatest achievement, to have persuaded the commercial premise to pay for *not knowing*.

This repositioned the artist within a wider social context and it was pioneering work which has emerged in mainstream art as apparently 'socially engaged practice'.

VL: What was the process of the acquisition of the APG archive with Tate?

BS: Well, the process of the acquisition was that Tate told me they would be interested in the APG archive around 2000. We asked Louisa Riley-Smith, a twentieth-century archive specialist, to value the archive. It took four years to negotiate the word 'acquire' into 'purchase'. I was determined it had to be bought and in talking it through with APG artists it was felt strongly that it wasn't just going to be handed over. In many ways the archive represents rare tangible evidence of the art practice of that time. I think, at that time, Tate was beginning to expand its budgets to buy archives. People also donated their archives to the Tate. It was around the same time that Bill Furlong's Audio Arts archive was also purchased by the Tate.

As part of the acquisition, I negotiated that Tate would put on a public event about APG. This event was supported by the Arts Council, called 'Art and Social Intervention: The Incidental Person Symposia', in 2005. For this we brought together artists, critics but also politicians and representatives of those who hosted APG placements. The event sold out and has had a lasting effect. It was the first time that the APG archive came to the fore as a 'live' event. The only disappointment being that the Secretary of State for Culture who spoke had not read my brief on who the audience was, and delivered a totally inappropriate speech.

What was important about the APG was that the artists involved were part of a collective. A letter was written to each of them outlining the plan to sell the archive, asking if they were happy for the archive to go to Tate and offering a token payment to each artist. A special proviso in the sale stated that if anybody loaned it or published from it they had to acknowledge that APG was a collective and it belonged to the artists and that it was an artwork. There has been a continuing debate about whether APG was a strategy or artwork. A lawyer was used for the negotiation of the

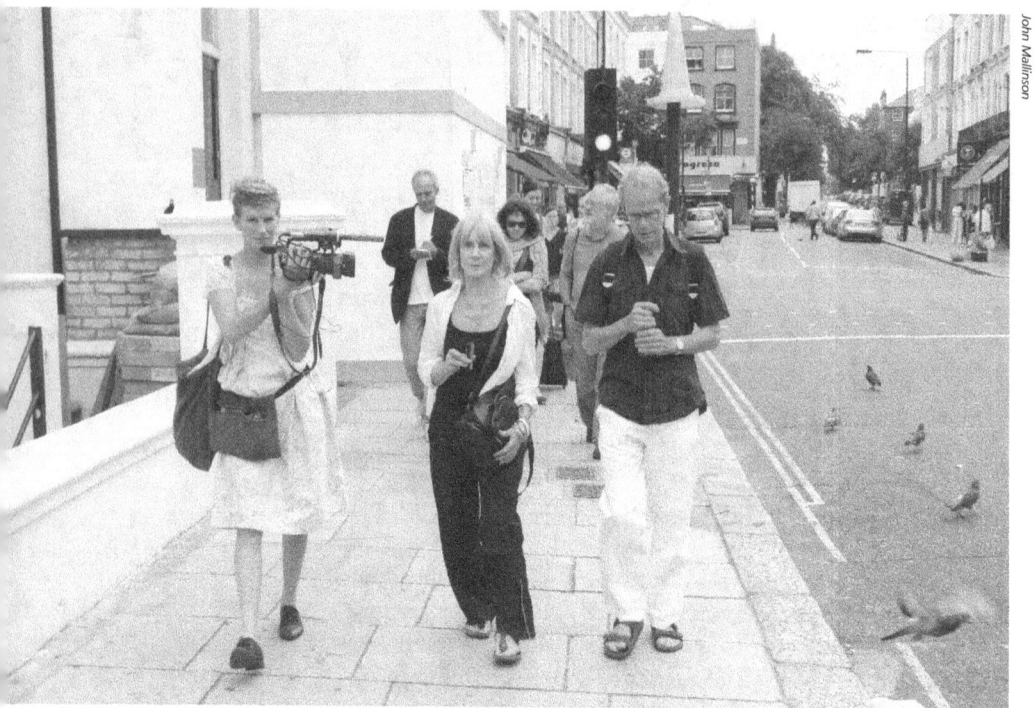

contract which was important to make sure such special conditions were binding.

Beginnings walk, Notting Hill, with Barbara, Guy Brett and Laura Prouvost.

VL: What does it mean to sell your own history?

BS: I felt the papers were going somewhere where [they] could be a resource and where [they] would be looked after. John and I had already buried a whole lot in the garden some years back because there was nowhere to put it. The money from the sale was used to carry on ideas and work on a next set of projects.

VL: Where was the APG archive, before it went to the Tate?

BS: It was around John's studio and in my house as it turned out. I've got pictures of it being taken from John's studio at Flat Time House by Adrian Glew of Tate. A lot of related material is still in my house but most of this is my personal archive which I am now cataloguing. There were the big boards and banners that were made for the Hayward exhibition. These were brought out for the first time in the Tate archive by Adrian Glew to provide a venue to end my 'I AM AN ARCHIVE' walks series. As Adrian put it at the time, "Welcome to an APG World". The Hayward was an important show called 'Art and Economics' in 1971 and John and I had kept some of the elements of the installation. When they went into the Tate they had mould so they were put in isolation; I felt this was so symbolic. They were put in isolation so that the spores wouldn't get onto other people's archives. And I thought this is just so symbolically typical of anything to do with APG – people were terrified of our spores!

VL: Did you edit the archive before it went to Tate?

BS: No, it was roughly catalogued by a student from Goldsmiths, Barnaby Drabble.

VL: What has happened with the archive?

BS: Alex Sainsbury, the owner of Raven Row Gallery, has given financial assistance so that it has been properly catalogued. The APG is to be the subject of an exhibition at Raven Row in September 2012.

VL: How did your work 'I AM AN ARCHIVE' develop out of these experiences of working with the APG archive?

BS: Well, going into Tate archives and seeing these rows and rows of material in boxes being wound out of endless shelves and these great drawers really got me associated with archives.
    Barnaby Drabble had roughly categorised types of material and put it in chronological order. Then when it went to Tate I was involved in going through the archive and realised how completely random the order of it was. Dates were wrong, whole chunks of stuff were in [the] wrong place and so I got very involved in looking in the files and rearranging the material to assist with the cataloguing of the archive. I'd have sessions with my white gloves on and it became a sort of mime which an artist, Laura Trevail, who was working with me, filmed for me. I gradually found myself talking the archive. I started to see it, the material I was looking at, as stories and I found myself telling these stories and realised I was a kind of database of memories and knowledge about the documents I was reading and looking at. Peter Cross, who was at the Arts Council at the time, (Peter had been behind getting the APG public event on when the Tate acquired the archive) said "Barbara, you've got to do your story, you know, it's your story".

VL: Where did the title for 'I AM AN ARCHIVE' come from?

BS: That came out of what I said in a rather bad temper when Barny and I were sorting all the papers out; I said "I am a bloody archive!" and so, from that moment my own project developed under this title.

VL: 'I AM AN ARCHIVE' has generated a number of works, most of which have been performance and time based; could you describe one of the first ones?

BS: One of the first ones I did was at the London Institute in 2002, although I had done small performances before that, with a small battered suitcase, out of which I brought my family history and personal archive. A photograph of me in India, how I would learn to climb onto elephants from their tail, and various other souvenirs. The performance charted a series of journeys, each of which were in the suitcase, which I would get out and present and then put them back; but I hadn't called it 'I AM AN ARCHIVE' then.

The performances that I started for 'I AM AN ARCHIVE' were around the time that the archive was going to Tate. I carried in an archive box and I took diaries from the '60s out of it, and read dates and pieces from them. The first of these at the London Institute was on the occasion of Chelsea College of Art moving to Millbank. Chelsea put on a series of events recalling both the early days of Chelsea Art School and also of the hospital at Millbank, Chelsea's new home. I had various documents from my archive, including photocopies of the actual letters that Tony Benn had written to me when APG were making the proposal to the Department of Health that recorded how he decided to involve Barbara Castle. I took things out of the box and I talked about each item and told its story. Then I built it up from that, so when I was invited to Kunstfabrik in Berlin [2005] my performance for 'Produkt und Vision', I used a crate with the Civil Service Memorandum banner in it which I pulled out and I talked about. The banner had been returned from a show in Barcelona in a crate and I was making the analogy or story that I had sent the banner as a rolled-up piece of canvas and it had been returned to me in a crate as a product but it had been sent to Barcelona as a vision.

I have also done this kind of performance more recently, in my exhibition at the Arnolfini, 'Beyond the Acid Free' [2009–10]. As part of the show, I had a dirty wheelbarrow, I insisted on a dirty wheelbarrow, as the Arnolfini had given me a nice clean one and

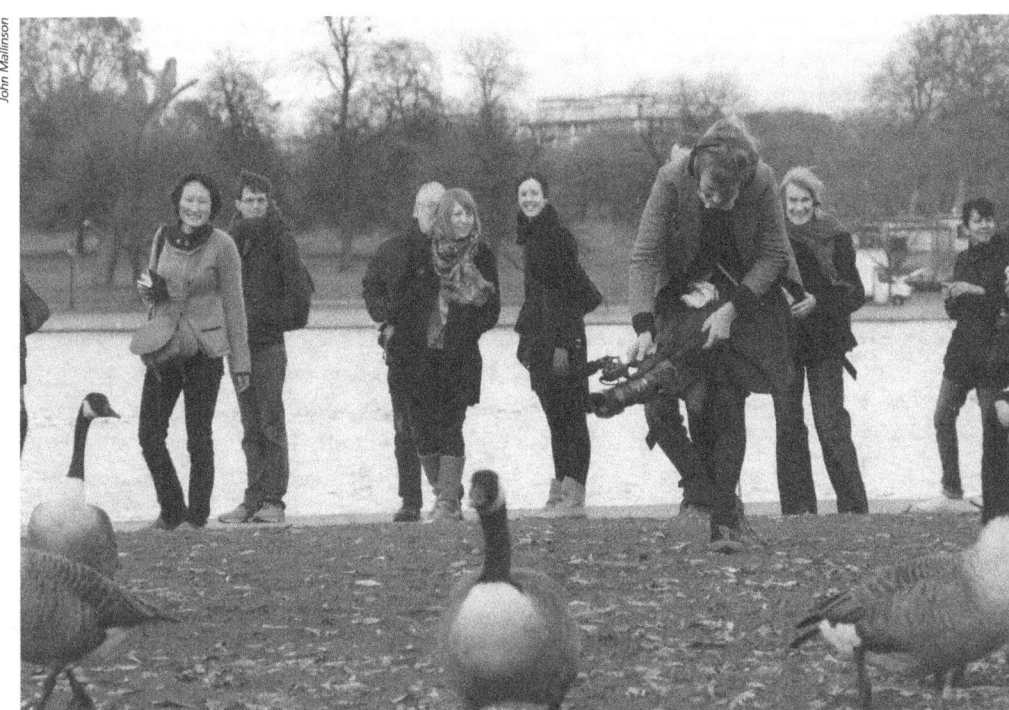

I said "No, take it away, it's got new clean yellow wheels, I want one with dirty wheels". And they said "Oh no, you'll get your files dirty", which was the opposite of the point I was making with the exhibition.

Westminster Walk 1 – walkers short cut past the Serpentine.

In the wheelbarrow were degradable leaf bags and I had '60s and '70s diaries. I would take out a little bit and read it. I also had the old files from the APG archive that Tate was throwing out. I asked Adrian Glew to give me all the files as they repackaged the archive material into the acid-free preservation packaging. I used these dirty old files as part of the work, to make other works, and I'd had photocopies of the archive made and put them in the files. I'd read these out and I'd chop them up and put them into the leaf bags and I'd hang them up. And then gave the bags to James Marriott, from Platform, to go and plant these bags so that they would grow.

VL: Part of 'I AM AN ARCHIVE' [is] the walks which retrace significant events in the history of APG. Could you describe the ideas behind the walks?

BS: The idea was to do five documented and participatory walks, which would be onsite, to recreate context. The five locations were chosen both for their significance in the development of my practice, from Happenings to industrial and government APG placements, but also, each context was specific to a change or a shift in the perception of the role of the artist in society at that time. From a supported role using industry and government intervention solely for materials and funding, to a role where the artist acts as a carrier of specialist information and methodology in the socio-political sphere.

The first was called 'Beginnings Walk' and retraced the genesis of the APG in the 1960s and it took place in west London where John and I lived in the late '60s, early '70s. The second walk covered Westminster and Millbank and the industrial and government placements. To end this walk, Adrian Glew brought out all these boards and stood them up against the walls of the archive reading room and laid out all of the APG archive contents on the tables to create, as Adrian put it, an "APG world" as the end venue for the participants on this walk to actually peruse the documents of the APG journey they had taken part in. The third was the Scottish Office Placement of the 1970s which John Latham undertook; the fourth was based around Southwark, an educational research project of the 1990s and 2000s. I included coverage of John's 'Flat Time House' in Peckham. The final one, the German walk, stems from Joseph Beuys' invitation to APG to discuss artist-with-government placements in his Honey Pump at Documenta 6 in Kassel, Germany in 1977. APG had had an exchange with German industrialists in Dusseldorf in the early '70s, on the invitation of Jurgen Harten, then director of the Kunsthalle Dusseldorf. APG went on to hold a series of podium exchanges with the German government and secretaries of state in Bonn which led to the first international artist-with-government placement and I am just back from Bonn, having completed the last in my 'I AM AN ARCHIVE' walks series, the German walk.

The walks involved the participation of artists I have worked with originally, the new generation of artists interested in engaging with this journey and key figures from the socio-political-commercial spectrum. I saw myself as both receiver and transmitter, tapping into pools of memories and anecdotal exchange with other walkers. The idea of physically moving around the sites was pivotal, with assemblages from archive material and found objects to trigger discussion. So they were and are a kind of spontaneous group storytelling, interviewing, filming and recording, setting the past against the present.

There was such an interest, especially from people who are doing what is now called this 'socially engaged art practice', in its various ways. APG had a definitive notion about context as half the work and what context actually consisted of. The component parts of a context, not only the place but also the people and, if it's a hosting organisation, the intention of that hosting organisation.

I found in doing the walks they became much bigger than I'd anticipated. I hadn't factored into the walks the interest from galleries in various areas, who offered to be part of the event. The Serpentine participated in my Westminster walk and Stills Gallery for the Edinburgh walk where we could meet at the beginning and end of each of the walks. For the Beginnings Walk we started in the Talbot Tabernacle, Notting Hill Gate, because we'd done the events and Happenings there. The walk visited Portland Road where Yoko Ono stayed with us during the Destruction in Art Symposium whilst she was developing works such as her *Cut Piece*.[2] I helped her with this piece by, for example, sourcing the dress from Biba.

The walks generated a mass of documentation. Not only was it filmed and recorded but I'd ask participants to record as well, so I've got a whole lot of extra images and material. However, the sound on some of the film is not good throughout but we were very limited by budget.

VL: What was the experience for you and the participants on the walk?

BS: I felt rather pleased when the people I worked with said "that was brilliant, Barbara" and I got the feeling they were very interested. David Harding commented on the importance of the APG placements and the way those placements had been done and why they were different to any other type of engagement. He also said how I'd made the placements happen. It was wonderful for me to hear him say that. I felt very pleased to have done the walks, and that there was a lot of material there for the development and dissemination of the ideas of APG and my practice. But I did feel that there was a bit of a breakdown between people walking with me when I'm telling the story and say a group of people telling their own stories to each other that maybe didn't get captured, so maybe a lot was missed.

VL: I also wanted to get a sense of what it felt like for you walking in the same place as the past events?

2   Two performances of *Cut Piece* took place in September 1966 at the Africa Centre London – see Kevin Concannon's 'Yoko Ono's *Cut Piece*: From Text to Performance and Back Again' (*PAJ: A Journal of Performance and Art*, PAJ 90, Volume 30, Number 3, September 2008, pp.81–93).

BS: Well, when it came to doing the walk in Scotland, when we were overlooking the Niddrie Heart, that upset me and I did cry, possibly because we'd also scattered John's ashes on the Niddrie Heart, I'd choreographed that also. But walking over the same stuff, I was so conscious, I suppose, of telling the story. I got much more of a feel about the time and the events when I was doing individual interviews. When I was actually walking, you had the present day, like the group weren't allowed to be outside the headquarters of the present Steel Board because you'd be told to move on and ridiculous sorts of things, so it was coping with the present. Some participants were new younger people who'd never heard of any of this before, so I was very conscious of telling the story rather than what I was feeling. I loved doing it.

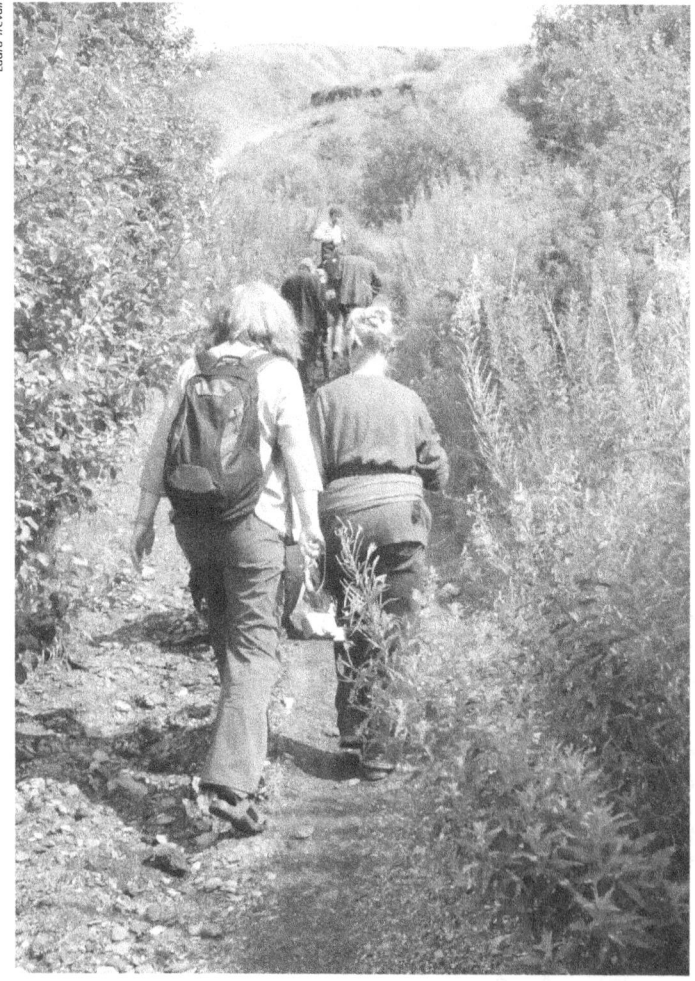

Laura Trevail

Scotland Walk 2, West Lothian – going up to the Niddrie Heart.

VL: What was it that you loved about doing these walks?

BS: I think I loved it because it was doing, and it was real, in two time spans. It was bringing together and it was apparently really interesting to younger artists. It was being in the two places, the past and present. It is really odd walking around London, being in my body, with my total age span, knowing that the world is the way it is now. It's very strange being in my body, being held by this husk of my body, and when I'm feeling very tired the thing that gets me going again is when I'm telling the story and where there's a reciprocal interest in receiving it.

VL: It's really interesting that this very active, performative piece 'I AM AN ARCHIVE' came out of looking at these static bits of past, the actual archive. I think these two competing forces come together so that you have created something that's alive and active.

BS: Well this is why I called my Arnolfini exhibition 'Beyond the Acid Free', because I wanted it to not go into the acid free and be dead, and in the studio I make the static into the alive. Though I haven't spent enough time on that as yet.

Officially in the art world the APG and its activities were suppressed, and that's why there was never this material put out about us. People looking up and researching APG tell me they couldn't find anything. It wasn't until it got to the archive at Tate that it has started to become more widely known, as before it only would have existed in the artists' own archives or files.

VL: How did you feel about the work you were doing with APG in terms of documenting it at the time?

BS: My sense at the time was, I suppose, very much that it was a continuous performance, it was an assemblage from the assemblages that I made out of people and my actions. It became a social sculpture. Though I don't like to use this term as it has its Beuysian origins. It has been adopted by Shelly Sachs at Oxford Brookes with her Social Sculpture programme there.

VL: Was there a different sense of the relationship between the present and the past at that time to what there might be now?

BS: I think at that time I was very much in the present and in the future. I would look at a bit of history. I did want to do a West

Country walk based on my earliest memories and where I grew up. I had the last bit of the war as a kid. There'd be times my father would be asked to go to meet with Churchill – as a kind of advisor. He'd arrived home in a taxi pretty spaced out, because Churchill could drink anyone under the table. I remember my sister and I would fight for the cigar stubs in the morning. So I had history in me and I've got a chunky piece of history in Devon with dance and the Ballet Russe at Dartington Hall. I stayed in Devon with my grandparents when I had rheumatic fever as a child and was sent to dance classes to make me strong. When I was doing APG, I met Whitney Straight who was the son of the Elmhirsts who started Dartington. One of the places I wanted to get involved with APG was the Post Office and Whitney Straight was the Chief Executive, who supported an APG feasibility study with the Post Office.

But, all these stories are what actually happened. At the time I was doing it. Now there's all sorts of research assistance, and at the time there were no arts and humanities departments to support my activity. I was putting one foot in front of other and getting into new contexts and then having to deal with that context. I wouldn't be conscious of being historic, although history was one of my best subjects at school.

VL: What is the difference between approaching the archive through the APG pieces of paper that are now at Tate, and doing the 'I AM AN ARCHIVE'?

BS: Well the difference is in the doing 'I AM AN ARCHIVE', I utilise a lot of the stuff that's in the Tate. Like at the Alnolfini where I used the leftover files from the APG archive as part of the performance.

VL: Can you define the difference between the APG archive and John Latham's archive at Flat Time House?

BS: There's been a difference drawn between the practice, APG and John's work and ideas. It's the latter which is at Flat Time House. Because John did a lot of the written material on APG, it is heavily influenced by his use of language and his ideas of time base and his ideas on art and science. But people automatically thought that John was APG they didn't realise he didn't conceive the idea.

VL: In putting your APG archive in an institutional context, can

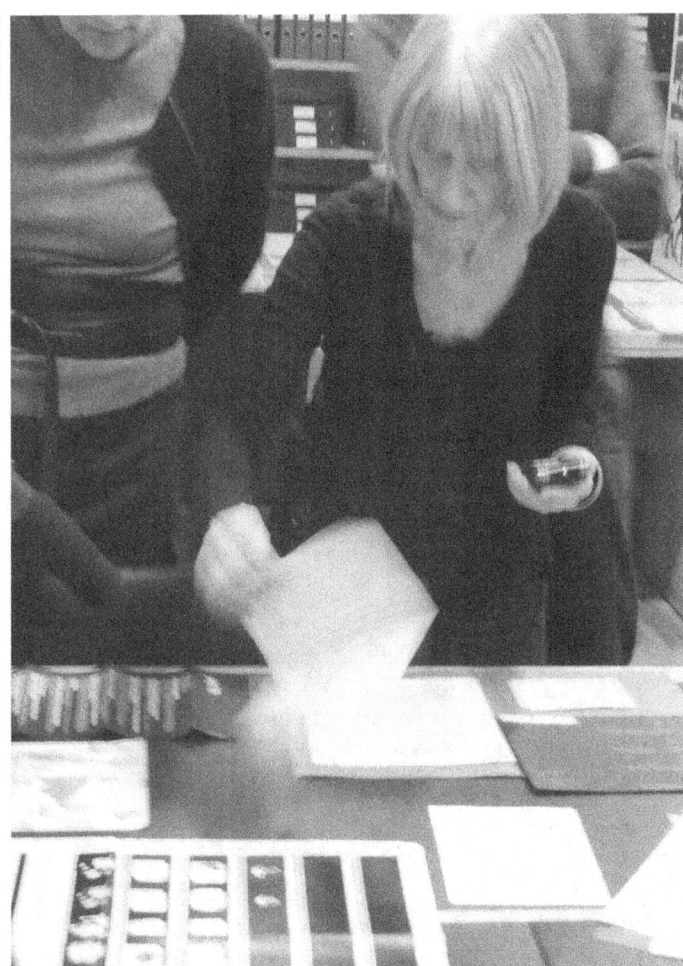

Barbara takes participants of the final walk, Westminster Walk 2, through some of the documents in 'APG World' at the Tate archive.

you explain what it means when it is transferred from the private to the public?

BS: The professional to the personal, in relation to archive, is very obscure. It is constantly being reviewed by me all the time because I've made my life a work.

VL: It's interesting that people assumed John Latham was the APG. What else has been suppressed by history that is revealed in the archive?

BS: Anthony Hudek, who was a Research Fellow at Flat Time House, started to draw out where the practice was with APG and my role in running it, and where John put his ideas across into the APG placement. There's a point at which I stop being Barbara Latham and I become Barbara Steveni. In Berlin, 1977 it was commented on that I was the only woman on the platform, so I suddenly called myself Barbara Steveni, and I realised that I'd hidden myself behind the letters APG. I mean, I hadn't noticed that I had, it was an unconscious suppression. At that time, all the artists associated with the APG were men. I had suggested Marie Yates, for the Peterlee Placement, and then there was Anna Ridley who was in the BBC so they were in there but not on the recognised level of the men. When I started doing the walks I wanted to track the gender differences involved in being an artist at that time, especially those who, like me, were women artists living with male artists, like Felicity Sparrow [Ian Breakwell's wife] and Caroline Coon. I've got more stories to tell in little chunks, which are to do with the women at the time. I was incredibly naïve in, you might say, in terms of gender politics and left–right politics. I was just going ahead and doing it.

In working on the exhibition for Raven Row, in 2012, on the APG, I am questioning where do I lie in all this, where was the art, where was my art? And I feel very much like an assemblage, because that's what I did, I put pieces together and I performed and made something.

VL: So, for you, what is the future of the archive?

BS: Well, this is heavy because it's all about being dead. The future of the archive is, I hope, that it will be an active resource.

VL: What hints or tips would you give for other artists who are starting a negotiation with an institution for their archive?

BS: I would tell them they need to work out what would they like their archive to do and for whom. It's actually the same questions I would ask when going into any institution or doing a placement – what is the context? What is the motivation I have for a placement there? What is the motivation of that hosting organisation to receive it? Is there any fusion of appropriately motivated endeavour from which something can happen from the placement of an archive here, for both parties concerned? I think those are the questions to be asked about doing anything at all, otherwise you're contaminating the planet, aren't you?

And another thing is, why are we digitising all these things and keeping all these things and for what? To just digress into a story, I was at a dinner and sitting next to a man who ran a firm that buried nuclear waste in the Alps. When he heard about my practice, he thought artists might have a good idea of what design or icon or mark should be put on this nuclear waste so that whoever was coming afterwards would not get contaminated and harmed! (Creatures from another planet?!) I feel this relates to archives, what are we doing with our archives, what are we keeping and what are we not keeping, and what can the planet hold?

VL: That's very interesting; because it's about how and what society is deciding to keep and what we choose to forget. Going back to the start of our interview I wanted to ask how you perceived your archive, both your personal archive and the APG archive, before the Tate asked you for it.

BS: I wasn't looking at it. One just knew stuff was there, taking up all this space, and it wasn't in any order. So it hadn't been thought of with the word 'archive' attached to it at all.

VL: What word was attached to it?

BS: Nothing! It was just all this stuff! It's detritus or stuff and some of it isn't even a document, it is some ashes left over from book burning, for example. So it was nothing. Before the word 'archive' came in and people from institutions conjured up the word 'archive' for it, because it now is a funding stream, nobody had thought about it. I certainly hadn't and John hadn't either.

ARTISTS AND ARCHIVES: A CORRESPONDENCE

6

The following letters continue a correspondence between the artists Uriel Orlow and Ruth Maclennan that had a starting point in their mutual interest in the archive and which was published in their book Re: the archive, the image and the very dead sheep.[1] *The new letters continue their interrogation of the position of the artist in relation to the archive.*

Dear Ruth

Since our conversation the other day I've been thinking about what got me interested in archives and the archival. Apart from my first brush with systematic accumulation as an avid collector of numerous useless things such as erasers, bells etc. when I was a child, I also remember that my first studio was a bit like an archival ante-chamber of organised junk. But it wasn't until later, when I was asked to accompany a film-maker friend of mine on a trip to archives in Germany, that I began to think of them more consciously. My friend was writing a script about Herschel Grynszpan, the Jewish boy who shot a German embassy official in Paris in November 1938, in exasperation at the news of the deportation of his family from Germany to Poland.[2] Because I understand German, French and Yiddish, my friend asked me to co-ordinate and lead the research at various archives in Germany. We visited archives in Hanover, where Herschel's family lived; the photo and film archive in Koblenz; and various departments of the Bundesarchiv in Berlin. My role was strange in that I was facilitating someone else's research rather than doing my own. This meant that I was focused on procedural aspects of navigating catalogues and ordering documents but I also had to locate relevant information in them. What struck me while doing this research was the level of detail preserved – we saw taxi and dry-cleaner receipts from the murdered, minor embassy official. We also came across a number of documents that hadn't been consulted since 1945, some of which had only recently joined the archive from the former GDR [Deutsche Demokratische Republik]. Not working academically, I began to think about our roles as witnesses of these documents and about the sheer materiality of the collections, beyond the specific information its documents contain. How are we to imagine or comprehend such a collection, if the extent of its size and subject matter exceeds our grasp? Indeed,

1 Uriel Orlow and Ruth Maclennan, *Re: the archive, the image and the very dead sheep*, London: School of Advanced Study/The National Archives/Double Agents, 2004

2 This was the first deportation and was organised in haste, as a response to an ultimatum set by the Polish government which threatened to strip all Polish nationals living abroad of their nationality. Herschel's desperate and impulsive act of revenge was of course construed by the Nazis as part of a conspiracy and used as the pretext for the already planned November pogrom, the so-called Kristallnacht, which a few days later saw synagogues and Jewish shops all over Germany go up in flames.

what is the meaning and status of the archive as a whole, operating as it does like a memorial behind closed doors? And how do we engage with the dialectics of documents with seemingly pointless detail and others with huge historical or emotional significance? Historians and other academics that use archives for their research have developed strategies to deal with these questions. But beyond the specificity of a research project, the questions remain largely unanswered, waiting for a different approach, an entrance through the back door of the archive, as it were… Perhaps this is where artists come in. The freedom from pursuing specific research in the archive allows the foregrounding of other, material and conceptual aspects of the archive. But then again, every time I do go to an archive, even if my focus is the archival itself, I get drawn to the documents, to browsing the catalogue and letting myself be directed by associations, which often produce the most amazing constellations, where, for an instant, things connect in the strangest and most meaningful ways. Perhaps this associative principle is what is at work in artworks in general – and so the archive operates both as a model and as a prompter for art.

Uriel

Dear Uriel

It is great to receive your letter and to feel the beginnings of a new correspondence. As I read about your first encounter with the archive, I am reminded of my first encounter with what retrospectively has become an archive. Just after I graduated from university, I went on a trip to Western Siberia with a group of five Cambridge students and our teacher. We joined academics and students from the University of Sverdlovsk (now Ekaterinburg again, its Tsarist name, and the site of the execution of the last Tsar and his family). In exchange for bringing an enormous computer for the history department, they took us with them on an archaeographic expedition to Old Believers' villages in remote areas of Western Siberia. The word 'archaeographic' is a transliteration of a Russian word that doesn't exist in English, but which certainly has a ring to it, and draws together many of the strands that we discussed in our book.[3]

This field trip, expedition, ethnographic survey, scavenge, was an annual event when twenty or so students and faculty would pile into an armoured truck and drive out into the wilderness to set up camp and do hands-on research and conservation work with Old

3 Orlow and Maclennan, op. cit.

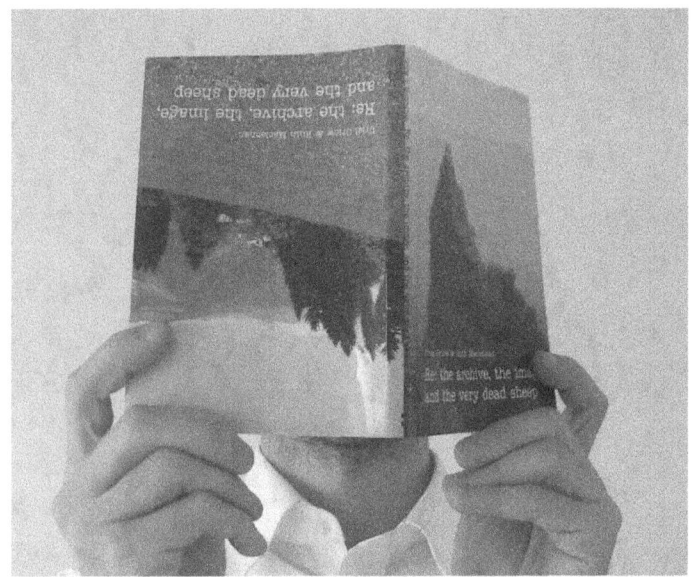

Re: the archive, the image and the very dead sheep, Uriel Orlow and Ruth Maclennan, published by Double agents, London, 2004

Believers. We would meet with an elder of one of the Old Believer sects and find out who had died, and who was still around in the village. The purpose was to establish whether the deceased, or the near-deceased, had left any religious books that could be given to the University's collection, to be preserved and studied, and saved from thieves or from the children and grandchildren who might sell the books, thus committing a mortal sin. For Old Believers' devotional books and manuscripts are passed down the generations, and are the sacred foundation of worship. They are even more important than icons, in that they are the means of communicating and preserving a religion which has few if any churches, no priests, no seminaries, and no official, formal means of teaching and keeping alive its doctrines and traditions.[4]

By 1991, there weren't many Old Believers left in Western Siberia; we made it our business to track them down and help them with small amounts of money and food, in return for relieving them of their books in order to preserve them for posterity. Was it a fair exchange? One seventeenth-century illuminated manuscript, two early printed Bibles from the eighteenth century, and half a dozen nineteenth-century texts, for a couple of tins of tushonka (tinned beef), a tin of condensed milk and the knowledge that their books would be poured over by academics and students for years to come, and their religion would not be completely forgotten.

On this expedition I used a video camera for the first time. It was lent to me by a keen BBC cameraman who asked me to take

4 The Old Believers originate in a schism in the Russian Orthodox Church in the seventeenth century, following reforms to Church ritual and texts. Those who refused to accept the innovations became known as the Old Believers. There are numerous sects, some with only a handful of worshippers. Persecuted under the tsars and then under Stalin, many of them ended up in Siberia, working in Peter the Great's steel factories or living as subsistence farmers.

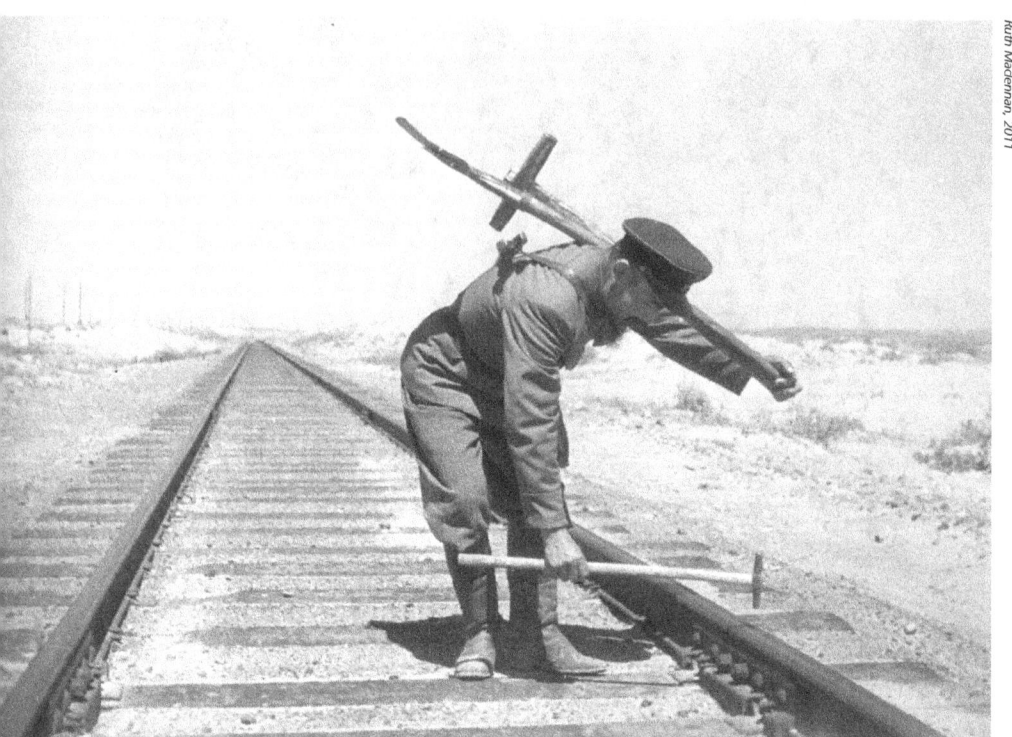

Ruth Maclennan, 2011

lots of footage that could go into their archive, and might be used for some future story. I filmed several old women, a few of their grandchildren, some scenes of izbas and rural dilapidation. Many of my subjects had never even seen a photographic camera. I had the strange and disturbing feeling – which I've also read about – of being a cause of the destruction of their way of life; that filming them in their traditional clothes, posing for the camera, or hiding behind a glass door, or singing psalms, was turning their precarious lives into a performance, an image of a way of life that vanished as soon as it was fixed. At the same time, their way of life was pretty tough, and perhaps wasn't worth preserving. Much of what I saw and heard wasn't picturesque, just grim.

This journey to Siberia is very important to me, to the story I tell myself of my life, and more nebulously perhaps, to my work, to the way I think and see and put things down. There is a tension between the idea of Siberia and the physical reality of being there. We camped, sleeping three to a two-person tent, cooking cabbage and potatoes for twenty, fighting the mutant mosquitoes and hornets. We drove long distances along impassable roads, in an armoured truck designed to resist chemical attack. One felt lost in

From the series 'The Railway Workers', anonymous archival photographs from the State Documentary Film and Audio Archive of Kazakhstan, 1939–61 the unencompassable hugeness of the land. The Old Believers carried on practising their faith, despite every obstacle, and despite the fact that there were hardly any other believers to practice with them, and yet they were still persecuted, despite barely existing, stranded – or rooted – in this vast landscape, cut off from the rest of the country.

This is a digression that has taken me back to the archive. My interest in the archive and the archival derives from this experience of the archival in extremis: the Old Believers' near extinction and the preservation of their culture in their stories and their manuscripts; the deep connection between geography (on a big and small scale) and the archive. Geography here means the way the landscape affects the stuff of the archive – the people who make it, the way things are stored, the way stories are told, the way they are forgotten, and the way they are put back together again for someone else to read and interpret.

Our new correspondence I think takes us beyond the book, beyond our experiences of the familiar landscapes of our childhoods, and our daily lives, and into other places. Perhaps this is important to us now because of the work we each are doing in Kazakhstan and in Nigeria.

Ruth

Dear Ruth

It's wonderful but also chilling to read about your extra-archival experience in Siberia. Your account points to the other side of the materiality of the archive I was describing in my first letter, namely the archival in the world at large. To be sure, the dialectics of storage and retrieval and the master-discourse of classification operate in an altogether more opaque manner out there; histories are stored in oral testimony, dilapidated buildings, mould-infested books, and the landscape itself is a document waiting to be consulted. On the one hand, these archival ephemera elude the domiciliation or house arrest that for Derrida defines the archive: documents being localised and given a guardian.[5] Yet, on the other hand, in their non-intentionality they operate exactly like archival documents: they are unpublished, raw traces of life which were never expected to be read out of their original context, in the archival realm.[6] Sophie Calle following unknowing strangers and recording their every move creates an instant archive of the everyday (for example in *Suite Vénitienne*). Mark Dion's *Thames Dig* retrieved from the

5   Jacques Derrida, *Archive Fever*, trans. by Eric Prenowitz, Chicago: Chicago University Press, 1996, p.2

6   Arlette Farge, *Le goût de l'archive*, Paris: Editions du Seuil, 1989, p.12

Uriel Orlow, 2010

From the series 'The Bitterlake Chronicles'; document by Horst Wagner, 1967

river outside the Tate Modern a heap full of unintentional documents, a lost-property cabinet of curiosities, ranging from bicycles to sets of false teeth. The artist and the archaeologist seem to share an insatiable curiosity and sense of adventure. Like the pre-archival documents they attempt to read and retrieve, both artist and archaeologist are exposed to the elements. Arlette Farge, in her book *Le goût de l'archive*, describes working with archives as a rendezvous with the sea or extreme weather conditions: a dive into immeasurable depths, the joy of immersion, the fear of drowning...[7]

Think of Tacita Dean's epic archaeology/archivology of Donald Crowhurst's failed circumnavigation of the globe without stopping in 1969, her documents being the sea itself, the stranded trimaran, the logbooks. There is no space here to describe any of these works further so I might as well give myself over to the list, that oldest

7 Arlette Farge, *Le goût de l'archive*, Paris: Editions du Seuil, 1989, p.10

form of collecting (words) and describing collections (property): Bernd and Hilla Becher's water-tower photographs, Peter Greenaway's 'Physical Self', Gerhard Richter's *Atlas* are all strategic collections, retrieving non-documents, digging for unmined sources. Another list would include Christian Boltanski's and the Atlas Group's pseudo-archives, or Michael Landy's anti-archive *Break Down* which creates an inventory of destruction rather than preservation.

I am beginning to imagine an über-archive of archival artworks and wonder what its organisational principles might be: artists' collections, artists' histories, artists' classifications, artists' meta-archives, artists' anti-archives, artists' invisible collections… The list could go on endlessly.

Uriel

Dear Uriel

Your last letter brings up many thoughts about why artists are lured by the archive and its effects. The works you describe point to the age-old question of the relation between an artist's life and the art works that she makes. It is almost banal to refer to this art-historical truism, and I don't wish to analyse the psychology of any of the artists you list. I can't speak for anyone else, but my feeling is that the power of the archival for artists lies in this tension between matter and meaning: does the stuff that I accumulate mean anything, and how much control can I, or do I want to, have over that meaning? The archival document is a seductive metaphor for an object/fragment/trace that is not yet (and may never be) an art object, or an art idea. Artists are surrounded by potential things that carry meanings which they may or may not put to use in a context that will endow them with many other meanings, through association, and make them art. The artist senses the power to choose to make meaning out of the seemingly random thing that she encounters. As you say, the archival carries within it the idea of space, and placement within it, which is so important to artists, particularly since they have had more control over placement after the separation of art from cult. And since Dada and then Minimalism, Fluxus and conceptual art, the context has become more and more important in the making of the work as well as the reception of it.

But more important than the analogy between the archival document and the stuff with which the artist works, I think the archive is a central component of the ambivalence that artists can feel towards making things at all, and situating them in the world at large, and within their own story of their life and work. At some point in their life artists usually confront, and answer in their own way, the following questions: "Why add anything more to the already overburdened culture?" And, "Why produce more stuff, which is going to become a commodity and lose all its original, critical meaning?" And then there is the urge to clear the decks, to destroy old work, to destroy the archive in order to start afresh and be free of one's past works and the future they seem to determine. Michael Landy's *Break Down* is perhaps the most systematic and consistent work to enact this desire and evoke the pathos and liberation of the destruction. But other artists have destroyed their work only to be reborn as a different kind of artist altogether. This need to destroy the archive in order to start again is felt by other people too (with sometimes radical results: emigration, changed identities, or the more routine divorce or plastic surgery), but with the artist's destruction of artwork, the archive is being directly invoked.

I didn't mean to end with artists destroying the archive. But perhaps I've arrived here because it is the most dramatic encounter of art with the archive. The deliberate destruction of the archive has very dangerous connotations as far as politics and history are concerned, but that is dealt with elsewhere. And with the Old Believers it is they themselves who disappear as their archive comes into existence – not the cause of their demise, but the testament to it. Within art however, to destroy the archive can be a more subtle, playful or radical experiment, a means of disrupting orders and plans, beliefs and expectations (in the audience, and in the artist herself). There is of course always the chance that the phoenix won't rise again from the flames, but the thrill is in the risk.

Ruth

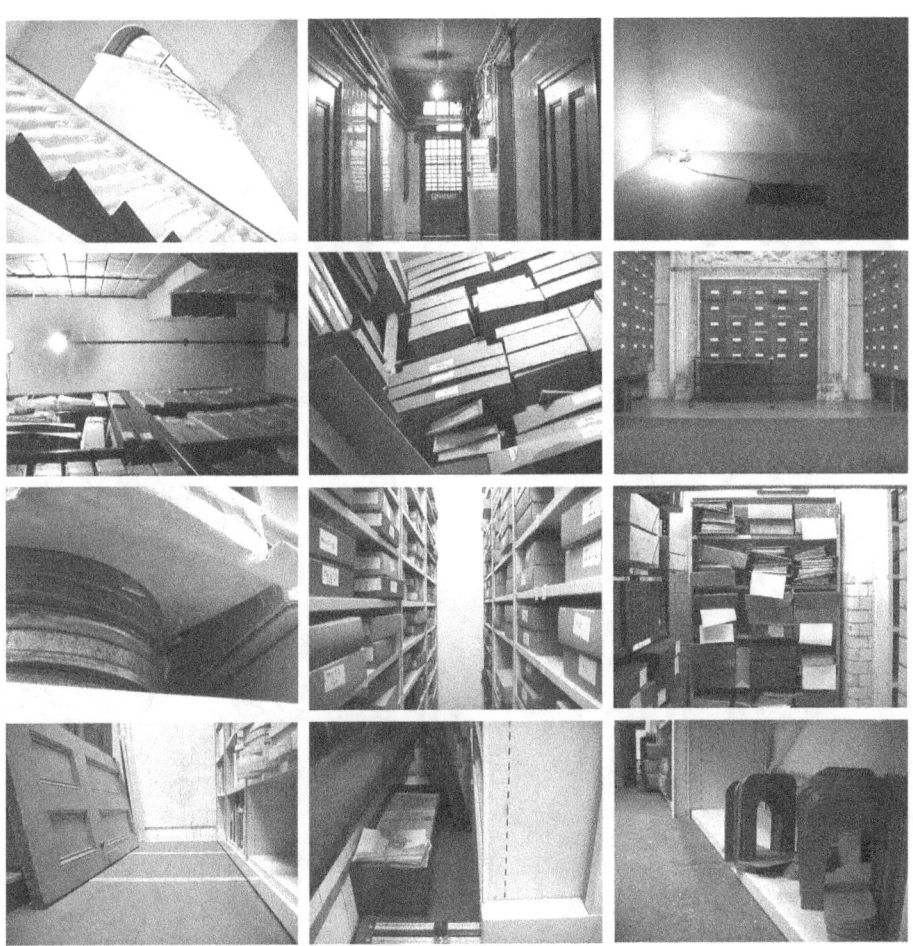

Uriel Orlow, Inside the
Archive, 2005–7

THE ARTIST IN THE ARCHIVE: FREDERICO CÂMARA

Victoria Lane

7

In 2006, I was introduced to the artist Frederico Câmara who was starting a fellowship at the Henry Moore Institute in Leeds, where I was the archivist.[1] The Institute hosted a steady stream of curators, academics and artists, all of whom had an interest in the history and practice of sculpture. As a general rule, I would introduce visitors to the archive collections by presenting parts that related to their interest in sculpture. Sometimes researchers became fascinated with what might seem to an outsider to be the esoteric props of the archivist's trade: the white cotton or latex gloves, the cushions for resting documents on or the weights used to hold down unwieldy drawings that have been rolled up for many years. But Frederico made a request that had not been asked before. He had not come to explore the contents of the collections or discuss the nature of archives with me and was already certain of his agenda. He quietly asked me if I would allow him to take photographs inside the strong room of the archive.

This might not sound controversial. However, for an archivist to let anybody who is not a designated keyholder across the threshold of the archive store is against normal practice. The strong room is a highly secure place, a modern equivalent of the medieval common chest. The latter had a complex set of keys and locks that could only be opened when the selected keyholders were all present. In a similar way, the documents that the archive store contains are usually unique and need to be protected in a supine state with steady environmental conditions that prevent fire, decay, dust, dirt, infestation and theft. Policies and procedures stipulate and protect who may go into the space of the store – usually only the archivist(s), director and a buildings manager. There are also measures in place that involve systems of locks with several keys or with codes only known to the chosen few. What Frederico had asked for was a security risk: not only did it involve being let inside the sanctified space, it also meant he would document it and possibly show these pictures in public.

What was it that Frederico wanted to photograph in the strong room and why? It is a space that he would have to request permission to enter and to occupy under supervision. This type of criteria starts to define the place's characteristics. It is a hidden and

1 During this period, Penelope Curtis was the Curator of the Henry Moore Institute where she instigated a programme of fellowships. These could focus on any aspect of sculpture but were unusual in that they included the archive collection as part of their potential scope. She actively encouraged the use of the archive in both traditional ways through research but also through non-traditional routes with its use by artists.

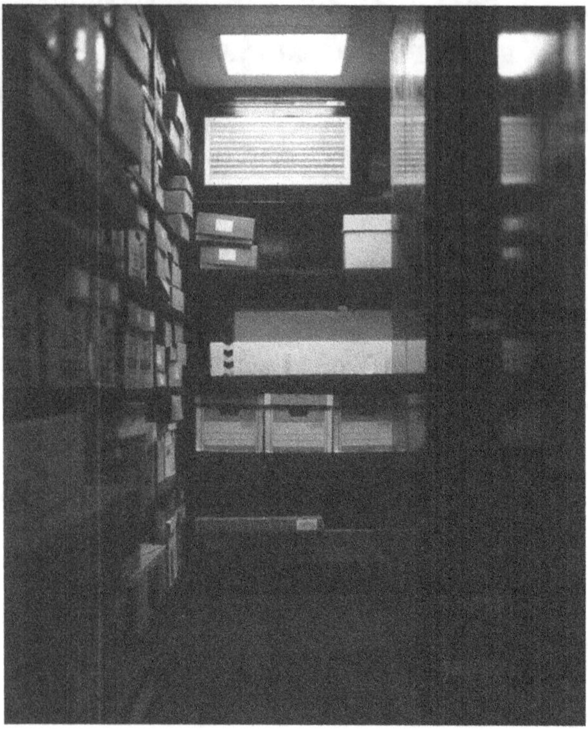

Photograph, 120 cm x 150 cm, 2006; © Frederico Câmara

Figure 1: Archive, Henry Moore Institute, Leeds, UK

isolated space containing material which is formally presented in public – in the gallery or reading room. In many ways it is a kind of non-space, generally unseen, in which the locked-up items play a silent waiting game, sitting in readiness to be chosen. Or it could be viewed as an 'off-stage' room, concealing precious artifacts in a behind-the-scenes mysteriousness. Frederico's request drew attention to the actual space of the strong room and questioned what it was and how it functioned.

This was part of a wider project that Frederico was undertaking, to photograph any type of store in museums and archives. During his fellowship at HMI he not only produced images of the archive strong room but also the sculpture stores and libraries. The photographs have an exquisite and haunting beauty. What is seemingly banal, such as sets of boxes on shelves, is reinvented through his imaging of the spaces (Figure 1). Empty of humans they become dramatic stage sets that seem to suggest that an incident of pathos has just occurred or is about to happen. They become spaces which invite the viewer to project their own narratives onto the photographs. The image of the abandoned library is a store without function (Figure 2). All the books have

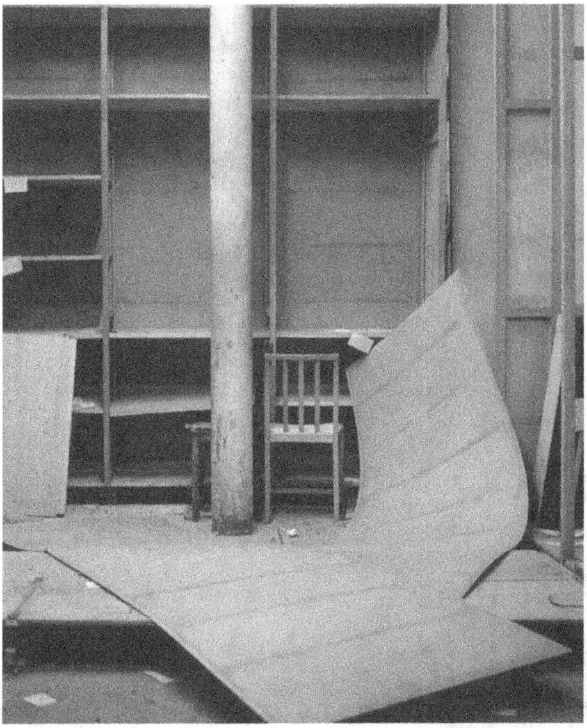

Figure 2: Vanitas: Old Library, Leeds Art Gallery, UK

Photograph, 120 cm x 150 cm, 2006; © Frederico Câmara

gone and it is empty, appearing as if it has been harshly dismembered in the process so that knowledge seems to have been violently done away with. Frederico's photograph reinvents the accident of a broken, disused store into something that takes on a carefully planned installation and a site of anticipation.

The figuring of these spaces in Frederico's photographs recalls Foucault's theory of heterotopias, which are counter-sites that attempt to represent the unreal vision of utopia whilst simultaneously contesting and inverting the ideal realm.[2] Foucault posits that utopic spaces do not exist and are unreal, and contrasts them with heterotopic spaces, which are real spaces that combine with the mythic qualities of utopia. This could find its parallel in archival theory where the intellectual and physical controls of documents are accepted as two separate but related realms. The intellectual control of documents is the description of the ideal arrangement of papers in a catalogue and is utopic. It presents an archive in a logical order, either in the given and original order that the papers are presented or, if there is no discernible order, one that the archivist constructs; for example, in a chronological or alphabetical sequence, thus allowing the papers to be searched with

2 Frederico Câmara cited Foucault's 'Of Other Spaces' (Michel Foucault, translated by Jay Miskowiec, 'Of Other Spaces', *Diacritics*, Vol.16, No. 1, Spring 1986, pp.22–7) as an influence in a conversation with Jo Longhurst at Pavilion, Leeds in relation to his commission there, *In an Ideal World* (17th March – 30th April 2010, see: http://www.pavilion.org.uk/pavilion.php?pid=119).

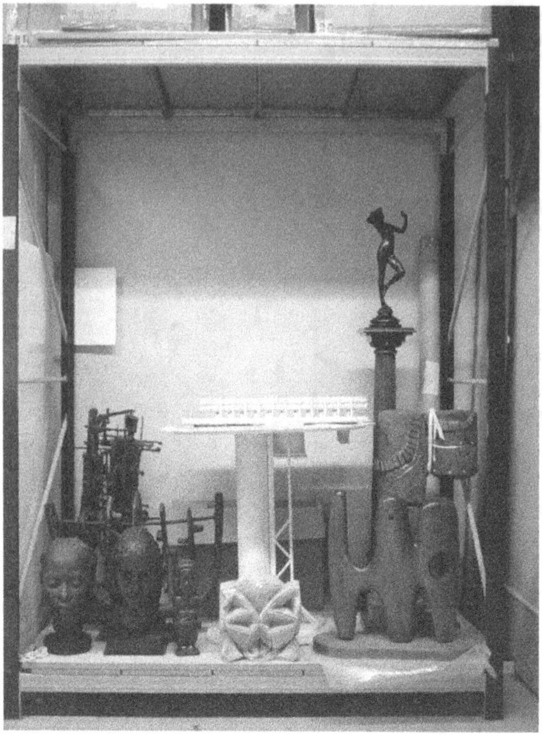

Photograph, 120 cm x 150 cm, 2006; © Frederico Cámara

Figure 3: Vanitas: Sculpture Store, Henry Moore Institute, Leeds, UK

fluidity. The physical control of archives is something altogether messier and real which does not simply reflect the model of intellectual controls. The physical control of archives involves how each item, folder and box sits on the shelves and is tied to the pragmatics of the size of items and space available. Very often items which appear as part of a series in a catalogue might not sit next to each other on a shelf because one might be a large bound volume and the next item might be a tiny piece of paper. Therefore items with no other similarity than their size might get placed on the same shelf. The physical controls of archives are located in the archive store and this, as is the case with all museums and archive stores, is a heterotopic space.

In Foucault's terms, archives, like museums and libraries, are examples of heterotopias as they are spaces that exhibit a "perpetual and indefinite accumulation of time in an immobile place".[3] The store is neither here nor there; accessible only to certain people, inaccessible to most; it is an in-between space. Heterotopias are also "capable of juxtaposing in a single real place several spaces, several sites that in themselves are incompatible."[4] In the archive store, for example, a nineteenth-century, right-wing sculptor's

3 Foucault, op. cit., p.26

4 Ibid., p.25

papers might sit alongside those of a twentieth-century artist with communist leanings. The neutrality of the territory of the store contains all competing, contrary and similar subjects and people and puts them into an accidental and irrational relationship with each other through their coexistence in the space. This is what Frederico represents within his images of these places.

The context of the museum store makes this principle of heterotopia more obviously manifest as the objects are not confined to boxes. Different cultures, times and types of object become a microcosm of the subject and Frederico's image of the sculpture store (Figure 3) enacts the heterotopic through framing the bizarre accidents of placement on the shelves. The muddle and jumble of the store comes to the fore. Modernist pieces are placed next to portrait sculptures with their heads bowed; leaving the viewer to make sense of these relationships or provide the narrative or suggest the unexpected metaphors. In the gallery space, the curated vision would never allow such random associations of disassociation. In the archive, the anonymous character of the boxes belie the content and even then most of the content has to be carefully studied and examined to bring its potential fully to light. Some of Frederico's images of other store rooms (figures 4 and 5) focus on the ordered

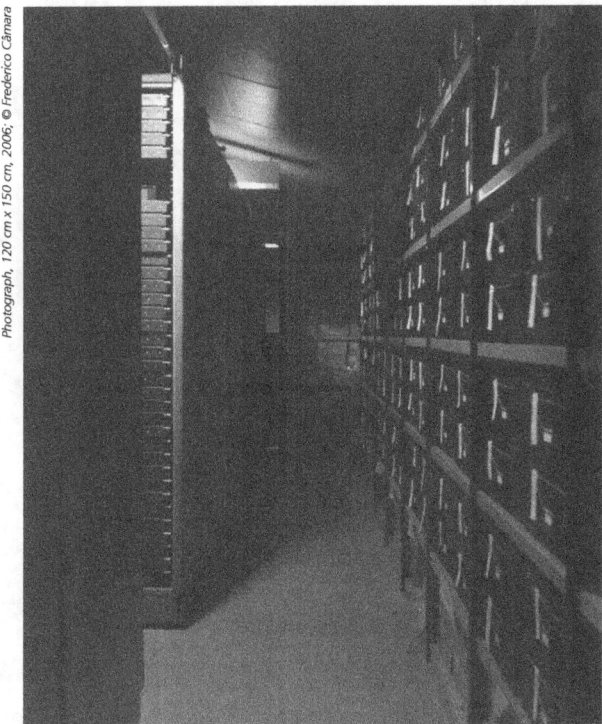

Figure 4: Yeaden Museum Resource Centre, Leeds, UK

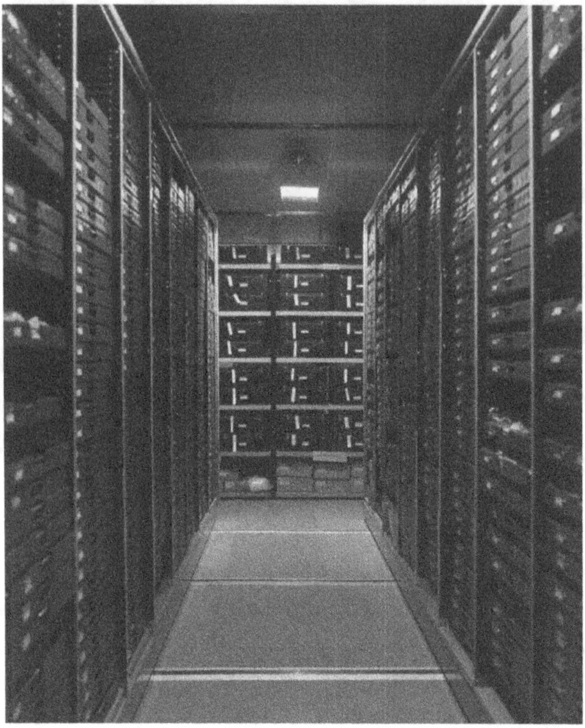

Photograph, 120 cm x 150 cm, 2006; © Frederico Câmara

Figure 5: Yeaden Museum Resource Centre, Leeds, UK

regularity of these spaces. The dark and regular acid-free boxes parade across the shelves with only the label to indicate what might be inside. Boxes upon boxes are draped in Hitchcockian lighting, giving a sinister framing, evocative of a secret Stasi-like archive which controls through order.

Frederico's photographs are made in a documentary fashion which leads Stephen Feeke to an interpretation in which his work "remains neutral, without passing judgment… he records what he finds there leaving us to respond in whichever way we feel… In fact Câmara talks about his work as reportage and it can have a cool, dispassionate edge."[5] However, through enacting the heterotopic potential of these places, the images are invested with an emotional and aesthetic intensity. The spaces, beautifully framed and exquisitely lit, take on a dramatic tension. Perhaps this feels less like Foucault's real heterotopic space and more like the interior realm of space described by Bachelard?[6] Is it rather the poetics of the heterotopic that Frederico exposes in his images of the spaces of the store; presenting the space between the real and the ideal?

5   Stephen Feeke, 'Beauty and the Beast', at: http://www.frederico camara.com

6   Gaston Bachelard, *The Poetics of Space*, Boston: Beacon Press, 1992

SECTION TWO
Archivists

ALL THAT STUFF!
ORGANISING RECORDS OF CREATIVE PROCESSES
Anna McNally

8

An inquiry around archive[s]... demands an attempt to understand the conditions and circumstance of preservation of material as, and the exclusion of material from, the record as well as attention to the relations of power underpinning such inclusions and exclusions.

Carolyn Hamilton, Verne Harris and Graeme Reid[1]

Using an archive in a reading room is never an unmediated experience, yet very few researchers are aware of the archivist's hand in the process. What happens to an artist's papers, the remnants of a life and work, between leaving the studio and arriving in the reading room in acid-free folders? Although archives are primary sources, they are sources that have been selected, arranged and described by an intermediary. In particular, the type of papers in an artist's archive and the manner in which they arrive have often required more interpretation on the part of the archivist than the catalogue might imply.

Although there are increasing moves to work with artists to organise their own archives, the majority of collections are acquired from an artist's family after his or her death. Even if archivists have been able to work with the artist and their family prior to the death, that doesn't mean the papers arrive in any kind of order. Archives usually arrive in an assortment of carefully labelled boxes, random carrier bags and even old washing-powder packets, depending on how fastidious the person packing them was feeling. Sometimes the acquisition of the collection can be painfully negotiated over a couple of years, particularly if the taxman is involved; at other times, it's a case of a phone call asking if we can pick it up before the house is sold on Friday. Even with their increasing financial value, the archives are understandably the last thing on the family's mind at that time.

That's because, at this stage, archives are not a carefully organised collection – an Archive with a capital A – but whatever you can find in the drawers and cupboards, in an artist's studio and office. They are whatever happens to be leftover from someone's life, usually with a bias towards the end of their life. Researchers often comment on the scarcity of papers documenting an artist's early

1 Hamilton, Harris and Reid, 'Introduction' in C. Hamilton, V. Harris, M. Pickover, G. Reid, R. Saleh and J. Taylor (eds), *Refiguring the Archive*, Kluwer Academic Publishers, 2002, p.9

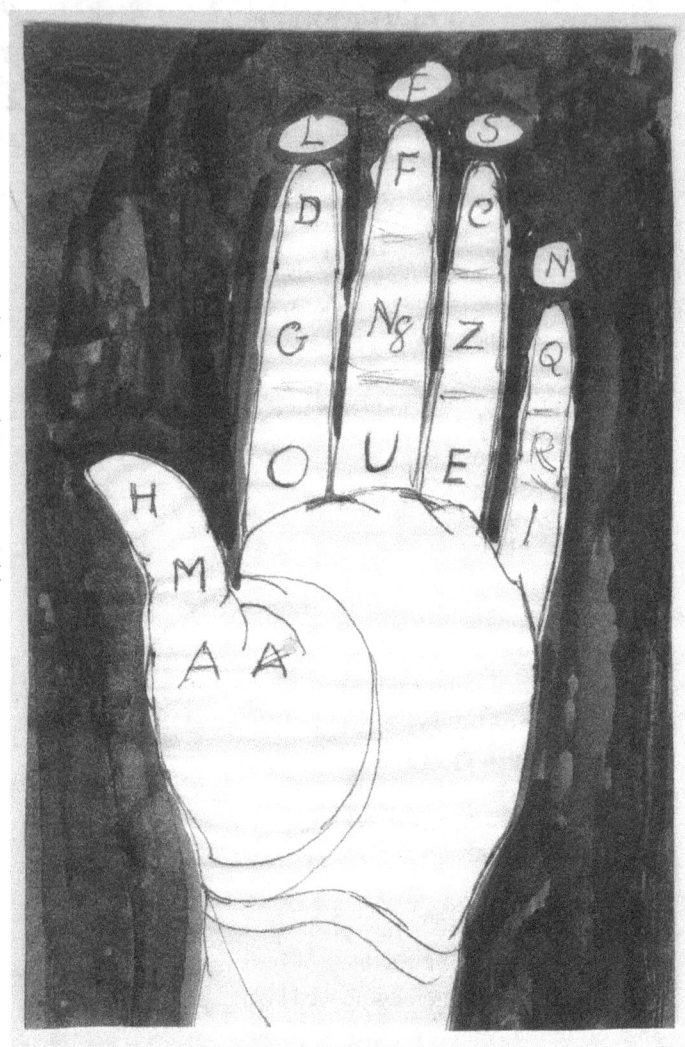

Ithell Colquhoun,
Drawing of a hand

career; but at that time of their life they were often living in rented accommodation, moving around fairly frequently, and inevitably things got lost or didn't seem worth packing up – we all know the temptation to throw previously cherished mementoes into a black bin bag when you're moving house. By the time an artist has made enough money to settle down, buy a house and accumulate, often he or she has passed into the more established, less avant-garde phase of their work and archives tend to tell us more about this time of their life.

There can sometimes be surprisingly little about art in an artist's archives, and a lot about business. Archives are traces of processes and transactions. Artists might do a lot of thinking about art but rarely do they document it. Correspondence with artist friends tends to be more social than theoretical, and that with galleries and museums tend to focus on the practicalities of transporting and paying for works. As a result, artist's personal papers are usually missing the very things that academics are looking for – the moment of inception, the change of style, the formative influence of other artists, the time before they were famous – whilst being rich in shipping invoices.

> The Archive is not potentially made up of everything, as is human memory; and it is not the fathomless and timeless place in which nothing goes away that is the unconscious. The Archive is made from selected and consciously chosen documentation from the past and also from the mad fragments that no one intended to preserve and just ended up there…
>
> Carolyn Steedman[2]

An archive can never be complete, but to say it is lacking items is also to miss the point. An archive is what it is: it is what is left, no more and no less. However, whilst those early moments might be unrecorded, conversely archives usually include documentation of their later life that the artist didn't get around to throwing away. Ingrid Schaffner has said that "the artist's life is a grand archive, in which every discarded receipt, marginal note, or studio scrap might someday be deemed tremendously significant."[3] It might, indeed; but for now it is a pile of papers and, until the archivist has looked through, sorted and described them, such scraps remain unfindable, amongst a wealth of rather less significant remnants of their life. So, where does the archivist begin when they're faced with all this stuff?

Once the material arrives in the archive repository, the first step is to check for mould, creepy crawlies and anything else you'd rather wasn't there. Papers have often been stored in garages and lofts and it's important to quarantine them on arrival so as not to put the rest of the collections at risk. If they don't require any treatment then the cataloguing process can begin in earnest with a thorough look through the collection. Most artists' personal papers consist of a combination of letters (received), photographs (of their work, of themselves, of unidentified people), sketches, any writings they might have drafted or published (autobiographies, articles, dubious poetry), printed materials about themselves or their interests. There might also be papers relating to projects they've been involved with (Naum Gabo's archive includes both

2   Carolyn Steedman, *Dust*, Manchester University Press, 2001, p.68

3   Ingrid Schaffner, 'Deep Storage', *Frieze*, issue 23, Jun–Aug 1995

theatre and product design, for example) or their wider interests and influences (Ithell Colquhoun's papers document her extensive occult studies).

Archivists need to have a good knowledge of the artist's work to understand the potential significance of what they find but, as the first person to look at the papers, you are also often seeing previously unknown elements of their life. Archives often contain documentation of projects that either never quite got off the ground or were never seen to fruition. In this case, there is nothing in the external, real world that relates to the documentation and you can only work from internal evidence – a file title (but what if the folder had been re-used?), an annotation on a drawing (is that a date or a telephone number, scribbled down when the sketch was close at hand?), a chance reference in correspondence. As you work through the boxes, items that had seemed unimportant or inexplicable at first glance can suddenly begin to make sense.

This process of 'appraisal' gives you a chance to start thinking about how to arrange the collection, but also what you're going to keep. Although everything has a potential research value, this has to be weighed against the cost of preserving it forever, bearing in mind the financial and environmental burden of a climate-controlled strong room. Archives continue to accumulate and every year they require more space. There are some things in a collection that are just never going to be looked at by anyone, and so there is no point in keeping them.

There are no hard and fast rules about this. It's something that you have to develop a professional feeling for, and is very much dependent on the archive. For example, if there is one unpaid dry-cleaning bill in an archive, dated three months before the artist died, then you're probably going to throw it away. If the artist had lived a little longer he probably would have thrown it away himself. But if there are 30 years of unpaid bills in a person's archive then this really tells you something about their character and it's worth keeping at least a representative selection of them. A good archivist would never dispose of something just because they didn't know what it is; but you have to consider whether it really evidences or demonstrates anything.

Although controversial, this process is really a service to the researcher, reducing the sheer quantity of paper they have to wade through for little reward; but it has the unconscious side effect of making everything else in the archive gain a little more prestige. From this moment, all items in the collection appear to have been carefully selected when actually it's just that they weren't thrown

FROM
HENRY MOORE, HOGLANDS, PERRY GREEN, MUCH HADHAM, HERTS.
MUCH HADHAM 66

8523/12/143

23rd.December.1948.

Dear Michael,

Thank you for your very nice
Christmas card and the invitation on
it to come to lunch one day when I'm
in London, – which I'll be only too
delighted to do.

I'm not likely to come to London
much now until the New Year so I'll
drop a p.c. or ring up early in 1949.

Hope you both have a very Happy
Christmas and a good 1949.

Yours ever, Henry.

away. It is also the case that we'd never throw away any drawing by an artist, even if it's just a doodle, so it's the practical side of their life that disappears and tends to leave them looking as if they ate, drank and slept Art, lessening the picture of them as ordinary human beings. Archivists try not to predict research interests but inevitably end up privileging the biographer over the thematic research – and hoping that no-one ever gets funding for a PhD titled 'Artists and Dry-cleaners: an awkward relationship, 1940–1970'.

Printed notecard from Henry Moore to Michael Ayrton, accepting his invite to lunch, 23rd December 1948

…I walked into the archive with all the trepidation of the academic apprentice, worried that I would never penetrate the secrets of the archive, and worse that the secrets of the archive were impenetrable not because of the daring originality of my line of research but because of my fundamental ignorance of the archival structure of the conditions of historical knowledge.

Nicholas B Dirks[4]

4   Nicholas B. Dirks, 'Annals of the archive: Ethnographic notes on the sources of history' in B.K. Axel (ed.), *From the Margins: Historical anthropology and its futures*, Duke University Press, 2002, p.47

After sorting through the papers and removing anything he or she has decided not to keep, the archivist can then start to arrange the collection in a meaningful way. The key concept in archival theory is 'original order', which holds that an archive shouldn't be re-arranged in such a way as to lose its original context. So, if the papers in a file have been arranged in date order, you wouldn't re-arrange the contents by correspondent, or re-distribute their contents across a number of new thematic files. The order tells the researcher how the file's creator (either a person or an organisation) used the information, however inconvenient it might prove for their own enquiries. The theory of original order works well with the records of an organisation but in practice is often meaningless when it comes to personal papers. Few artists have their correspondence in any kind of order, let alone their sketches.

If you're lucky, when the boxes arrive at the archive they might have some note of where the papers within were found – "2nd drawer study", for example – but this is rare. The archivist of personal papers must proceed with caution and not re-arrange anything physically until confident that any interrelationships between the items are understood. This is why we don't like to let researchers look at an archive until it is catalogued, in case they disturb any order that is there but not immediately apparent.

If there is no discernible original order in the papers then the aim is to arrange them in a meaningful manner that reflects the context of their creation and/or for ease of use by researchers. This means that similar items are grouped together by theme (such as the working papers for a book) or by format (for example, photographs). This is rarely easy because artists tend to have messy lives and even trying to separate the personal and professional can involve some rather arbitrary decisions. While cataloguing Ithell Colquhoun's papers[5], I had to decide which drawings were artworks and which were occult diagrams, always being aware that most researchers will see the catalogue as authoritative and treat an item according to the category the archivist has placed it in. The cataloguing process does not allow for uncertainty or indecision.

Ernst van Alphen discusses how the act of archiving introduces "meaning, order, boundaries, coherence and reason into what is disparate and confused, contingent and without contours". However, he goes on to discuss how this coherence has a price. In the process of categorising individual items you take away all the uniqueness from the objects within the collection and assign them one particular value, allowing them only the context you have designated for them within a series of other items you have deemed similar. "Unique objects become representative of the category within which they are included," van Alphen says; "they become

5   Tate Gallery Archive, collection TGA 929

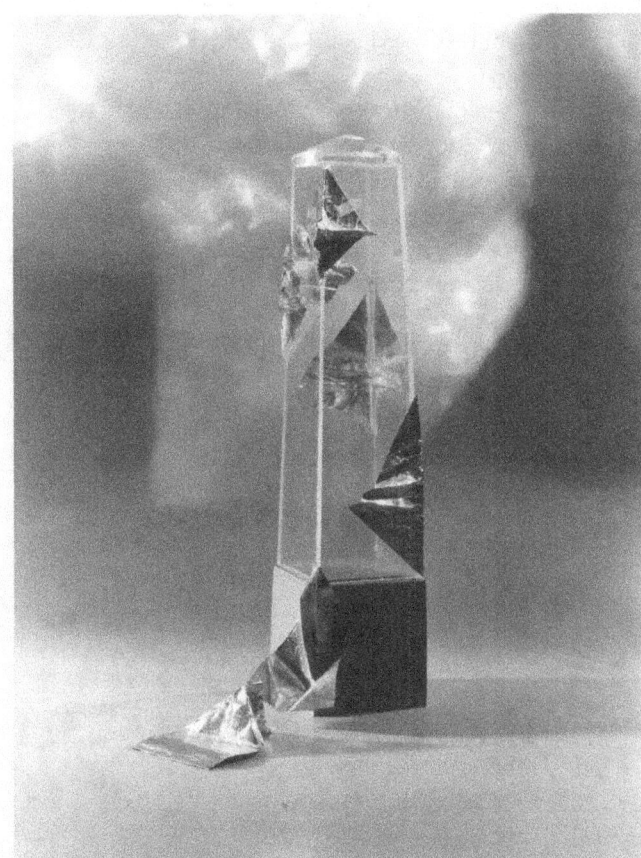

Photograph of Peter Startup's maquette proposed for the Art Council's Southbank Commission, photographer unknown

another expression of those objects that surround it"[6]. Matthias Winzen has called this process "protective destruction" and talks about the inherent violence "in all sorting, re- and devaluing, fixing and defining"[7].

So much archival theory comes from business records where it makes sense to say "this file was created for this purpose, stored in this order and used in this way". Often with personal papers, it's not possible to say for certain how a document was used or why it was kept. Instead of organising items thematically, we might perhaps catalogue items according to the frequency with which they were used. So perhaps the appointment diary an artist always kept in a jacket pocket would belong to one series and the official award certificate they barely looked at would belong to another. Yet in a conventional archive catalogue, both those items would come under the heading 'personal items'. The current system is certainly

6   Ernst van Alphen, 'Archival Obsessions and Obsessive Archives' in Holly and Smith (ed.), *What is Research in the Visual Arts?*, Yale University Press, 2008, p.66

7   Matthias Winzen, 'Collecting, so Normal, so Paradoxical' in Schaffner and Winzen (eds), *Deep Storage: Collecting, Storing and Archiving in Art*, Prestel, 1998, p.22

the most practical and the most useful for researchers, but we should not pretend it reflects the context in which those items were used during the artist's life.

The art historian Ann Reynolds published a 'morphological' reading of Robert Smithson's archive[8] in which she sought to situate him within the theoretical frameworks of his time. Rather than working from his art back to the archive and concentrating on preparatory sketches and drafts, she started from what she found in the archive: "a large variety of magazines, tourist pamphlets, postcards, books and records" which, because they "were a part of a large number of people's lives and, consequently, part of a particular period in history that extends well beyond the personal history of the artist"[9], allowed her to place Smithson's work in a broader historical context. "To discover what Smithson actually did with these documents and images, rather than what they appear to express as isolated things," she says, "one has to reconstruct Smithson's patterns of use"[10]. Reynolds then uses the documents in the archive to learn about Smithson's working process and to discover the connections he created between thoughts and images that wouldn't have otherwise been obvious. Her approach mirrors that of the archivist, working with the material towards an understanding of the artist's life and work as a whole. However, where Reynolds has the luxury of writing a book to discuss the links she has found between items, the archivist must work within the convention of hierarchical cataloguing and the limits of international archival description guidelines.

> Those who work at the archivist's trade must take on some otherwise unedifying characteristics. They should have the gossip's urge to pry, the snob's delight in name dropping, the miser's insatiable greed. They freely indulge the temptation to open other people's mail. They are helpless romantics, sustained by infinite reserves of optimism and curiosity. If they hope to avoid despair or insanity in the face of ever growing mountains of paper, they must live by Mr Micawber's eternal refrain "something will turn up".
>
> Garnett McCoy[11]

After the items have been arranged into series, the cataloguer then describes (depending on time and resources) each file or individual item within the collection. The aim of description is two-fold. Firstly, to minimise the number of times archives are called up from the storeroom unnecessarily. Calling up items only to find that they are irrelevant is annoying for researchers, because it wastes their

8 Ann Reynolds, *Robert Smithson: Learning from New Jersey and Elsewhere*, Cambridge, MA: MIT Press, 2003

9 Ibid., p.xiii

10 Ibid., p.2

11 Garnett McCoy, 'Ten of the Best: An Archivist's Choice', *Archives of American Art Journal*, vol. 19, no. 2, 1979, pp.2–18

precious time in the archive. It also hastens the physical degradation of the paper, because of the fluctuation in environmental conditions and the unnecessary handling, thus conflicting with one's responsibility to preserve the archive for future researchers as well.

The second aim of cataloguing is security, so that the archive knows what it owns. You need to be able to identify each item individually and differentiate it from other similar items within the collection and so you try to record enough information about each item to enable you to do this. With correspondence this is reasonably simple because the correspondent and date on a letter are usually enough to differentiate it from any other letter (although you are always left at the end with letters signed by "M" and dated "Tuesday").

Notebooks and sketchbooks represent a challenge, unless the creator has been very particular in his/her labelling and dating. Discussing the writer Nellie McClung's notebooks (held by the British Columbia Archives), Carole Gerson describes how they were used by not only McClung but also her six children and comments "Whatever her personal system of organization may have been, it has not survived. The institution to which her son delivered many cartons of these notebooks in 1953, two years after his mother's death, did not attempt to reconstruct it, either chronologically or thematically".[12] While this might be frustrating for the researcher, there's an honesty to this approach. Any attempt at thematic organisation of notebooks is bound to fail, as by their nature they are likely to cover a number of topics. Chronological ordering, whilst the ideal, can only ever be tentative at best and there is always the risk that the researcher will take it to be authoritative. If the contents are similar across all the volumes, archival description often falls back on a detailed narrative of each notebook's cover. This might enable the archive to keep control over its holdings but doesn't help the researcher.

On the other hand, cataloguing notebooks looks like child's play compared to sketches. It's hard enough describing a sketch in two or three lines anyway, since they're usually not titled and not dated; but it's even harder if you are trying to differentiate it from other sketches, because artists tend to be rather repetitive and also to return to themes over a matter of decades. With an artist like Naum Gabo, this problem was confounded by his tendency to re-use whichever scrap of paper was closest to hand. This put paid to any hopes of dating the several hundred drawings in his collection by guessing at the age of the paper.

Cataloguing is supposed to be objective but it's hard to be

12 Helen M. Buss and Marlene Kadar, *Working in women's archives: researching women's private literature and archival documents*, Wilfrid Laurier University Press, 2001, p.12

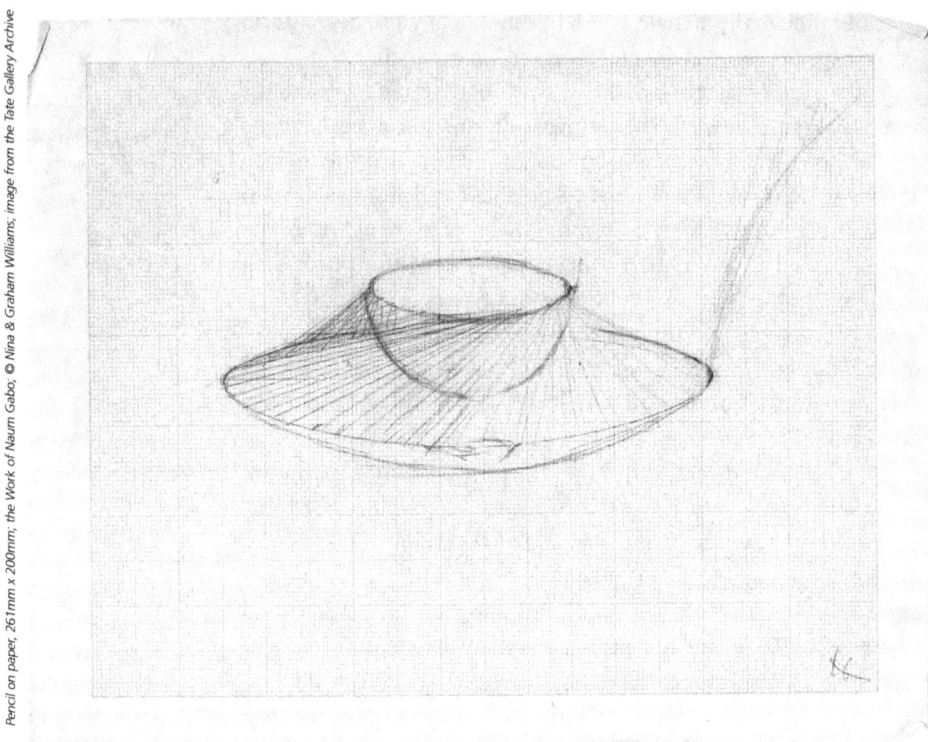

objective when you're trying to describe art. You find yourself looking, understandably, for similarities to works by the artist. Even if you know it's supposed to be abstract, you still find yourself turning it upside down and wondering if it's meant to be a cat. Yet if you describe a drawing as "possibly related to x", you've put the seed of the idea in the researcher's head and influenced how they will look at the sketch. However, at the same time, it's your duty as a cataloguer to record any information you might have gained about the archive during the cataloguing process, thus helping researchers to find any archives that might be relevant to them. So you find yourself walking a fine line and using lots of word like 'probably', 'possibly' and 'appears to be'. It's these tentative expressions that mark out archival cataloguing from library classification and should remind you that there's a human involved in the process.

Naum Gabo, Drawing of a construction

...[I]t's important to understand that even a descriptive document so apparently straightforward as a list of folder titles is a report on the archivist's examination of the materials and has been shaped by the sense the archivist is making of the apparent order and organization of the folders. A finding aid is a text that is not transparent but must be interpreted by the researcher.

Sammie L. Morris and Shirley K. Rose[13]

Researchers are used to questioning the implicit bias in a first-hand source but usually take the objectivity of archival description for granted. In his discussion of "the textuality of archives", Andrew Prescott states of the archives themselves that "Text is always biased, always limited and always deceptive"[14]. However, he never considers that this might be the case for archival catalogues as well. Even with items that might seem more straightforward, such as correspondence, it's easy for the archivist to miss allusions where people are referred to by nicknames, or have signed off with their initials only. An archive catalogue can never be comprehensive. Similarly, the conventions of hierarchical arrangement and objective description prevent the cataloguer from including information he or she might have liked to. For example, how amusing a particular letter is, or how different a particular sketch is to the rest of the artist's work.

Once the archive is arranged and every item within it has been described, more or less successfully, the archivist puts each item into smart new acid-free folders and writes the reference number on each piece of paper in 2B pencil. These are now no longer the remnants of someone's life but their Archive, numbered, filed, boxed and preserved for future generations. The transformation is complete. The catalogue is uploaded to the Internet where it goes to meet a public who have no knowledge of you as an archivist – your interests, your bias, your abilities – or what a sorry state this collection was in when you first laid eyes on it.

When a researcher looks at that catalogue they will see your brief description of the archival item and rarely stop to question it. They will order it up in the searchroom and receive not a bundle of papers held together with an elastic band in a fruit crate but a neat set of papers in a folder, tied up with archival tape. And unlike the poor bewildered cataloguer, they will know in advance, or think they know, what they are getting. They will come to the archive with the preconception that it is valuable because it has been selected and described and packaged, but also that it is valuable because it is a direct link to the artist. But we should question just how direct that link really is.

When we think about artists' personal papers, I believe it's helpful to consider the debate around the documentation of live art events and happenings, and the extent to which they can ever

13 'Invisible Hands' in Ramsey, Sharer, L'Eplattenier and Mastrangelo (eds), *Working in the Archives: Practical Research Methods for Rhetoric and Composition*, Southern Illinois University, 2010

14 Andrew Prescott, 'The textuality of the archive' in Louise Craven (ed.), *What are Archives? Cultural and Theoretical Perspectives*, p.33

accurately represent the event itself. Speaking about Allen Kaprow's archive, Alex Potts describes "the blurring... [which takes] place between the archival traces of the work and the work as such, which exists now in highly mediated form."[15] Similarly, I think it's easy to blur the documentation of the archive with the archive itself and, by association, with the artist's life that the archive represents. It is important that researchers always keep in mind how mediated their access to the archive is. Ernst van Alphen concludes that "uncritical belief in the importance of the archive is ultimately blinding because it closes off certain perspectives, it discourages the asking of certain questions"[16]. I think the same could be said of blindness to the archival process.

15 Alex Potts, 'The Artwork, the Archive, and the Living Moment' in Holly and Smith (eds), *What is Research in the Visual Arts*, Yale University Press, 2008, p.124

16 Ernst van Alphen, 'Archival Obsessions and Obsessive Archives' in Holly and Smith (eds), *What is Research in the Visual Arts*, Yale University Press, 2008, p.82

ARCHIVE AS EVENT:
CREATIVE ARCHIVING FOR JOHN LATHAM
Athanasios Velios

9

John Latham often struggled to communicate his ideas and ironically the same applies to me. My difficulty stems from the fact that most of the people involved in this project are outside the archive profession and therefore, despite some initial positive remarks, it is difficult to confirm that the concepts and guidelines described here are useful. It is appropriate that the readers of this publication may be archivists or related professionals who work closely with artists or artists' archives. I hope that I share their concerns when approaching an archive and that what I am proposing will be useful for them.

Creative archiving was introduced recently[1] to describe the process by which the archivist openly contributes to the interpretation of an archive. The result of creative archiving is an additional layer of interpretation, typically through an online interface, which illustrates the archivist's ideas about the core concepts kept within the archive material. This delivers a result which is unique to the specific archive rather than a standardised view of the collection as presented by popular library or archiving software. The proposal of creative archiving comes as a result of recent discussions in the archiving profession. These are outlined next.

Up until the 1980s, important publications have been setting standards to ensure that material kept in archives reflects historical truth and therefore can be used as evidence. These include the founding publication in the archiving profession, the *Manual for the Arrangement and Description of Archives*[2] and *A Manual of Archive Administration*[3], which emphasise *provenance, original order (description)* and *selection* as the core principles in archiving practice. With the exception of *provenance*, which is, perhaps, the least disputable principle, archivists have been criticised on the validity of their methodology in that both *selection* and *original order* allow the archivist to be subjective, thus distorting evidence and historical truth. Postmodern thinking (for example, Hardiman[4] after Derrida[5]) made that argument clear by concluding that there is no exclusionary truth in accepted meanings. In other words, the archivist (or anybody in that role) is unable to approach the archival material objectively. To overcome this de-facto limitation,

1   Athanasios Velios, 'Creative Archiving: A case study from the John Latham Archive', *Journal of the Society of Archivists*, Vol. 32, No. 2, October 2011, pp.255–71

2   S. Muller, J.A. Feith and R. Fruin, *Manual for the Arrangement and Description of Archives; drawn up by Direction of the Netherlands Association of Archivists*, translation of the 2nd ed. by Arthur H. Leavitt, New York: H.W. Wilson Co, 1968

3   Hilary Jenkinson, Carnegie Endowment for International Peace, Division of Economics and History, *A Manual of Archive Administration: Including the Problems of War Archives and Archive Making*, Oxford: Clarendon Press, 1922

4   Rachel Hardiman, 'En mal d'archive: Postmodernist Theory and Recordkeeping', *Journal of the Society of Archivists*, 30/1, 2009, http://www.informaworld.com/10.1080/00379810903264591

5   Jacques Derrida, *Archive Fever: A Freudian Impression*, University of Chicago Press, 1998

chapter 9 / archive as event: creative archiving for John Latham

109

postmodernists propose to *deconstruct* archival practice by only approaching archives through the accepted subjectivity of the archivist. While postmodernists developed these ideas about archival practice, an historic shift was about to take place on the Internet where disputes and discussions about any matter were recorded openly through forums and social networking websites. Ketelaar[6] describes how *provenance/description* can be debated online, thus addressing the problem of the archivists' subjectivity. In theory this is a good alternative for archival practice, but in practice archives are published online using software tools setup by administrators and archivists. As such, these are by definition subjective because they follow a specific structure and format. Also, a visitor often contributes data outside the official record (for example, a free-text comment on a date entry) and therefore the contribution is not *archival* data, but instead a comment about that data.

The conclusion to the above is that archivists are still the safe-guards of historical *truth*, either directly or indirectly (through web-archives). This unique position, combined with their inevitable subjectivity, leads to criticism against the archiving profession. When no alternatives seem to have emerged, creative archiving offers a new angle to this discussion.

Archiving is an interesting profession because of the combination of skills required:

- Partiality and consistency: Experienced archivists are able to maintain a consistent quality in their descriptions. Even with a partial understanding of the situation, their practice is systematic and therefore the resulting records can be used in research. Such quality is rare in community descriptions (e.g. in a web archive with open contributions) unless tight restrictions have been placed by the archivist.

- Partiality and authority: Specialist archivists working for years in an archive often have a better understanding of the material than researchers who visit the archive to consult specific resources. Archivists suffer in that their education, social background, religion, ethnicity and so on influence their descriptions and result in a biased version of the truth. This, however, does not deny them authority on the subject area.

- Partiality and classification: Researchers who are willing to use an archive for their research benefit from important assistance from the archivist in the form of a classification index and a

6　Eric Ketelaar, 'Archives as Spaces of Memory', *Journal of the Society of Archivists*, 29/1, 2008, http://www.informaworld.com/10.1080/00379810802499678

finding aid. These demonstrate the archivist's ability to correlate and organise information. Indeed, the way the index is built is again biased, but it is the only entry to the archive and is another point where the archivist influences research.

Because partiality is unavoidable in *archival description* and since the perceived truth according to postmodernists may be changing anyway, let us turn partiality to an advantage. Creative archiving is taking the inevitability of partiality to an extreme and celebrates the archivist's role in interpreting history while at the same time clearly admitting that this is only one version of the truth.

Ketelaar[7] was able to introduce postmodern practice to archiving through social networking because the technology which allowed such a proposal was becoming increasingly widely available. Social-networking tools were mature enough to be used efficiently in an archiving context. Creative archiving is a timely proposal for the same reason: the online software available for its implementation is now mature enough to undertake a formal archiving role. In fact, software may be the answer to some of the postmodern concerns about archiving. A common standardised structure and appearance of archives appears to implement the *universal truth* idea of the archive, where all implementations of digital archives – both digitised and born digital – adhere to the same processing techniques. If this universal view of the archive is removed then it is arguable that there is no single truth in the profession's methodologies. The archivist can then pursue his or her own interpretation of the material and declare it as such. Online systems that allow such a personalised view of the archive exist and, as well as offering interpretation tools, they maintain important standards for search-engine discoverability.

In a recent publication[8], the Drupal content-management system was discussed as an excellent tool for implementing online archives using creative archiving ideas. Drupal's standardised database ensures compatible data sharing with other systems, while the so-called theming layer allows for any type of presentation and examination of this data to match the archivist's views. Drupal was used to deliver the online archive of the artist John Latham and this case study is described in the following sections.

In 2008, Ligatus initiated a project to produce an online archive of John Latham's papers with the support of the John Latham Foundation. The proposal for the project was built around the concept of creative archiving whereby the material of the archive would first be studied by the archivists[9] and then a new

7 Ibid., p.17
8 Athanasios Velios, 'The John Latham Archive: an on-line implementation using Drupal', *Art Documentation*, 2011
9 Antony Hudek and the author

classification system based on John Latham's work would be used to organise the archive. Although initially this work was planned to be implemented only online, two publications[10] accompany the online archive.

John Latham's artwork is difficult to interpret. A newcomer may appreciate the work aesthetically, but the underlying ideas are not immediately obvious. In order to digest these ideas and be able to propose a reasonable model for the classification of Latham's papers, a set of key documents were identified from the archive which could explain Latham's ideas.

Once these ideas were fully understood and following discussions with other parties who had previously worked with Latham, the core concept of mapping the archive based on the brothers Karamazov evolved. This was a daring take on Latham's work and archive but it has always been clear that it is only an interpretation and not necessarily the *official* Latham view. Technical methodologies of digitisation, metadata creation and classification followed and the resulting online version of the archive was developed. The artist's ideas and their interpretation for the archive are explained in the next section alongside the corresponding features of the online implementation.

John Walker[11] has written extensively on John Latham's work and the artist himself has outlined some of his ideas in his *Report of a Surveyor*[12], among other publications. Below, these are presented somewhat chronologically in the sequence in which the ideas were conceived.

One of the most important concepts of Latham's work is the *Least Event*, which was initially expressed in the 1950s. Critical to that concept was the use of a spray gun and the realisation of the blank canvas as the potential of becoming any artwork. The concept of the transition (or event) of the canvas from a non-existing artwork to the finished work was simplified to the minimum possible event by the use of the spray gun: the appearance of a single droplet of black paint on the white canvas – the *Least Event*. The well-known one-second drawings illustrate this concept (Figure 1[13] and *Two Noits – One-Second Drawing, 1970*[14]). In later years Latham replaced the canvas with glass because he wanted to emphasise the idea of the potential of events to happen. Later artworks where glass is juxtaposed to a white solid surface can offer the same interpretation.

In July 1983, Andrew Dipper and John Latham published a paper[15] explaining this concept by comparing the state of non-existence (*O state*) and the evidence of existence (*I state*) which

10 Antony Hudek (ed.), *Sun Times*, London: Occasional Papers, 2009; and Antony Hudek and Athanasios Velios (eds), *The Portable John Latham*, London: Occasional Papers, 2010

11 John Walker, *John Latham: The Incidental Person – His Art and Ideas*, London: Middlesex University Press, 1995

12 John Latham, *Report of a Surveyor*, Stuttgart: Hansjorg Mayer, 1984

13 Antony Hudek and Athanasios Velios (eds), *The Portable John Latham*, London: Occasional Papers, 2010, p.64

14 Walker, op. cit., p.109

15 Andrew Dipper and John Latham, *Sub Quantum: Notes towards a concept*, 1983

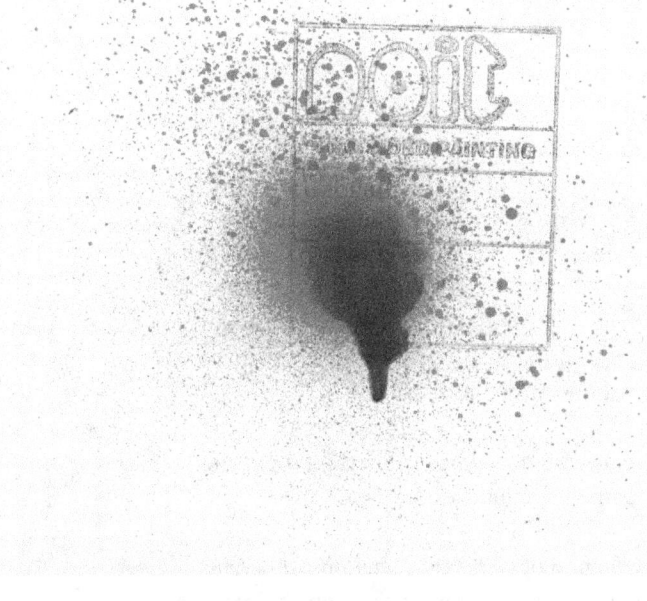

formed *OI-IO* or *OHO*, including the idea of cyclical changes of state.

By using the *Least Event* as a unit, Latham further developed the concept of event on different scales by suggesting that complex events are built by a sequence of *Least Events*. To organise these events a scale was necessary and, in 1975, Latham[16] proposed the use of the *Time-Base Spectrum* as a filing system for classifying these events and their frequency. The *Time-Base Spectrum*, featured in the *Time-Base Roller works* (Figure 2), was created to illustrate that function. It sorts events from high frequency (shorter – *low-base*) on the left (point A) to low frequency (longer – *high-base*) on the right (point Z). While both extremes of the spectrum are occupied with events outside human perception, events in the middle of the

16 John Latham, *State of Mind: John Latham*, Dusseldorf: Stadtische Kunsthalle, 1975, § 3.3

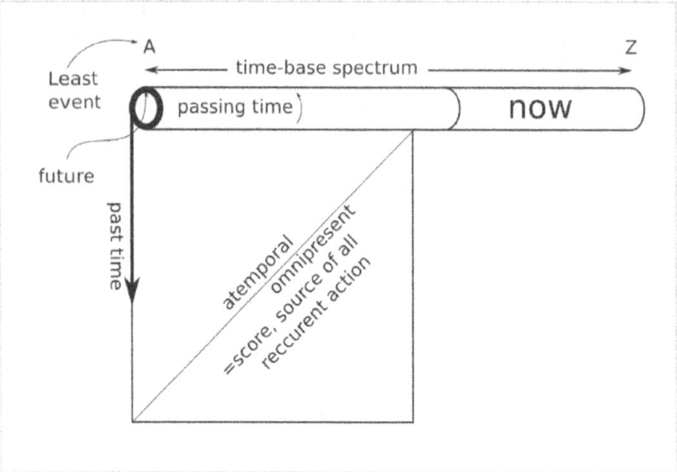

Figure 2: *Time-Base Roller*, after John Latham

spectrum are possible for humans to experience. In 1976, Latham[17] defined a terminology for these events:

1. *Bio-physical events*, for events which relate to human life (such as birth, death or illness)

2. *Socio-political*, for events concerning society and politics which span much longer periods than a human life (such as institutions, organisations and political parties)

3. *Geo-political*, for events related to almost permanent social and political constructs (such as countries or religions) and

4. *Geo-physical*, for geological or planetary alterations and events caused by human activity with a long-term impact on the environment (such as the melting of the ice caps or the movement of tectonic plates).

The *Time-Base Roller* encapsulates another important idea in Latham's work, that of the omnipresent time, which is discussed next.

The *Time-Base Roller* holds canvas rolled around a cylinder. It was designed to be viewed whilst being unrolled, whereby the drawn content of the canvas is shown to the viewer momentarily on the cylinder, before it disappears and the viewer is only able to see the rear. Unrolling the canvas takes a given length of time and this is the time we normally consider: the passing time. While this canvas is being unrolled, events are experienced momentarily at

17 John Latham, *Time-Base: And Determination in Events*, London: Tate Gallery, 1976, p.16

the basic .(T) diagram

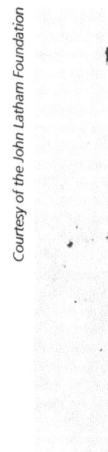

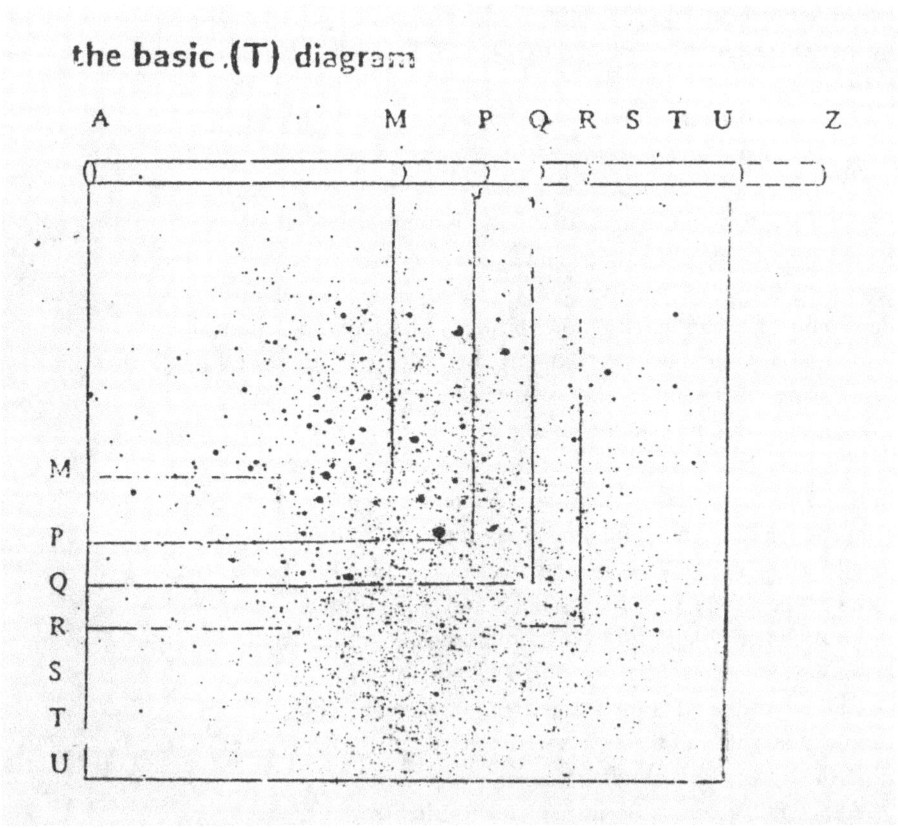

Figure 3: John Latham, 'The basic (T) diagram'

the front of the cylinder in the form of painted areas on the canvas. *Low-base* events depicted as narrow stripes pass quickly (and more often) while *high-base* events are wider and take longer to complete (less often). This indicates a different type of time: frequency. The third type of time is depicted from the beginning, since the canvas has always held events in the spectrum. The third type of time is the atemporal/omnipresent type of time. Latham used another metaphor to describe this: music. Music is performed over a period of time, a song lasting, for example, two or three minutes. Musicians play instruments to perform the music and the notes they play have given frequencies. The music itself is prearranged in a score and in theory its potential to be played exists prior to the specific performance. This omnipresent nature of time materialises through the performance.

Because of Latham's interest in merging sociology and psychology with physics under a common event base system, he focused on the part of the *Time-Base Spectrum* which concerned human activity in social constructs. Latham indicates three key positions for classifying characteristics of people which are inspired by the characters of Dostoevsky's *Brothers Karamazov*. Dimitri (Mitya), the oldest brother, is depicted as an impulsive and cyclothymic person whose main concern is himself. Ivan, the middle brother, is a well-educated and controlled person able to observe his older brother's attitude, rationally explain it and often avoid it. Latham underlines that Ivan is limited by his own framework of logic and, although intelligent, is unable to surpass his reasoning capacity. The youngest brother, Alexei (Alyosha), is depicted as the intuitive and more spiritual character who, despite his good but limited education, approaches a situation in the best way, having observed the other two characters[18,19], (also referred to online, for example, by Latham[20]).

The three brothers represent different levels of human existence in the *Time-Base Spectrum* and indicate different points of view of a situation and different understandings of the *truth*. This triplet of *impulse, reason* and *intuition* is more evident in Latham's Observer series[21]. Mitya takes the form of a bulky and rather scattered group of books. Ivan is depicted by a more canonical arrangement of books and is always connected to Mitya by a wire. Alyosha is consistently depicted as the smallest group of books, reduced to a simple indentation of the canvas in *Observer IV*, and disconnected from the other two brothers.

Although Latham's work includes many other aspects, the above description represents some of the main ideas in his work which were used in constructing the interpretation layer of the online archive.

John Latham's archive online[22] has been implemented by describing every item in the archive using the Drupal content-management system[23]. An extensive review of the advantages of Drupal for creative archiving has been published previously[24]. It is important to emphasise that Drupal allows the publication of structured information according to given standards and has recently included extensions for implementing the Resource Description Framework[25] which allows the semantic publication of archival material for intelligent machine searching. To satisfy further technical requirements of archival data, records consist of fields chosen after investigating both the ISAD(G) and Dublin Core standards. These fields include what is generally accepted as useful information such as title, author and date; and also a small set of fields inspired by Latham's work as described in the following sections.

The online representation of the John Latham archive keeps the

18 John A. Walker, 'John Latham and the Book: The Convergence of Art and Physics', *The Burlington Magazine*, 129/1016, 1987, http://www.jstor.org/stable/883213, p.718

19 John Latham and Charles Harrison, 'Where does the collision happen?', *Studio International*, 175/900, 1968, p.260

20 John Latham, Letter to Brian Flowers, http://www.ligatus.org.uk/aae/node/2799, 1975

21 Walker, op. cit., pp.47–9

22 www.ligatus.org.uk/aae

23 www.drupal.org

24 Velios, op. cit.

25 RDF Working Group, RDF – Semantic Web Standards, http://www.w3.org/RDF/, 2004

traditional concept of the home page as a starting point for navigation. The visitor is presented with three links – MA, IA and AA – arranged in a triangle. If a visitor is already aware of John Latham's categorisation of social characters according to the brothers Karamazov, the meaning of the links is obvious:

1. Instinctive/impulsive Dimitri (Mitya – MA)

2. Rational/structured Ivan (IA)

3. Reflective/intuitive Alexei (Alyosha – AA)

For the uninformed visitor, activating the links (by moving the focus or hovering with the mouse above them) reveals an extract from Latham's interview published in *Studio International*[26] indicating the different approaches to searching the archive for each link. By following any of these links the visitor is able to search the same archival material in different ways. Switching from one version to the other, in other words making a shift from one character/state-of-mind to the other, is possible. However, having to choose an initial path already stimulates the visitor in their exploration of John Latham's ideology.

OI-IO
The choice of character from the home page introduces the visitor to a blank screen while the title of the browser window changes to *OI-IO*. The blank screen is presented to the visitor momentarily and automatically redirects to the archive's Mitya, Ivan or Alyosha version (according to the link initially chosen). It indicates the blank canvas on which the event of the online archive takes place. Having experienced the *Least Event*, the user is presented with different archival search tools for each version/brother.

Mitya
MA represents a state of mind to match the older brother in Dostoyevsky's novel. Mitya approaches the material in the archive in a spontaneous and unorganised way, without any interest in analysis or examination of texts and related metadata. Mitya's attention is drawn to pictorial material in the same way he might look at tabloid newspaper headlines[27]. MA only shows the photographs of documents and returns no other data from the database. These photographs are shown randomly, as in a slide show, to emphasise the casual nature of the presentation. MA offers only

26 Latham and Harrison, op. cit.

27 Antony Hudek (ed.), *Sun Times*, London: Occasional Papers, 2009

an impression of the archive and the visitor relies on luck to identify an interesting document.

In MA the visitor is given the opportunity to stop the slide show. This action indicates the need for closer/lengthier examination of the record or document. By clicking on the photograph the visitor is able to visit the specific record in the database with an opportunity to find out more about the document and perhaps attempt a change of character from Mitya to Ivan or Alyosha.

Ivan

IA represents the structured, rational and methodical character of Ivan, the middle brother in the novel. The less passionate and more logical character of Ivan approaches the archive with the intention of performing systematic searching for results which will eventually allow him to reach some conclusions. Ivan is perhaps the closest character to an academic researcher who requires an organised index of the documents, similar to what traditional archiving practice offers. Controlled vocabularies and standardised metadata are employed to fulfil this requirement.

IA reflects the ultimate index for an archive and offers advanced tools for faceted searching for most of the available metadata. Another technique for searching the archive under IA is by simulating the original location of the documents in the physical archive in boxes and folders, thus offering the principle of *original order* online.

Alyosha

AA represents the reflective and intuitive character of the youngest brother in the novel and is perhaps one that requires more thought. Alyosha is charismatic, able to observe a situation and react to it, not necessarily in an informed way, but successfully through intuition. Latham sees the artist in our society as the person closest to Alyosha. To emphasise this intuition, AA is implemented based on Latham's own classification system – the *Time-Base Spectrum* – and, as such, users can only begin to use it meaningfully after having studied Latham's theory, unless they are intuitive. Items in the archive are assigned a score for each category (*bio-physical, socio-political, geo-political, geo-physical*) based on their content. For example, a utility bill scores high on the first categories as it refers to events which are rather short (*low-base*) and do not concern major political or geological events. Similarly, an essay about theoretical physics scores high on the last category because of cosmological references (*high-base*), but is not as relevant to the other ones.

Classifying records using these time-base scores subsequently allows searching by selecting scores and retrieving records. Although the choice of scores could be implemented as a simple choice of numerical values in each category, the interpretation layer implements this choice using sound. A specific sound has been matched to each numerical value of the different categories. The visitor plays a sound and, by selecting that sound intuitively, is also choosing its corresponding value. Choice of multiple sounds is possible for combinations of values in the four categories. When the selection of sounds is complete, all documents linked to these sounds are retrieved.

Replacing numerical values with sound was done for three reasons: a) by making the choice of a value less accessible (i.e. through sound), the emphasis is on intuition which better represents Alyosha's character; b) sound, as explained earlier, is a good metaphor for describing the different types of time which are related to the *Time-Base Spectrum*; and c) since, according to Latham, the artist in society is closest to the Alyosha state, arguably, an artist should be involved in producing that part of the archive.

Implementing the sound-based search of Alyosha was made possible by the contribution of the sound artist, Professor David Toop. During a performance at Whitechapel Gallery entitled *FLAT TIME/sounding*, four performers investigated John Latham's ideas of time[28]. The recording of that performance was subsequently edited by David Toop into a body of work called *FLAT TIME Particles*, with extracts of the performance representing different time-bases for Alyosha. The FLAT TIME Particles have been used as sound values for AA.

While MA, IA and AA are the archive's different retrieval tools and somewhat independent of each other, Latham always explored their relationships and often linked them in his artwork. MA, IA and AA intersect in a common interface online, which functions as a presentation page for the document record. Therefore, following the retrieval of items with one of the brothers, the resulting clickable list of items leads to individual item pages. This includes the photograph of the document and also features a switch for the *IP box*. The abbreviation *IP* stands for *Incidental Person*, which is another term that Latham used to describe the intuitive person, the Alyosha state, the position of the artist in society. By clicking on that switch, a panel appears with metadata about the document which includes IA and AA details, making the document record the

28 Performance by John Butcher, Aleksander Kolkowski, Phil Durrant and David Toop, 4th September 2010, recorded by David Hunt, funded by PRS for Music

meeting point of the three different versions of the archive.

The main criticism of creative archiving is that the proposed interpretation layer could be considered as an additional barrier to accessing information on an online archive. It is important to clarify here what a barrier is. In most cases, a barrier delays searching and retrieval of data. However, creative archiving is not meant to replace traditional or current searching techniques. Machine indexing and searching is increasingly becoming the de-facto way information is accessed online. With the gradual transformation of the web to a space where data is offered to and indexed by large search engines, users are directed to retrieval portals; they identify results and are then redirected to individual resources and archives which hold the primary information. Any barrier to searching is due to technical reasons which can be resolved relatively easily. Such a barrier is irrelevant to the interpretation of the material because searching should be seen as a separate function of an online archive.

If the interpretation layer itself is seen as a barrier, then it has been unsuccessful in communicating the archivist's ideas about the underlying records, possibly because the visitor disagrees with that interpretation. We should, however, see this as an advantage, because such disagreement can lead to dialogue which may improve the archivist's view of the material and also attract interest to the resource at a time when exposure and impact of resources is crucial for their survival.

Another, perhaps more philosophical, point about creative archiving can be made by postmodern thinking: although creative archiving is meant to provide an answer to the archivist's concerns about keeping the *truth*, by admitting the subjectivity of one's view, any implementation of creative archiving requires the use of software which is itself a structural constraint and can thus only offer one version of the truth in archiving practice. To some extent this is true; however, the argument does not hold because the archivist is not concerned with the tools which help manage data, but rather with the data itself. In order to communicate one's ideas, the use of a structure is required. In a gallery this structure is the artwork; in a library this structure is the book; and on the Internet this structure is the software. Moreover, extensive work on ontology in computer science and philosophy allows abstraction of data which can then be digested in any desirable way.

Creative archiving should be seen as an extra tool in the archivist's hands with which a clear interpretation of the available records can be communicated while keeping the validity (although still subjective) of the underlying data. The archivist will then be able to justify their subjective views based on their background by contributing their expert view to the research community instead of trying unsuccessfully to erase any sign of their existence from the archive.

Acknowledgements

The author thanks Antony Hudek, with whom the John Latham interpretation was jointly developed, and Karyn Stuckey, formerly of the Archives and Special Collections Centre, University of the Arts London, for recommending appropriate archiving standards.

10

BARRY FLANAGAN'S ARCHIVE: INTERCONNECTIVITIES
Jo Melvin and Meirian Jump

A website comprising a catalogue of the archive of artist Barry Flanagan (1941–2009) and a database of his artworks and exhibitions went live at www.barryflanagan.com in June 2012. The site includes links between pages for artworks, publications, exhibitions and archive files. Related archival documentation is tied to artworks and exhibitions, while exhibited and published works are connected to shows, books and journals. It is this interconnectivity that sets it apart from other online archival resources. The artwork and archive catalogues can be viewed together, thereby experiencing an interconnecting network as a total exhibition. The site also brings the archive into the open, away from access difficulties, and into the domain of an art exhibition. Conceived by Flanagan and begun during his lifetime, the project has been a number of years in the making. Here, art historian Jo Melvin opens by examining Flanagan's questions and concerns for his archive, raised in conversation with her. These discussions led to the exploration of models and to the development of subsequent strategies and decisions. This is followed by archivist Meirian Jump's account of the project itself, combined with an analysis of the ways in which the site might be used by researchers.

Notes on the Archive of Barry Flanagan

"Interpretation or any form of meta-language is at the best of times a hazardous exercise."[1] Simon Critchley's observation offers a caution to flights of fancy and reinforces a regularly used directive of Flanagan's: "examine the evidence". This reassuringly straightforward statement indicates a pragmatic attitude to the strategies one might invoke when facing unanswerable questions.

What courses of action are available to an artist when considering where to deposit their archive? The first consideration is whether the archive should go to an institution or remain in the control of the artist or their estate. This may be determined by a number of factors, such as access, space, storage conditions and financial resources. Posthumous representation, legacy, data protection and privacy and their control are all factors that may affect the decision-making process. For any archive, the question of access is a paramount concern, as this determines its use value.

1 Simon Critchley, *Very Little Almost*, Routledge, 1997, p.141

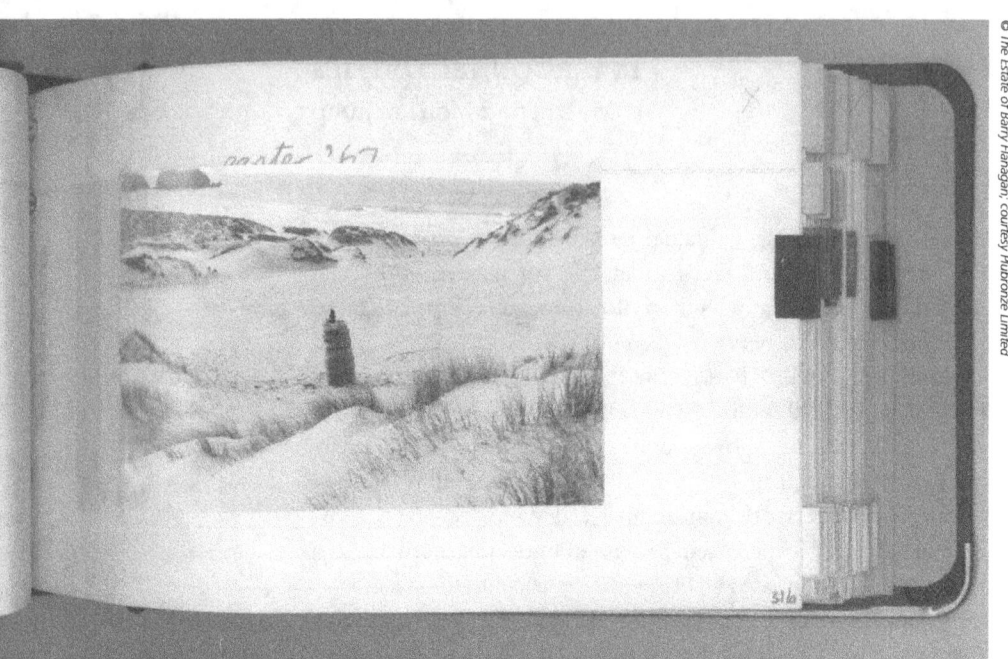

Although the topic addresses the concerns of many artists today, the decisions and actions outlined here are those specifically set in motion by Barry Flanagan. The case examples presented are tangential metaphors for the decision-making processes and were points of discussion between Flanagan and the writer.

The ideal rendering of an archive with exhibition display was a central topic of conversation. It was intended that the display be navigated through salient moments, works and exhibitions, whereby the individual artwork is the starting point for a visual web of interconnectivity. A particular exemplar from 1969 in methodological terms was Seth Siegelaub's calendar exhibition, 'One Month', which he referred to in his correspondence at the time as his "international" show. The publication is relevant to Flanagan's ideal model of archive–exhibition as both presuppose free distribution, easy access, design cohesion, uniformity and equality. Significantly, though this information is anecdotal in relation to its application, Flanagan was one of the 31 artists invited by Siegelaub to contribute to the exhibition.[2] In January 1969, Siegelaub wrote to 31 artists allocating each alphabetically a day of March. For instance, Carl Andre was given 1 March and Flanagan 11 March. Their contributions were printed on the allocated day, the letter sent to the artists served as a frontispiece for the project

Stock book entry for Easter 1967 (JBF/6/1/1.1)

2   The invited artists were Carl Andre, Mike Asher, Terry Atkinson, Michael Baldwin, Robert Barry, Rick Barthelme, Ian Baxter, James Byars, John Chamberlain, Ron Cooper, Barry Flanagan, Dan Flavin, Alex Hay, Douglas Huebler, Robert Huot, Stephen Kaltenbach, On Kawara, Joseph Kosuth, Christine Kozlov, Sol LeWitt, Richard Long, Robert Morris, Bruce Nauman, Claes Oldenburg, Dennis Oppenheim, Alan Ruppersberg, Ed Ruscha, Robert Smithson, De Wain Vallentine, Lawrence Weiner and Ian Wilson.

and those who chose not to participate were not removed. That is to say, their name remained beside the date on the list and, when their date came, the sheet was left blank. Andre was one of the eleven who decided not to participate. Flanagan's submission was an annotated response to Siegelaub's questions and instructions. It raised the question of copyright, as one of Siegelaub's conditions was that the printed submissions would belong to him. Siegelaub transcribed Flanagan's annotations for the calendar.

Douglas Huebler's date was 14 March. He instigated a synonymous project, 'Site Sculpture Project Duration Piece 10'. Huebler divided the 24-hour period into equal intervals and invited the same group of artists to note their "physical location in space when that actual moment occurs." The instruction statement printed in 'One Month' noted that "all locations that are actually reported will serve as a document that will join with this statement to constitute the final piece". It is relevant to note that Huebler sent this work to Barbara Reise "as a trade for a subscription to *Studio*", along with the documentation of several other of his works. It is included in Reise's Douglas Huebler file.[3] Barbara Reise was an art historian and critic from the US who came to London on a Fulbright scholarship. She taught in art schools and became a contributing editor of *Studio International* magazine and decided to stay in the UK. On her return to London after a visit to New York, Siegelaub wrote to remind her to pass on the invitation letters to the British-based artists for their contributions to his "international show".[4]

A core component of Flanagan's archive is his group of logbooks.[5] These provide a visual model for building the www.barryflanagan.com website and, crucially, this gives open access to the data for all researchers without having to travel to an institution. Flanagan began the logs while a student on the Advanced Sculpture Course at St Martins School of Art in 1965. The records track the sculptures by name, date and medium and are usually accompanied by a photograph. Entries include exhibition histories, collectors' names, whether or not the item was purchased and the sale prices. Flanagan entered the information by hand, until 1970, when his assistants took over some of the tasks of data entry. His first solo exhibition at the Rowan Gallery in 1966 instigated the use of a new black plastic covered notebook with the handwritten label, "rowan take in book" stuck on the front.[6] This systematises all records of works that passed through his gallery dealer and documents a shift in the way information was processed from that date onwards. The "take in book" cross references with

3 TGA 786/5/2/81 Barbara Reise Douglas Huebler file
4 TGA 786/4/3 Barbara Reise personal correspondence to and from family and friends
5 JBF/6/1/1
6 JBF/6/1.2

the logbooks and provides a complete sequence of the changing provenance. This first exhibition was also the occasion when Flanagan began to order the presentation of press cuttings which he stuck in scrapbooks, often keeping only the text, without date or source. It was a practice he maintained until 1976 after which point his press files became somewhat randomly compiled as no one person oversaw the process.[7]

At times, the aesthetic decision of newspaper cutting becomes a partial record as, without the author, title, name of paper, page or date, its reference function is compromised. The document is fragmentary and elliptical like those items that are not present in the archive, such as the lost correspondence and subsequent missing links. This practice is not peculiar to Flanagan. For instance, MoMA New York's press records from the 'Information' show in 1970, curated by Kynaston McShine, create similar frustrations in attributing authorship or even locating where the article appeared. The 'Information' show was one of the first large-scale exhibitions to include a significant amount of documentation as an artwork in itself. The catalogue then became an archive of this process. The collage of press records for the exhibition can be seen as a work in itself and one wonders whether an unacknowledged artist working in the library was responsible.[8]

One of the major reasons why an artist may decide to maintain control of his or her archive, once questions of legacy become a concern, is that of access. This is a two-fold situation as, on the one hand, there is the ease with which a researcher can view material and, on the other, the case that uncatalogued archives are of questionable value. Tate Gallery Archive is a research-rich resource but gaining the necessary permission to view uncatalogued papers may take a great deal of time and, in some instances, permission may not be forthcoming. Such papers often remain unsorted if an archive has been deposited with conditions or without a legacy, or when it is on loan to the institution, pending its deposit or its acquisition.

Frank Martin's archive was given to the nation in lieu of taxes and is deposited in Tate Gallery Archive. This is not yet catalogued and its viewing depends on application to the archivist. Much of the material originates from Frank Martin's time as head of sculpture at St Martins School of Art, 1952–1979. Arguably, some items may belong in the School's archive. In practice, though, it is only because Martin kept this documentation that it is now available to researchers. For years, St Martins did not have the systems in place to look after its records and the storage boxes were

7   JBF/5/1/1
8   Museum of Modern Art Archives New York, PI II.A.441

1969	MARCH				1969	
SUN	MON	TUE	WED	THU	FRI	SAT
						1
2	3	4	5	6	7	8
9	10	11	12	13	14	15
16	17	18	19	20	21	22
23/30	24/31	25	26	27	28	29

Front cover of Seth Siegelaub's One Month calendar exhibition, published in 1969

frequently raided for trophies. The Tate's archive description states that the papers are the "Personal papers of Frank Martin" and the definition raises questions of what is 'personal' in a working/professional context. Greater accessibility of these papers would enable this question, along with other more tangible ones, to be considered.

Amongst Frank Martin's student files was one on Flanagan. In 1965 Flanagan was heavily engaged in concrete poetry, both as a practitioner and a promoter. He had printed and published sixteen issues of the magazine *Silåns*, with two colleagues from the school, sculptor Rudy Leenders, a member of staff, and Alistair Jackson who was a fellow student. Flanagan was interested in the poetic stances of speaking and writing. The relationship between the sound of words and letters, sound and their shape, the space between words, letters and the way their utterance left the body to be projected into space and received by their hearer. He experimented with these ideas in concrete poetry and on several occasions performed kinetic poems where the absence of sound was an integral part of the total experience of sculptural phenomena.

Frank Martin's Flanagan file reveals his contribution to the exhibition 'Between Poetry and Painting', organised by Jasia Reichardt at the ICA in 1965. Flanagan's name does not appear in the catalogue although there is a catch-all acknowledgement at the end of the list of artists: "and many, many others."[9] This exhibition is noted in the Rowan Gallery catalogue for Flanagan's first solo exhibition in 1966. Frank Martin had cut out a review by Anne Davison from an unnamed magazine. It was accompanied by photographs documenting Flanagan's performance. Davison selected Flanagan's contribution, noting: "I found the most striking poem one which lasted only about 8 seconds, and which was completely silent – a sort of hand sculpture through space... The two hands, developing from separate entities into a complete and natural unit, gave new and direct meaning to a theme often inadequately expressed in words."[10] During the summer that year, a group of poets gathered in Oxford for the Second International Exhibition of Experimental Poems at St Catherine's College, when Flanagan performed the silent lip poem, 'O for Orange, U for you', 1965. The work was published in *Silâns* 15, 1965.

The experimental magazine *Silâns* enabled Flanagan to engage directly with silence and the absence of sound as a form of sculptural presence. *Silâns* is the phonetic spelling of the French word for silence. It is difficult to define a lack of sound or noise without a framework to contain the enquiry, for which the magazine provided a discursive space. Distinctions in the unseen are delineated in the opening issue 'A prelude to a sculpture that has never been seen' and 'A prelude to a sculpture that has never been seen before'. They follow an epigraph from James Joyce's *Ulysses*, when he coins the expression 'Sllt', the sound made by the printer and by the creaking door, objects in animated conversation; "everything speaks in its own way."

Sllt. The nethermost deck of the first machine jogged forward its flyboard with sllt the first batch of quirefold papers. Sllt. Almost human the way it sllt to call attention. Doing its level best to speak. That door too sllt creaking, asking to be shut. Everything speaks in its own way. Sllt.

Barry Flanagan gave his original copies of *Silâns* to St Martins

9 'Between Poetry and Painting', 22 October – 27 November 1965, ICA catalogue, unpaginated
10 Frank Martin archive TGA 201014 Barry Flanagan file, Anne Davison review

School of Art Special Collections; a set of photocopies remain in his archive. There is also a set in Frank Martin's archive and isolated copies elsewhere, including in the Themerson archive. Judy Lindsay, Head of Special Collections at Central St Martins, University of the Arts, supported a plan to print a facsimile that would be faithful to the original ideology of a fast, cheaply produced, experimental art magazine. Because Flanagan had donated his copies for safe keeping and with the intention that they would be available for research purposes, it was necessary to get a licence from the University of the Arts to print the book. A thousand copies were printed last year and its availability gives a fresh look at the collaborations between poetry, the visual arts and the ferment of ideas, between art practices, which embrace concrete poetry as a sculptural form, the beat and underground scene during the 1960s. Significantly, the Royal Academy shop considers the book "too avant garde" to stock. This demonstrates that, for the RA, the twenty-three-year-old Barry Flanagan in 1964–5 was producing work of a more radical nature than the Young British Artists, showcased at the RA in the Sensation exhibition in 1997.

Archival crossovers and networks frequently raise the spectre of ownership and questions of copyright and data protection become of paramount concern in many of these instances. There are items originating with Barry Flanagan amongst Peter Townsend's editorial papers that comprise the *Studio International* Archive.[11] One day in April 1969, Flanagan turned up unannounced at the offices of *Studio International*, 37 Museum Street, London WC1. He had a bundle of papers which he wanted to discuss with the editor, Peter Townsend, who suggested they adjourn to the Museum Tavern, the pub next door. Flanagan was motivated by the current magazine issue, which was dedicated to minimalism. One consequence of their conversations was the publication of Flanagan's 'An Old New York Letter', in which he questioned the motivation of the "gallant studio" in giving so much space to scandal. At a later date, when Eva Hesse died in 1970, Flanagan approached Townsend with the proposal for a homage to be published in *Studio International* that would be formed by Hesse's writing on her work. He brought the catalogue for the 'Art in Process iv' catalogue, held at Finch College, New York in December 1969 from where her statement was taken and left it in the office with his introductory note.[12] Authorship and ownership do not necessarily go hand in hand: archives frequently contain papers with different copyright statuses and data-protection concerns.

11 Held at Tate Gallery Archive, TGA 20028
12 TGA 20028 *Studio International* July/August 1970 for Flanagan's annotated copy. The Flanagan Archive holds a replacement copy purchased recently as part of the policy to obtain items Flanagan had lost.

Flanagan was continually seeking out strategies for compilation and used questions to devise plans for denoting systems of reference, which might lead to the incorporation of 'imaginary solutions'. An introduction to Alfred Jarry's writing by means of a gift of *The Evergreen Review* from a poet friend, Nick Wayte in Bristol in 1963, resulted in a meeting of minds. Flanagan referred to Jarry as his anti-artistic father figure, a historical hero and a symbolic figure emblematic of the individual imagination in revolt. In the archive Flanagan's discussions on Jarry are to be found in the interview with Lynne Cook and in Alex Turnbull's film interviews. Throughout his life Flanagan paid homage to Alfred Jarry, the playwright and inventor of 'pataphysics', which is "the science of imaginary solutions". It is a sensibility evident in Flanagan's thesis from St Martins School of Art 1966. He writes:

Perhaps the question is how I absorb, correlate, sense and continue to do so. How may I spend this accumulation that is absorbed, correlated and sensed. A person may walk, talk, breath, hear, see, eat, feel, and he must make sense. The person is aware and accounts.

My hand touched the table for the very first time, for all it know [sic]. My brain seems to have a strange unreal life of its own: it will remember many other time, times. Time and times, timing timing times timing timing, and rather over qualify the touch. Its [sic] just not good enough, my conduct does not add up to the simple demands of this digression and wondering situation. The sheer adventure and life of the touch is the only relevancy.

These ambiguous thought processes and Flanagan's elliptical forms of expression featured heavily in conversations and shaped creative ways of approaching the archive project.

The Archive Project

Barry Flanagan's archive is a unique collection of papers that provides a broad contextual backdrop to the artist's work. A mix of sketchbooks, diaries, correspondence, writings, photographs and casting records, the archive spans the whole of Flanagan's career from the late 1950s to 2009. Documentation including sketches for sculpture, letters on commissions and photographic source material all give a fascinating insight into the artist's practice. As a coherent body of papers it is of value in itself, embodying a case study of the working life of an artist and the creative process in action.

In 2009 the archive arrived in large cardboard boxes at the estate's offices in AB Fine Art Foundry, east London. The sorting process began. As with other artist's archives, the division between personal and professional was ill defined and, in common with many non-institutional archives, Flanagan's papers often lacked a clear filing structure. At times the original order was difficult to detect. Additionally, the line between an artist's 'archival' working papers and the work itself is often blurred. Grappling with these issues during the cataloguing process was a fascinating learning experience. The cataloguing project was undertaken alongside the compilation of information on Flanagan's works and exhibitions; these complementary tasks fed into one another.

Creating an integrated website at www.barryflanagan.com meant that data on the archive and artworks had to be inputted on a single system. Information on some exhibitions, artworks and items from the archive had been entered on a pre-existing database using TMS (The Museum System) software. Indeed, the establishment of this database, along with a number of other efforts made to inventory Flanagan's work, is documented in the archive. On TMS, all entries, whether for an exhibition or a document such as a press cutting from an archive file, were treated as 'objects'. They could not be properly defined, adequately described, nor understood in the context of their relationships with other entries. The software would not support the mapping of a hierarchical structure for the description of the archive – multi-level description is customarily used in the cataloguing of archives. Nevertheless, the database proved a very useful resource; data could be transferred with relative ease onto the new system. Rather than muddle through making compromises using established museum or archive cataloguing software, Filemaker, a versatile database programme, was selected for the project. Different layouts, functionality and data fields were generated for all sections of the database, including the archive catalogue. With reference to ISAD(G), an international standard for archival description, and in collaboration with the database designer, the catalogue was created with a hierarchical structure and core metadata fields at each level.

A central concern was the usability of the archive catalogue, particularly for visitors to the site unfamiliar with archival research. A clear, simple design was prioritised with a user guide free from confusing jargon. Also, the hierarchy opened left to right, like a computer folder structure, and the selection of a search result always brought the user back to the file's place in the hierarchy structure. Small sacrifices were made to accommodate this design – text fields were limited, as were the number of levels in the hierarchy structure. Both allowances, however, were generous and caused no major disruption to the description process.

Crucially, the use of Filemaker software allowed dynamic links to be created between entries for artworks, exhibitions and archive files on the website. It is hoped that enabling users to weave through the two sections of the website will encourage new and creative ways of thinking about Flanagan's work. Descriptions of, and scans from, archive files can be linked to artwork entries, complete with photographs and full specifications, and to exhibition entries that include lists of works and exhibiting artists. These links serve a number of functions in the archive catalogue. Firstly, they have a similar role to authority files, ensuring that accurate data on subject matter featured in descriptions of archive files is consistently referenced. Data entries on artworks and exhibitions provide archival descriptions with important supporting information. Secondly, they encourage users visiting an artwork or exhibition page, perhaps new to archival research, to examine related documentation, promoting awareness of the archive.

Linking archive file descriptions to related artwork and exhibition entries brings together files on specific subjects that are not necessarily closely related in the hierarchy structure. Similarly, the linking system enables archive files from different series to be linked to one another as 'related files'. For instance, a poster marking the centenary of the birth of Joan Miró featuring *Homage*, 1988 by Flanagan (JBF/5/6/1.14) is linked to a file of letters from the Fundació Joan Miró, Barcelona regarding the commissioning of the project in a separate series of correspondence (JBF/6/2/4.20). These relationships provide the archivist with a way of imposing new orders and different groupings on the archive, which might be of interest to researchers, without upsetting the original order and hierarchy structure.

In the first instance, links have been made referencing names, subjects, artworks and themes. It is anticipated that this network of relationships will be built upon as the site evolves. There is potential for user navigation, feedback from readers and new research interests to contribute to the development of this aspect of the online resource. The scope of the archive and the site's functionality are best demonstrated through an examination of a couple of Barry Flanagan's exhibitions on the website. Here follows two case studies that, using the exhibition pages as starting points, show how one might browse across the site to explore related archival documentation.

Exhibition poster for
'Barry Flanagan, Stone
and Bronze Sculptures'
at the Venice Biennale
in 1982

BARRY FLANAGAN
SCULTURE IN PIETRA E IN BRONZO
PADIGLIONE DELLA GRAN BRETAGNA
XXXX BIENNALE DI VENEZIA
13 GIUGNO – 12 SETTEMBRE 1982
THE BRITISH COUNCIL

'Barry Flanagan, Stone and Bronze Sculptures', British Pavilion, Venice Biennale (1982)

Barry Flanagan represented Britain at the Venice Biennale in 1982. This retrospective, like the recent Tate show 'Barry Flanagan: Early works 1965–1982' (September 2011 – January 2012), included work crafted in stone, canvas, sheet metal and bronze spanning his career from the early 1960s to 1982.

On the exhibition page, one is provided with comprehensive information on the exhibition including dates and a list of works shown, along with other touring venues, namely the Whitechapel

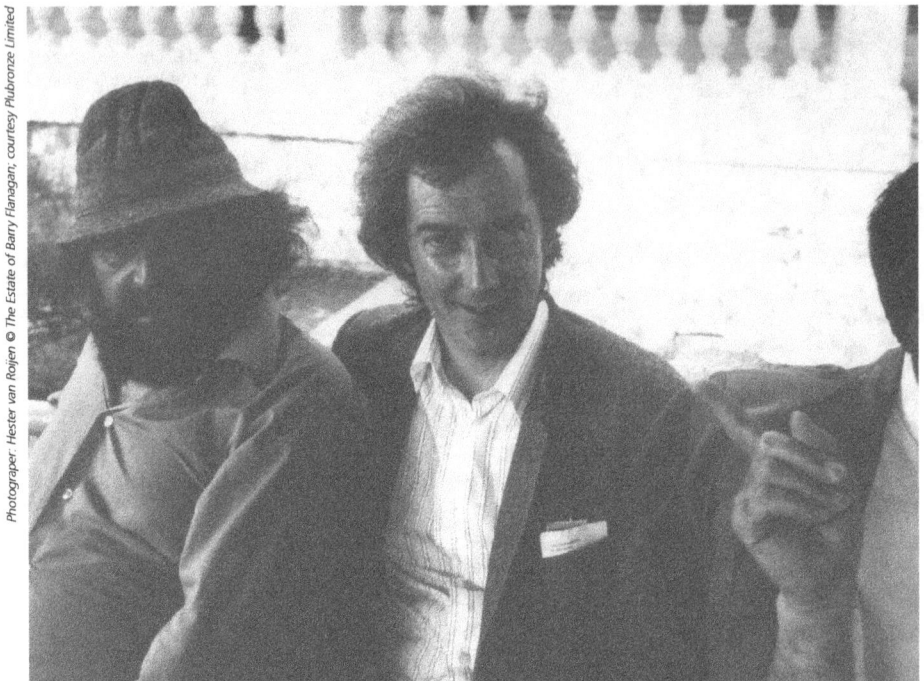

Photographer: Hester van Roijen © The Estate of Barry Flanagan; courtesy Plubronze Limited

Art Gallery, London and Museum Haus Esters, Krefeld. Scrolling down, the page displays a list of 20 archive files containing material related to the exhibition, complete with reference numbers and thumbnails of any scanned images. These links take the user away from the artworks section and into the archive catalogue.

Barry Flanagan (centre) with David Brown (left) at the Venice Biennale, 1982

The first two files listed are posters (JBF/5/6/1.8 and 9) for this exhibition and the touring show at the Whitechapel. One is in Italian and shows one of Flanagan's hare drawings, while the other is illustrated by an installation shot showing *Soprano*, 1981 in the foreground. The poster, in turn, is linked to this artwork, enabling further related browsing. These files form part of a series of posters acquired by Flanagan featuring his work and promoting his exhibitions, providing an insight into how they were presented to the public.

Visual material, in particular photographs, forms a central component of the archive. A wide variety of prints, in addition to slides and negatives, ranges from installation shots and studio shots of work, to source material for work and photographs of trips and events. Files of photographs linked to the exhibition include images of a gathering held in AB Fine Art Foundry prior to the Biennale (JBF/3/4/2.6). Flanagan maintained a life-long connection with the east London foundry and these images show him socialising with friends and colleagues in amongst his work. Installation shots by Anthony Stokes (JBF/3/6/1/3.3) give an insight into how the show was curated. A file of photographs compiled for publication in the exhibition catalogue for a retrospective at the Irish Museum of Modern Art, Dublin in 2006 (JBF/3/7/1/2.2) is also linked to the exhibition page. These include a photograph of Flanagan with David Brown of the Tate Gallery and the British Council, at the Biennale by Hester van Roijen, who owned her own gallery and used to work for Waddington Galleries, London.

Administrative papers, while less visually appealing, arguably provide researchers with a better impression of how the artist operated behind the scenes. They map out the organisation of exhibitions, the scheduling of media appearances and the proofing of publications. Many of these kinds of papers, including correspondence, invoices, drafts and inventories, are arranged in a category called 'Operational Papers' (JBF/6). Here one can find a chronology of Flanagan's life drawn up for the Biennale catalogue by one of Flanagan's assistants (JBF/6/2/8.4). A file of correspondence with the British Council regarding the return of photographs used in the exhibition catalogue (JBF/6/3/1.4) is also linked to the exhibition page.

Audio-visual material forms a small but exciting portion of the archive. Flanagan rarely made media appearances but some of the recordings held in the archive are linked to the Biennale exhibition page. These include Lynne Cooke's 1982 interview with Flanagan (JBF/4/1.1). The audio recording formed the backing to a slide show featured in the show when it toured to the Whitechapel Gallery. An episode of the *South Bank Show*, broadcast in 1983, included Melvyn Bragg's interview with Flanagan that references the exhibition in Venice (JBF/4/1.2). Clips of other audio-visual material can be accessed online in the 'Media' section of the website.

'Barry Flanagan on Park Avenue', 54th to 59th Street, New York (1995–6)

This outdoor exhibition involved the installation of some of Flanagan's later work – bronze hares – along Park Avenue. Flanagan is best known for these large bronzes which feature in public places across the world and which dominated the later part of his career. He exhibited a number of times in the US, including at the Museum of Modern Art and the Solomon R. Guggenheim Museum, New York.

Leaping Hare on *Crescent Bell* installed on Park Avenue, New York in 1995

An exploration of links to the archive catalogue from this exhibition page brings to light different kinds of archival material. The photograph files show the installation process (JBF/3/8.20 and JBF/3/8.21). These dynamic, black-and-white images by Jessica Craig Martin show sculptures including *Hare and Bell*, 1988 and *Hospitality*, 1990 being hoisted, set down and unveiled. Additional related photograph files include those of AB Fine Art Foundry staff in New York (JBF/3/9.19). These images tell their own story; Flanagan took the group out to the US to see the works in situ.

One of the richest sources in the archive is Flanagan's writings, most of which can be found in the series called 'Writings with related papers' (JBF/1/2). These include notes on his thoughts, artist's statements and drafts for correspondence, in addition to related papers including press cuttings. One such file (JBF/1/2.42) is linked to the Park Avenue exhibition. It contains notes on the hare as a chosen subject entitled 'Why the Hare?' and a biro drawing for an armature, alongside small photocopies of the aforementioned Park Avenue installation shots. This file, like many in the archive, is linked to other archive files in different series, but covering similar themes. Here one can navigate to a file of digital printed images in a series of source material for work (JBF/3/3/2.1) that includes additional documentation on the hare. A file of press cuttings, including reviews (JBF/5/1/2.3), also contains reference to the Park Avenue exhibition. From the early 1970s Flanagan accumulated reviews, alongside other press cuttings that took his interest, in loose files like this one.

Hospitality, 1990 is one of the artworks on exhibition at Park Avenue. Browsing onto the artwork page, the user is once more encouraged to delve back into the archive. A couple of correspondence files are referenced including (JBF/6/3/1.33) a file of letters on the gift and sale of work. In terms of images, not only can one see photographs of *Hospitality*, 1990 installed elsewhere, for instance in Knokke in Belgium (JBF/3/8.26), but also of work in progress at AB Fine Art Foundry in London (JBF/3/4/2.7). These show casts of the leaping hare alongside foundry machinery and staff. In bringing together these archive files, a photographic diary of the life of the artwork is compiled, backed by a network of information from written sources. One can navigate back to the archive catalogue and still understand this documentation in its archival context.

The artist is confronted by numerous options when considering how to deal with their archive including legal issues, where to deposit it, how to make it available and their legacy. The path taken by Barry Flanagan and, later, his estate – to retain custody and take the initiative by creating a combined online archive catalogue and artwork and exhibition database – serves both to promote access and to encourage a fresh examination of Flanagan's life and works. Archive and artworks are exhibited side by side on the website, creating a visual web of information and providing comprehensive contextual data on both sides. The user is able to navigate across the site, searching and browsing for connections and related information. The website will eventually embody an online catalogue raisonné with the archival documents and references forming a key part of the network of interconnectivity. The resource is open to all researchers online at www.barryflanagan. com. Appointments can be arranged through the Estate of Barry Flanagan.

WITNESSING THE ARCHIVE: ART, CAPITALISM AND MEMORY
Sas Mays

11

Introductory Remarks: Witnessing Material

> Invention, it must be humbly admitted, does not consist in creating out of the void, but out of chaos; the materials must in the first place be afforded: it can give form to dark, shapeless substances, but cannot bring into being the substance itself.

Against the romantic presumption that invention is a faculty of genius, a godlike creation ex nihilo, from nothing, Mary Shelley's introduction to *Frankenstein* (1818) appears to argue that invention, perhaps as the monster is assembled from existing body parts, is rather a matter of the collection and reordering of existing material. Shelley's argument might provide a general model for the production of knowledge, the new emerging from the re-arrangement of the existing. It could also provide a model for art making and art practice, considered generically as a form of collage, as much as it also then gestures to what in the art world is called 'curation' and to what might also be called, given the diffusion of the term into contemporary art parlance, 'archiving'. But how might 'the archive' be understood here?

In Derrida's *Archive Fever* (1996/1995), the archive in its Classical form requires a number of basic elements: a substrate, an inscribed material; its consignation or ordered gathering within an arkheion, a domicile or housing; and its protection and interpretation by an archon, a magistrate of state law (Derrida 1996: 1–4). Through Godzich's introduction to de Man's *The Resistance to Theory* (1986), we might add to this schema, or theory of the archive, the figure of the theoria (Godzich 1986: xiv–xv) – those who, in Classical Greece, witnessed and attested to events, so that they could be brought into public discourse for a process of deliberation, toward a consensus that would be in itself taxonomic and ordering, such that the event might be recorded, drawn into state history and thus be ratified by normative archival inclusion. In their witnessing, the theoria rely on perception – on aesthesis, the historical and etymological basis of the term 'aesthetics' – so perhaps we should think of the relation between artist and archivist within this schema: the artist as a figure of the theoria, the process of consignation and domiciliation enacted by the archon or archivist. We must consider, however, the complexity of these figures, recognising that each performs the other's functions. Just as the artist negotiates existing (archival) rules and laws for the production of art, so the archivist is also a witness to the work. And testimony, as indicated through the figure of the theoria, is archival: it produces documents, material – so in addition, we should also mark here the condition of the archive for Derrida: each attempt to witness the archive, to account definitively for its subject, or finally to produce the very stuff of its subject, at once, and at the same time, adds more stuff to the archive (Derrida 1996: 68). It is in this sense, then, that the archive cannot produce a finite index of its subject; but such finality is endlessly deferred. As Derrida wrote in *Archive Fever*:

> By incorporating the knowledge deployed in reference to it, the archive augments itself, engrosses itself, it gains in auctoritas. But in the same stroke it loses the absolute and meta-textual authority it might claim to have. … The archivist produces more archive, and that is why the archive is never closed.
>
> (Derrida 1996: 68)

To desire the closure of the archive, or to desire the absolute fit between the archive and the thing archived, and thus finally to wrest the very stuff from all this stuff, without remainder, without more stuff, is to fall into the condition of archive fever. The impulse to finalise the archive is, in the end, one that can be compared to Lyotard's term in *The Postmodern Condition* (1984/1979) for the attempt to shut down on the production of new meanings and discourses: terror (Lyotard 1984: 46). It is, finally, and in its desire for finality, totalising, and totalitarian.

A book, whether printed or digital, likewise, is at once an ordered collection of accounts, witnessings – an archive of a kind (in being constructed through archival orders: index, taxonomy, consignation and so forth) and a witness that must also open itself to further connections, developments, disagreements – so that its finality is endlessly deferred. Such deferral is also a matter of the materiality of the book: whatever its structural, internal or physical relations to commensuration and finality, it is also, and at once, an object that comprises more stuff which must itself be archived – in libraries, galleries, retail outlets, homes and other institutions – and that will also be subject to perishment and dissolution. The book, then, gestures beyond itself and toward the world. As Gerhard Richter indicates, in his introduction to the interview with Derrida published as *Copy, Archive, Signature: A Conversation on Photography* (Derrida 2010/2000), such gesturing to the world is also a function of the photograph in its witnessing. And it is a world defined by a pervading economic problematic: in discussing the gifting of autographed photographs, Derrida suggests that such objects may be both a repetitive sign of "capitalisation, at once infinite and derisory", to which it "bears witness", and its difference – the possibility of an interruption of technological capitalism (Derrida 2010: 23, 26). The issue of the witness and the record, the theoria and the archon, the event and the arkheion, is thus not simply a question of subjects, but of the matter that they archive, and which then also concerns the witnessing produced by material objects. The witnessing of the archive must thus be understood in its genitive and accusative senses. It is specifically through this double genitive of witnessing material that this chapter addresses relations between art, archive and capital – firstly by discussing in more detail the relations between capitalism, archive and memory in the contemporary situation; secondly by turning toward a particular art-historical and theoretical account, or bearing witness to, relations between art, archive and economy. As Derrida also argues in 'Copy, Archive, Signature', the testimony of witnessing is complexly related to an act of invention that both finds, or receives, and creates or produces (Derrida 2010: 43–6). Hence, if the idea of the archive here is constructed, or invented, through the generalisations of critical theory and art history, this attention to 'the archive' generally conceived will nevertheless turn, finally, to archives more specifically indicated.

Capitalism and the Archive

Broadly speaking, we appear to live at a time witnessing an intensification of issues of, questions about, and recognition of, archives and archiving. This intensification can significantly be understood as a result of the socio-cultural, political and economic changes brought about by developments in capitalism and, more specifically, this apparent intensification can be argued to result from the development and spread of technologies of communication and storage, from the shift from the analogue to the digital and from analogue to digital institutions. These shifts raise a glut of complex, interconnected questions.

Firstly, given the apparently massive rise in technologies of memory – of digital documents and their storage – there is the question of over-accumulation. This issue surfaces in the prologue to Sven Spieker's *The Big Archive: Art from Bureaucracy* (2009):

"When an archive has to collect everything… it will soon succumb to entropy and chaos" (Spieker 2009: xiii). Western culture's fear of excessive accumulation has produced a variety of responses to this issue – for example: physical (destruction and perishment), editorial (cataloguing and selection), user-based (cataloguing, filtering and search criteria) and ideational (the privileging of experience, thought or organic memory over mnemotechnical accumulation). This latter issue then raises questions concerning relations between internal, organic memory and external, technological memory. Of course, 'technological memory' can refer to archaic technologies – writing, painting, sculpture – as much as to modern analogue forms – phonography, photography and film – but, with the spread of digital technology, memory appears to be ever more transferred to external devices: the issue of digital proliferation indicates the question of the transcription of memory from analogue to digital platforms and thus of what may be lost, transformed or created in such translation.[1] There is also the question of the stability of such external, technological memory (as much as the stability of organic memory), given the rapid production and obsolescence of digital memory formats – the floppy disc, the compact disc and so on – and their fallibility.

Thus follow questions concerning the remembering and forgetting of histories and traditions, and of the reclaiming, rewriting and reinvention of the past. Such reinvention or invention can of course be thought of positively, but it may also be performed for pernicious political and ideological gains. The right's attacks on trade-union power in Britain, for example, have included the rebranding of May Day as a bank, rather than a workers', holiday, thus effacing political memory in conjunction with the fabrication of 'heritage' as a marketisable, commodified and depoliticised form of history. This brings us, then, to issues of archival exclusion and reinscription, an activity that has of course characterised much feminist and postcolonial discourse in their reinscriptions of excluded voices, memories and experiences. This then in turn raises questions concerning the forms of and uses of public and private memory and archives, and thus issues of the ownership and control of archives and memory – particularly given that the apparent democratisation of the communication, production and dissemination of ideas in the digital sphere is clearly paralleled by intense capitalisation and mediated by demands of state control. We could think here, for example, of cuts to art funding and the demands for its quantifiable economic performance that will always be the desire of the neoliberal right

1   This question is central to the discourse of digital humanities – in terms of its aesthetic dimension, see the introduction to Drucker's *Speclab* (Drucker 2009: xi–xix).

in its withering away of the state.

This time is thus also one in which the conceptualisation and understanding of the archive and of archives, as constructed and performed in the practices of art theory, art criticism, art history and art practices – making, curation, collection – are of key importance. Indeed, if it should in this context be argued that the overriding issue for art and archiving is this relation to capitalism, this in turn raises questions of the possibility of evading its apparent hegemony, of a counter-force to its homogenisations and meager differentiations, of subversive art-practices and of counter-archives. Given the current rise in the market of archival studies within the institutions of the humanities, and of culture more widely, and conflicts of method and understanding between them, the politics of interpretation also devolves upon the conceptualisation of the archive in these disciplinary contexts; that is, not only the concept of the archive generally speaking, but of (relations between) archival types – the archive in its professional sense, the library, the museum and suchlike. We should also recognise, of course, that Western art has its own particular history of relation to archives, and to 'the archive' more generally thought, for example, in the Dada turn toward collage and print culture (as with photo-collages of Hanna Höch, among many others) and the turn toward the archive in Anglo-American conceptual art, as much as in the more recent turn toward 'art as research'.

But we should also recognise that art's relation to archival forms is not simply positive; indeed, the twentieth-century Western avant-gardes' antipathy toward the status quo, the outmoded and the repetitious, and the concomitant affirmation of novelty and futurity, has often been articulated through antipathy toward, for example, the state museum, figured as a mausoleum of dead forms.[2] We must then recognise, through such archival antipathy, the issue of the non-archival, the anti-archival and the extra-archival – the issue of that which does not emerge from the archive, or that which is not or cannot be contained within archives, and that which might refuse, reject or destroy archives – not necessarily in the name of mere nihilism, but in the name of futurity or in the name of difference to the past and present. The problematic issue of the extra-archival might be articulated through Foucault: while the essay 'Nietzsche, Genealogy, History' (1977/1971) argues that archival research may positively broach new knowledge, the later Foucault's insistence, in the volumes of *The History of Sexuality*, on doing rather than speaking, argues that to engage in discourse is to be open to examination and archivisation within normative

2 A key figure, for example, in Adorno's complex account of Valéry (Adorno 1967: 175–85).

constraints: the 'repressive hypothesis' is a fallacy, which means that the proliferating discourse of sex encodes, records and archives its 'deviants' as they speak their difference. This aspect of Foucault, then, appears to champion non-normative, different experiences as pertaining to the extra-archival, a positive exteriority in comparison to the apparent exclusion of marginalised social and political voices from history and memory.

There are, then, in this context, four key aspects for contemporary thought of the archive: the accumulation and limitation of archival material and the question of memory; the ownership of and access to archives; the politics of concepts of the archive; and the question of the unarchival. We might say, in generalisation, that the contemporary attention to the archive thus appears, paradoxically, as a symptom both of an apparent proliferation of technological memory and of a loss of memory; or at least, as a symptom of the technological and topological shift of memories and forms of memory.

But we must also recognise that this condition, while partly subject to fluctuation, has also always been the case, as is evidenced by Western culture's repetitive and intense interest in memory, tradition and history. Within this interest, we could mark two basic attitudes. On the one hand, art and culture have feared the loss of memory and tradition, as with, for example, Ruskin's thoughts on painting and architecture, in which capitalism and technology were destroying traditional social life and the landscape, and against which art might provide a memory of better times and values. On the other hand, the forgetting of tradition has been championed – and we could again think here of the European avant-gardes' antipathy to traditional forms of art, such as in Dada. These two attitudes might be understood in terms of Lyotard's 'Answering the Question: What is Postmodernism?', in *The Postmodern Condition*, not only as postures adopted by different cultural and political camps, but as two poles essential to, and thus traditional to, the modern condition. For Lyotard here the modern attitude is one characterised by a nostalgia for order and for the past; the postmodern by an affirmation of disorder and of the future. Yet Lyotard recognises that in modernity, these two attitudes are cyclically entwined – invention and disorder followed by canonisation and conservatism. What characterises the postmodern is the suspension of the second movement. In terms of the discourse of the sublime so familiar to art, and which clearly influences Lyotard's thought, these two attitudes may be mapped onto those of the first and second moments of the sublime: shock and disruption, followed by resolution. We might also map this structure, of excess and containment, novelty and repetition, onto the archival problematic of stuff, in terms of the transition from stuff to the very stuff, and to stuff again – thus recognising the circularity of the movement between the two poles. Thus, we should recognise the attention to memory and loss at least as far back as the text attributed to Longinus, *On the Sublime*, and trace the origins of its concerns in the Socratic philosophers. The movement, from disorder to order and to disorder again, must thus be seen not only as an issue of the modern in the sense of Modernism, but of Western culture from end to end – from Plato to NATO and beyond. Therefore, the current focus on archive and memory is a perennial aspect of Western thought; one determined in part by culture's continual adjustment to technological change, alongside our specific contemporary conditions, which are, to a massive extent, and as indicated, those of the capitalisation of technologies of communication and storage.[3]

Deleuze, Foster and the Archival Impulse

This question of art's relation to economy is something that significantly inflects Foster's engagement with art and the archive in 'An Archival Impulse' (2004), as it poses the difficult question of contemporary art's relation to global capitalism through Deleuze and Guattari's attention to that latter force in *A Thousand Plateaus: Capitalism and Schizophrenia* (2007/1980). I emphasise Foster's text here because it is both a description of and, perhaps more significantly, a symptom of the intense engagement with the archive in our time – a witnessing in the sense of a double genitive. And it is symptomatic in a number of senses other than in reflecting archival preoccupation: it appears to think 'the archive' by recourse to a critical-theoretical matrix that is almost entirely disengaged from archives as they are conceived in the professional practices of archiving, through a mélange of theoretical references that comprise a kind of loose collage – a mode of writing that has characterised so much art-theoretical writing; and it substantiates this activity of collaging through its utilisation of Deleuzian ideas, which in itself is significant of the spread of Deleuzianism in art theory and art history. Indeed, part of the point of this section is to offer a critique of the internal logic of Deleuzian thought as much, through this, as to offer a caution against art's impressionistic utilisation of philosophical figures: as I will eventually come to show, Deleuzian thought involves what can in fact be understood as an anti-archival impulse.

3 I discuss the relation between the sublime and the archive in more detail through Ansel Adams (Mays 2005: 87–108) and attend in more detail to the issues of technophobia and archival antipathy in the history of philosophy, through Plato, Kant and Hegel, and through Derrida and Badiou, in a longer discussion of philosophy and the legal archive (Mays 2009: 73–96).

Foster's account of the archive is based on the figure of the 'rhizome', which, in *A Thousand Plateaus*, is a figure of endless lateral connection that is opposed to vertical, hierarchical, centralised organisation. The rhizome, structured for example like the tubers and offshoots of the potato, figures endless, lateral, partially ordered connections between heterogeneous elements; the taproot, structured rather like a carrot, and like the traditional codex form of the book, figures centralised, replete knowledge and an ordered archive logically catalogued (Deleuze and Guattari 2007: 4–28). Likewise, Foster's account of archival art-practice is clearly couched in an idea of endless connectibility. For example, in his drive toward a "counter-hegemonic archive", Thomas Hirschhorn is cited as stating: "I want to use these forms to make spaces for the movement and endlessness of thinking" (Foster 2004: 6–9). Again, in Foster's description of Tacita Dean, the nonlinearity of the personal journey of the artist is "unchartered" – it "meandered... to no obvious destination". Dean's work for Foster is thus an allegory of the archive as "always incomplete" (Foster 2004: 12): "the work functions as a possible portal between an unfinished past and a reopened future" and is based on "enigmas without resolution" (Foster 2004: 15–16). Her utopia is "not as the other of reification (as in Hirschhorn) but as a concomitant of her archival presentation of the past as fundamentally heterogeneous and always incomplete" (Foster 2004: 16).[4]

Hence, despite the heterogeneity of the artists in Foster's consideration, there are general levels of comparability: each operates within the tension between archives of the private and the questioning of public archives (Foster 2004: 21). Indeed, through the concept of the rhizome, Foster proposes a general model for the archive: "Perhaps all archives develop in this way, through mutations of connection and disconnection" (Foster 2004: 6). While art here is "institutive" and "legislative" rather than "destructive" or simply "transgressive", it is also "indeterminant like the contents of any archive" (Foster 2004: 5). Generally speaking, then, the archive is defined in its endlessly partial indeterminacy. In this, Foster's description agrees with its theoretical source. Here, Deleuze and Guattari describe the rhizome: as having no beginning or end, only a middle; as a network of "finite" parts "forever rearranging" (Deleuze and Guattari 2007: 5, 19–23). The rhizome, in its lateral connectivity, is of course meant to exceed the stricture of the taproot, a figure of centralisation and unification; yet one that is also characterised by its "endless" (binarising) subdivision. The two forms are in fact aspects of "a model" that is "perpetually

4 A further development of the issue of archival antipathy might be noted in terms of the specifically utopian character of the archival impulse, as exampled by Foster's discussion of Dean (Foster 2004: 16). As Foster indicates, Frederic Jameson's work is key in this area of study (Foster 2004: 11, n. 25). Nevertheless, in Jameson's thought, as indicated by the collection of essays published as *Archaeologies of the Future* (2007), it is implicit that the archive generally speaking has a negative status – it represents the past as opposed to a utopian futurity. At least, such a negative valorisation might be noted, in recollection of the Shelley citation with which I began, where Jameson appeals to romantic thought, and the opposition between utopian fancy, which works with the memory of things given in the world, and utopian imagination, which has a greater shaping power (Jameson 2007: 43–56). Given that fancy attempts the formulation of "systemic schemes" (Jameson 2007: 56), which we might connect here to...

note continues on next page

in construction or collapsing… perpetually prolonging itself" (Deleuze and Guattari 2007: 22). The interconnection of these forms in *A Thousand Plateaus* is perhaps recognised in Foster's description of the tension between endless indeterminacy and "institution" and "legislation". Nevertheless, the effort, in Deleuze and Guattari as much as in Foster, is to attempt to maintain the rhizomatic without it falling back into centralising stricture. In overall terms, then, Foster describes the archival impulse as "a will to connect the unconnectable". In this sense, then, there is an evident antipathy here to the archive considered in its traditional sense as a replete, fully ordered, fixed repository – that is, considered as a form of epistemological or mnemonic stricture. As Foster's reference to Hirschhorn indicates, the stricture in question is of course that of capitalism and the state; a system of control that is to some extent associated with the taproot. But the relation between the two forms of order (rhizome and root) and capital is in fact more complex than this might suggest, as can now be indicated through historical changes in capitalism.

The historical issue could be indicated through one of Deleuze's texts referenced by Foster, 'Postscript on the Societies of Control' (1990). Rather than by the production, colonisation and concentration of capital, as in the preceding model of the 'disciplinary society' (as analysed by Foucault), the subsequent (and contemporary) model of 'control' works through assemblage and dispersion, and involves the transformability or deformability of entities such as the family and the factory (Deleuze 1990: 6). As Deleuze states, where discipline was "long… infinite and discontinuous", control is "short-term… continuous and without limit" (Deleuze 1990: 6) – and thus endless in its hegemonic extension. Deleuze's remark here that "Even art has left the spaces of enclosure in order to enter into the open circuits of the bank" (Deleuze 1990: 6) should lead us to question the relevance of such a description for contemporary art-practice; for example, in the context of short-term funding projects for art-as-research, etc. Indeed, if this gestures toward an identity between art-practice and capitalism, the art-archives that Foster discusses may be "perverse orders that aim to disturb the symbolic order at large" or indicators that the symbolic no longer operates through totalities (Foster 2004: 21). But as Foster also says, if the world is both connected and disconnected, and order is both incoherent and systemic, then this is something that archival art "seems to mimic" (Foster 2004: 22, n.60), but not to redeploy. Foster's point, here, and as directed by Deleuze and Guattari's insistent engagement with forms of

…"legal systems endlessly drafted and amended" (Jameson 2007: 10), the opposition can be connected to that between the totalising aspirations of the utopian programme and the more radical and open aspirations of the utopian impulse (Jameson 2007: 4–5). If such implications were to be consistently established in Jameson's text, it might be that Foster offers something of an inversion, given the affirmation of the utopian through the archival detour; yet, as indicated, the appeal to the rhizome would be ultimately contradictory to such an idea. In distinction from such archival antipathy, it is Derrida for whom the archive "opens out of the future" and which may potentiate a future that is different from the mere continuation of the normative present (Derrida 1995: 68).

capitalisation, is to gauge the relation of these practices to capitalism and its symbolic forms, or rather, to suggest that art of the archival impulse may offer the possibility of practices that may not simply be enfolded within the extension of capital.

There is thus an important qualification that needs be drawn regarding the extra-archival, previously registered here through the later Foucault. In order to indicate a form taken by the extra-archival in *A Thousand Plateaus*, the binaries through which it operates need to be further schematised. To the distinction of root and rhizome corresponds the difference between the 'smooth space' of statelessness that precedes the formation of the state, and the 'striated space' of state taxonomy and order. The former spatiality is the privileged one, which holds a kind of utopian or perhaps heterotopian possibility. But we should remember that in *A Thousand Plateaus*, while state capitalism is connected to striation, multinational capitalism is said to "fabricate a kind of deterritorialized smooth space... quite independent of the classical paths to striation". Hence, "the essential thing is... the distinction between striated capital and smooth capital, and the way in which the former gives rise to the latter" (Deleuze and Guattari 2007: 543). Capital thus operates through both forms of spatiality and in its multinational form returns to something like the originarity of the smooth. There is a caution then: "smooth spaces are not in themselves liberatory", just as in Foucault's 'Of Other Spaces' (1986/1967) the prison, as much as the nudist colony, stands as a heteroptopia (Foucault 1986: 22–7). Yet, with some similarity to Foucault's idea of the specific intellectual's engagement, smooth spaces are said to offer the possibility of changing the remits of struggle (Deleuze and Guattari 2007: 551).

Such a possibility is located in the way that smooth space is associated with stateless, 'nomadic', proximate, haptic thought, while striated space is associated with 'monadic', distant, optical thought. Clearly, then, the former mode of thought, less determined by centralising stricture, is connected to the rhizomatic principle of connection. This affirmation of thought is a particular example of Deleuze's general sense that the function of philosophy is to think new concepts – effectively, then, to be the theoria of new thought. Given that the 'archival impulse', considered as a rhizomatic activity, must therefore be a form of nomad art, we would thus need to consider Foster's archival artists here – we might remember then the necessarily haptic aspect of art-objects and Hirschhorn's emphasis on endless thought. As it is put in *A Thousand Plateaus*, nomad space and nomad art "give the eye that beholds them a function that is haptic rather than optical. This is an animality that can be seen only by touching it with one's mind" (Deleuze and Guattari 2007: 545). As this emphasis on animality connects again to the rhizome, figured as it is by rats and wolves, we should see then that the smooth space of haptic thought is offered as a mode of escape from the strictures of striation, and that, as far as the archive is associated, in its finitising taxonomy, with such striation, haptic thought is thus also offered as a mode of escape from the archive thus understood. The haptic thus gestures toward the extra-archival. It would be, then, that the rhizomatic model of connection might propel thought into a dimension exceeding traditional taxonomy. Such a desire can be seen where Kant and Hegel are cited by Deleuze and Guattari as exemplary of the philosopher as 'state functionary'. Thus, opposition is registered here to the Hegelian identification with state bureaucracy, for example, in *The Philosophy of Right* (1829). If thought is said to operate here within the striated space of the architectonic model or monument (Deleuze and Guattari 2007: 412–6), then the specific monument indicated is that of the archive in its bureaucratic or traditional sense. On the other hand, Artaud's affirmation of the formlessness of thought is linked to smooth space and to 'becoming' (Deleuze and Guattari 2007: 416–9). Just as Deleuze and Guattari deign to maintain the rhizome without it becoming rooted, they aim to maintain this violence of becoming without it crossing over into jurisdiction, legality and striation. The archive constructed through rhizomatic connections must not become an archive in the traditional sense.

However, in discussing the connection between the figure of the nomad, smooth space and the haptic, in *On Touching – Jean-Luc Nancy* (2005/2000), Derrida argues that the haptic tends towards a metaphysical desire for immediate proximity (Derrida 2005: 123–6) – such should be clear from its emphasis on closeness. Such a desire is, of course, one of the consistent objects of *Archive Fever*: it is discussed as the desire for the absolute proximity of the event of impression, that can be understood as the moment of inscription upon the substrate, the material of inscription, or as an absolute proximity of the impression or the document and the event to which it refers – a desire that is, however, always displaced by difference. The archive is, for Derrida, as much as a mark of the desire for original proximity, totalisation and finality, always in fact a site of endless deferral and displacement, that is, always an institution of différance. Thus, the privileging of the haptic in Deleuze and Guattari indicates an antipathy toward the archive: at the root of the Deleuzian thought of the rhizome is thus a kind of metaphysical anti-archival impulse: the fever of a desire for the absolute proximity of marker and marked. The rhizomatic, in terms of its association with the smooth and the haptic, leads back to the old philosophical dream of full presence. Or, rather, the desire for immediacy is thus, at one and the same time, an archival impulse in the sense that it is a form of archive fever, and an anti-archival impulse in the sense that it denies the différance of the archive. Indeed, in falling back into metaphysical desire, *A Thousand Plateaus* re-associates itself with the very state function it claims to exceed and thus the very archival model it aims to exceed. As Derrida emphasises in his citation of Deleuze and Guattari, the "continuous variation" of smooth space "operates step by step" – it does not escape segmentation. Hence, as Derrida says, smoothness is only given in a postulation that constitutes "an idealizing polarity, an idealizing tendency" (Derrida 2005: 125), which thus reiterates one of the fundamental divisions, or rather, fundamental striations, of philosophy: that opposition of the actual and the ideal. Thus, the argument, that from the striation of state capitalism, multinational capital produces some kind of simulacrum of smooth space, must be recognised in its reversal: smooth space returns to the striations associated with state capital. Indeed, it is the very idealising tendency of the attempt to escape archival stricture that, in its excess, propels it back into traditional taxonomic order, back into the archive traditionally thought. To the extent that Deleuze and Guattari position themselves, in *A Thousand Plateaus*, as the theoria of haptic thought, they must also, against themselves, become archivists.

The issue of the desire for totalisation in this context also bears on Foster's essay. Just as Foster generally refers to the rhizome rather than the root, the rhizome is the privileged term in the binary for Deleuze and Guattari – the good potato is opposed to the bad carrot. The rhizome represents a more originary form of connection, one that precedes and is freer than the centralising constraints of the root. Such privilege or binary hierarchy can also be read at the reflexive level of Foster's article. The evident heterogeneity of the artists named under the 'archival impulse' necessarily feeds into Foster's comment that the 'will to relate' or to connect the unconnectable is, of course, part of his own activity: it is rhizomatic and thus is possible through the precondition of endless connectability. In its rhizomatic connection of the rhizomatic connections represented by the artists of the archival impulse, Foster's paper is itself then effectively a 'plateau' (Deleuze and Guattari 2007: 24). But while primarily based in Deleuze, Foucault also appears (Foster 2004: 17) – the episteme is said to be always a matter of 'the archive' of existing knowledge – and Foster also mentions that Derrida may be relevant to the practices in question (Foster 2004: 5, note 8). This might in fact be problematic – because Derrida and Foucault and Deleuze are not ultimately amenable in terms of the systematicity of their thinking: to collate them may be to 'connect the unconnectable' within a rhizomatic model; to subsume Derrida and Foucault to Deleuze. Hence, Foster's connection of these thinkers would not be an act of relativisation (in which these thinkers would all play an equal or particular part): whatever its claims to detotalisation the rhizome would be here the colonising, hegemonic and hierarchical paradigm at work, and thus its figuring of opening would return to closure.

Concluding Remarks: The Agon of the Archive

Issues of the openness or closure of the archive, and conflicts between different accounts of such, are not merely philosophical. On the one hand, in the context of contemporary digital archiving, the market is marked by the politics of conflicts between totality and detotalisation – Google's attempt to gain the rights to digitise and profit from every book published in America, and the ensuing conflict with the Open Book Alliance, is a case in point. And such issues concerning the openness of the archive have been taken up by archival theory in the context of its professional practice through ideas of mobility, user-access and detotalisation (Cook and Schwartz 2002: 171–85); and the contemporary sociology of knowledge would provide another context for thinking the endlessness of the archive (Featherstone 2006: 591–5). On the other hand, then, with these different versions of what an archive might be or how it might work, this is a matter of the archive in terms of its conceptualisation, which is disciplinary, institutional, and thus political and material through and through – an issue of the institutions within which such conceptions operate. We have returned, then, to what were suggested as four key issues for art and the archive, by thus turning to conflicts between specific institutional-disciplinary understandings of the issue of archival accumulation, which institutional differences are of course issues of the control, preservation and dissemination of memory, as much as the claim to the extra-archival has, in this context, become significantly political. What this suggests is that how the archive is conceptualised, whether in the context of the professional practice of archiving or art-theory, is always a question, or rather a matter, of these kinds of complexities. This makes it incumbent on artists and archivists, theoreticians and practitioners, not only to recognise the imbrication of their roles, but to recognise that the theories of archives that are instanced or, rather, witnessed and invented by their actions matter.

By way of indicating how a model of conflicting conceptualisations of the archive might be formed, we might turn, finally, to Lyotard's 'Domus and the Megalopolis' (1993/1988) – a paper that discusses the problems of resistance to the technological archive. In archival terms, evidently connecting to technoscientific mnemonics, capitalist rationalisation "hands over the care for memory to the anonymity of archives" that obtain a meager qualification: "Libraries, museums: their richness is in fact the misery of the great conglomerates of council flats" (Lyotard 1993: 194, 197). The rationalisation of the technological archive appears to preclude its subversion: all that can be done is to attempt to witness the 'untameable' – that which cannot be identified, taxonomised and controlled by the techno-capitalist archive. There is, of course, a caution, since to bear witness to the disruption of order is to inscribe, it is thus to bring the untameable into articulation and into the remits of commodification. Yet if, thus, "the witness is a traitor", Lyotard indicates that the betrayal itself may not be complete:

> to say witness is to say trace, and to say trace is to say inscription. Retention, dwelling. … It is impossible to think or write without some facade of a house at least rising up. … And the dwelling of the work is built only from this passage from the awakening to the inscription of the awakening. And this passage itself does not cease to pass. And there is no roof where, at the end, the awakening will be over, where we will be awake, and the inscription will have ceased to inscribe.
>
> (Lyotard 1993: 197–8)

Witnessing, constructing traces, inscriptions, texts, creates an archive. There is some similarity in this image to the arkheion of the Classical archive, but it is one not limited or circumscribed, not final, replete and fixed, as in the ideal image of the state archive; rather, one that, in the necessary impurity of its witnessing, is endless. Elsewhere in this essay, Lyotard corroborates this sense in affirming the endless deconstruction of witnessings, referencing the Deleuzian terms 'deterritorialisation' and 'nomadism' (Lyotard

1993: 203).Yet, in difference to *A Thousand Plateaus*, I might argue that Lyotard's sense of the relations between witnessing, tracing, inscribing and archiving militates against the idea that theoria and archon are ultimately exclusive roles; against the idea that the witness as distinct from the archivist is the primary figure; and, indeed, militates against the capitalist state's synthesis of the two roles toward its own extension.

But such a claim to difference perhaps requires re-reading Lyotard's later essay through the earlier book: the megalopolis can be aligned to the condition of technoscience in *The Postmodern Condition*, in which there is a conflictual multiplicity of knowledge-producing institutions. In this sense, the later text is, I think, congruent with the former, in its reconfiguration of the sublime, and in its affirmation of dissensual paralogy – counter-talk – against the terrorism of consensus and the capitalist demand of effective economic performativity. In this sense the subversion of the megalopolis in the later essay can be thought of in a political context, for example, in thinking resistance to the violence of institutions of control, including those of archival order in its oppressive, capitalist function. Thus, rather than thinking the untameable only as a metaphysically inaccessible exteriority, we might think that we might 'speak', paralogically, of difference to techno-capitalism, through artistic and social activities.[5] Hence also, rather than thinking the process of archivisation as one directed toward consensus, and the ratification of unitary state law and history, as imaged by the normative order of the Classical archive with which we began, such a process might also be an agon, a conflict, which would concern dissensus, disorder, and that might resist inclusion within established systems of understanding. We might see in Lyotard an image of an impure, fractured and fracturing archive, or, rather, and significantly for this collection, the invention of a multiplicity of archives, or counter-archives, in endless agon; technological, witnessing memories, of political, cultural and, precisely here, aesthetic and social struggles.

5 This re-reading of the later essay in terms of the former book is a move intentionally made, for a politics of witnessing, against trends in trauma studies to speak of the priority of an ethics of the absolute other, as in Levinas, or to resacralise language, as in Agamben, in order to make of the archive of testimony a monument to the unspeakable (Agamben 2002/1999). Here, rather, the unspeakable is just what has not yet been articulated – a mediate figure of the otherness of the new rather than the other qua pure transcendental exteriority – which thus nevertheless invents (founds and finds) the untameable.

References

Adorno, Theodor (1967) 'Valéry Proust Museum', in *Prisms*, trans. Samuel and Shierry Weber, MIT Press

Agamben, Giorgio (2002/1999) *Remnants of Auschwitz: The Witness and the Archive*, trans. Daniel Heller-Roazen, Zone Books

Cook, Terry and Joan M. Schwartz (2002) 'Archives, Records, and Power: from (Postmodern) Theory to (Archival) Performance', *Archival Science*, 2, pp.171–85

Deleuze, Gilles (1990) 'Postscript on the Societies of Control', *October*, 59, Winter 1992, 3–7

Deleuze, Gilles and Felix Guattari (2007/1980) *A Thousand Plateaus: Capitalism and Schizophrenia*, trans. Brian Massumi, Athlone Press

Derrida, Jacques (1996/1995) Archive Fever: A Freudian Impression, trans. Eric Prenowitz, University of Chicago Press

Derrida, Jacques (2003) untitled essay, in Frédéric Brenner, *Diasporas: Homelands in Exile,* Vol. 2, trans. Peggy Kamuf, HarperCollins

Derrida, Jacques (2005/2000) *On Touching – Jean-Luc Nancy,* trans. Christine Irizarry, Stanford University Press

Derrida, Jacques (2010/2000) *Copy, Archive, Signature: A Conversation on Photography*, trans. Jeff Fort, Stanford University Press, pp.xxiv–xxv

Drucker, Johanna (2009) *Speclab: Digital Aesthetics and Projects in Speculative Computing*, University of Chicago Press

Featherstone, Mike (2006) 'Archive', *Theory Culture Society*, No. 23, Vol. 2–3, 591–5

Foster, Hal (2004) 'An Archival Impulse', *October*, 110, Fall 2004, 3–22

Foucault, Michel (1977/1971) 'Nietzsche, Genealogy, History', in *Michel Foucault, Language, Counter-Memory, Practice: Selected Essays and Interviews*, Donald Bouchard (ed.), Basil Blackwell

Foucault, Michel (1980/1977) 'Truth and Power', in *Michel Foucault, Power/Knowledge: Selected Interviews and Other Writings 1972–1977*, Colin Gordon (ed.), Harvester Press

Foucault, Michel (1986/1967) 'Of Other Spaces: Utopias and Heterotopias', *Diacritics*, 16, Spring 1986, 22–7

Foucault, Michel (1995/1975) *Discipline and Punish: The Birth of the Prison*, trans. Alan Sheridan, Vintage Books

Godzich, Vlad (1986) 'Foreword: The Tiger on the Paper Mat', in Paul de Man, *The Resistance to Theory*, University of Minnesota Press

Jameson, Frederic (2007) *Archaeologies of the Future: The Desire Called Utopia and Other Science Fictions,* Verso

Lyotard, Jean-François (1984/1979) *The Postmodern Condition: A Report on Knowledge*, trans. Geoff Bennington and Brian Massumi, University of Minnesota Press

Lyotard, Jean-François (1993/1988) 'Domus and the Megalopolis', in *The Inhuman: Reflections on Time*, trans. Geoff Bennington and Rachel Bowlby, Polity Press

Mays, Sas (2005) 'Ansel Adams: the Gender Politics of Literary-Philosophical and Photographic Archives', in Cunningham, Fisher and Mays (eds), Twentieth Century Literature and Photography, Cambridge Scholars Press

Mays, Sas (2009) 'Consigning Badiou to the Past: the Encyclopaedia and Philosophy's Gendered Relation to the Legal Archive', *Cultural Politics*, 5:1 2009, 73–96

Spieker, Sven (2009) *The Big Archive: Art from Bureaucracy*, MIT Press

"I CAN NEVER FIND ANYTHING AMONG THE PILES OF OLD PAPER AND GENERAL RUBBISH": EDWARD BURRA AND HIS ARCHIVE

Jane Stevenson

12

Edward Burra professed no interest in his own past. He reported on an attempt to interview him for a documentary:

> he came down yesterday or the day before to interview me on my past life the Chelsea P the Royal College & when this and when that & what date this & if I shat etc & this & that & done no good as I cant remember a thing, ever, or any date. So he didn't get very much.[1]

John Rothenstein fared no better when he was working on Burra: "I cant remember when Barabau was produced about 5 years ago maybe and as for tales of colege about 1927 or so I don't know".[2,3] However, due to a combination of his own indifference and the devotion of his sister and friends, he ended up leaving an enormous archive. The largest collection is at the Tate, but other sizeable deposits are with his gallery, the Lefevre and the Sussex County Archives. There are some smaller collections in his home town of Rye or in private hands. What all this material does and doesn't tell one prompts some general thoughts about artists and archives, from a biographer's point of view.

The main reason why someone's papers end up in an archive is that the person was important. There will therefore be a variety of journalism and critical writing about him or her. But the value of an archive is that it allows subsequent investigators to get underneath the public image, which would inevitably be some kind of simplification. Additionally, there are all kinds of ways that seeing an individual in context illuminates their work. Two thousand years ago in his life of Alexander the Great, the first true biographer, Plutarch, wrote that "often a man's most brilliant actions prove nothing as to his character, while some trifling incident, some casual remark or joke, will throw more light on what kind of man he was than the bloodiest battle, the greatest array of armies, or the most important siege… it is my duty to dwell especially on those actions which reveal the workings of my heroes' minds." That is as true now as it was then.[4] Once an individual is dead, for the "workings of [your] heroes' minds", you

1   London, Tate Gallery Archive (henceforth TGA) 779.1.106, EB to John Banting [JB], end of November 1971

2   J. Rothenstein, *Edward Burra: Penguin Modern Painters*, Penguin, 1945

3   TGA 8726.3.10, EB to J. Rothenstein, October 1942

4   Plutarch, *The Life of Alexander the Great*, Modern Library Classics

Photograph of Edward Burra by Barbara Ker-Seymer, 1933

cannot rely on what his agent, gallery and relatives choose to tell you. In retrospect, survivors will tend, naturally, to focus on your subject's reaction to crucial exhibitions or to major historical events. Archival material may very well tell you that your subject's attention was somewhere else at the time.

For example, Burra and Paul and Margaret Nash went on a holiday in France which was a turning point in both men's work because it introduced them to French surrealism. Nash's *Harbour and Room* and *Night Piece, Toulon*, and Burra's *The Common Stair* were all inspired by this trip. Burra had been drawn to surrealist art and writings since his first visit to Paris in 1925, but Margaret Nash notes in her memoir that it was during this 1929 trip that Nash himself began thinking seriously about surrealism: "Paul... became really interested in an aspect of Surrealist painting, namely, the release of the dream."[5] Burra, writing to his friend Billy Chappell,

5   London, National Art Library 86.X.29, Margaret Nash memoir of Paul Nash, p.43

fills in one important detail by recording their visit to the Léonce Rosenberg gallery in Paris, which was showing the work of Jean Viollier.

> Hey dey here we are in Toulon… Leonce R was very charming theres a lovely surrealiste peintre called Viollier all red plush birds nests in trees with the Venus de Milos head & shoulders coming thru the top I believe some of them may get shown at the Leicester. Now we know where John Armstrong has been says Margaret glancing round.

Otherwise, though, his correspondence is entirely devoted to the human comedy. On a postcard to Barbara Ker-Seymer, with a pin-up girl doing the splits in a sailor top and very short shorts on the other side, he observes:

> Well dear
> We have all moved to Pension des Lys et les Ruins. Tamaris [actually Pension Les Lys et les Roses], so jolly my dear my window looks on the farm yard such a din you never heard screeching cocks & quacking ducks I am doing to take Refuge in Harry Peil in the mystere du Train Bleu We have fruity drains in our pension we have to go down to lunch with pillow cases over our heads well dearie au revere yrs E

In 1969, a researcher asked Burra about that holiday. He was predictably vague:

> I let myself in for a young man who is doing a thesis on Pauls paintings & wants to see me about our little visit to TOOLONG & Nice as well. I don't remember much about the painting, but that he did an old steamer from the hotel window. Now all gone & by the wind greived.[6]

The only revealing thing here is the final quotation, which is from Thomas Wolfe's *Look Homeward, Angel* (1929):

> Which of us is not forever a stranger and alone?
> O lost, and by the wind grieved, ghost, come back again.

It suggests Burra's own emotional fragility towards the end of his life but also his love for Paul Nash, something he never touched upon directly.

6 AIK 3940–3942, EB to CA [Conrad Aiken] [1969]

From a biographer's point of view, the ideal artist was either extremely organised or, even better, a compulsive hoarder. The latter was true of Burra, who seldom threw anything away. In an absolutely ideal world, the subject of an archive dies at a very advanced age, not survived by lovers, a partner, warring serial spouses or, often even worse, by children. Burra is a very good subject from this point of view, because he was celibate. What biographers want most is maximum preservation and minimum censorship – that stuff has been kept and nobody has had a reason to censor it, because all the scandals the individual may have been involved with are so ancient they have ceased to matter.

This is because a biographer generally starts with wanting to find out about their subject's sex life and income, which between them explain so much about anyone's life, famous or otherwise. But these are generally the last things the people who deposit a personal archive will want to share with posterity. It is impossible to keep everything and the archivists themselves may make decisions, rational from their point of view, about how much they choose to accept. Additionally, before giving an individual's papers to an archive, whoever has made the decision to do so generally weeds it. For example, evidence for adultery tends to be discreetly binned, often to avoid hurting the living. However, the absolutely ideal archive has not been weeded, or at least, not systematically tidied. Lack of system is the biographer's friend. Even if obvious evidence of misbehaviour, such as inappropriate love letters, has been removed from the record, an attentive investigator often finds out where the bodies are buried from stuff that has been kept randomly, such as bits of old newspaper, bills or invoices.

In the case of Edward Burra, his sister presented his papers to the Tate. In some areas there has been a clear and very useful absence of weeding. Burra dropped everything on the floor and the Tate has not just ended up with letters but with a random selection of sweepings from his studio, which can be very enlightening. For example, anyone tidy-minded would surely have thrown away a mouldering copy of *The Queen – The Lady's Newspaper and Court Chronicle,* dating to around Burra's birth, which must have belonged to his grandmother. But it is a good thing that they didn't, because on closer examination half the advertisements are cut out and in fact it is the source of most of the found material in a collage now in the Scottish National Gallery of Modern Art in Edinburgh which he made while working with Paul Nash in 1929.[7]

However, on closer inspection it is possible to spot some gaps. For example, the circumstances around how Anne Burra's first

7 Untitled collage, ref. GMA 3948 – see http://www.nationalg alleries.org/collection/ artists-a-z/B/2859/ artist_name/Edward %20Burra/record_id/ 2232

marriage came about (one of Burra's friends refers darkly to "a bombshell"), just how and when that marriage ended, and how her second came to pass, are almost entirely obscure. It is not unreasonable to think that while Anne was admirably broad-minded about her brother's life and friends, she felt posterity could do without her own private affairs. It is an understandable point of view, but it is a clear indication that the surviving archival material has been selected more carefully than it might appear to be on the surface.

Another, and rather more important, example is the virtual disappearance of one of Burra's closest friends. Burra's lifelong companions, apart from his sister, were Billy Chappell, Barbara Ker-Seymer, Clover Pritchard and Beatrice Dawson (known as Bumble, or Bum). There are hundreds of letters from Billy and Barbara and Clover between 1924 and Burra's eventual death in 1976, but correspondence from Bumble for over more than fifty years is represented by a single postcard. A number of Burra's letters to her from the war years are preserved in the Lefevre; and a reasonable level of comments along the lines of "heard from Bum" in other letters make it clear that they did correspond.

There therefore must have been a reason why they all vanished; and I eventually found out what it was. Barbara Ker-Seymer's girlfriend, Barbara Roett (probably the last person living who knew this antique gossip), told me that Bumble separated from Gerald Corcoran during the war, a fact which is acknowledged in surviving correspondence, and had a long affair with A.J. MacNeill Reid of the Lefevre Gallery, which is not. Everyone remained on civilised terms. It's clear from other letters that Bumble and Gerald remained very much part of each other's lives. But presumably Bumble's letters referred to her private life and someone quite clearly decided that the world did not need to know any of this, in case it embarrassed the Corcorans, who were, and are, Burra's dealers at the Lefevre Gallery.

Censorship by children can pose a quite different set of problems. They may not worry too much about a parent's sexual life, but they may have a poor understanding of social norms and/or speech habits in their parents' young days. For example, Barbara Ker-Seymer reports spending an afternoon buying "glorious new nigger records" at Keith Prowse in 1927 (meaning, imported American jazz). Barbara, as she grew up, acquired any number of black friends and at least one black lover and was probably one of the least-racist people in the England of her day; but in 1927 she had not the slightest sense that 'nigger' might be

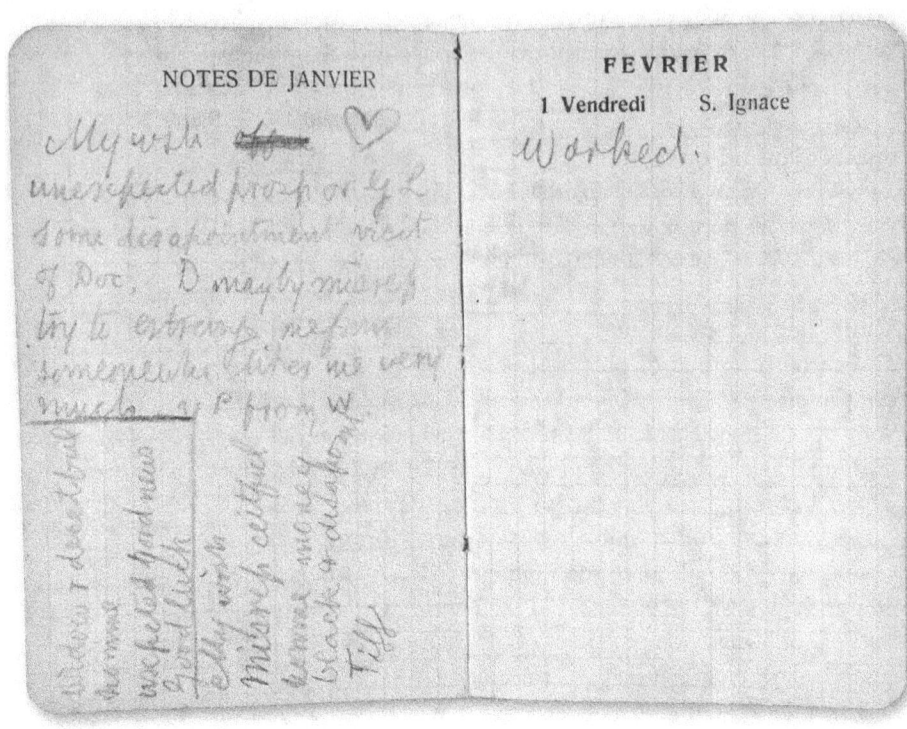

A page of Burra's pocket diary for January and 1st February 1929

an offensive word. Forty or fifty years down the line, something like this, which is perfectly reasonable in context, can be misunderstood and evidence destroyed in consequence. Other problems arise, though not in the case Burra, when descendants try to impose their own idea of what their famous forebear was like and to censor material not in accordance with the image.

Burra did not have a sexual life, but he did of course have an emotional life. However, he kept it to himself. He almost always wrote about what he had seen, seldom if at all about what he felt, or thought. Intensely private, he left no introspective writing of any kind and so it is particularly useful in understanding him that the Tate ended up with a dozen or so pocket diaries, the earliest of which is from 1929. One of the saddest things in the entire Burra archive is a tiny scrap of evidence that at twenty-five Burra was still having to work on his self-sufficiency. The diaries also reveal that he was superstitious. There is a pressed four-leaf clover in most of them, and they also indicate that through the twenties and thirties he was in the habit of telling his fortune from time to time with a pack of playing cards, particularly at the New Year. A fortune recorded in the 'notes' page for January 1929 runs:[8]

8 TGA 939.1.1, EB pocket diary for 1929

My wish ~~affair~~ ♥
Unexpected prosp or GL [prosperity or good luck]
Some disapointment visit of Doc D may by miss rep
[misrepresentation] try to estrange me from someone who likes
me very much & P [the person?] from me

There would be many visits from the doctor in 1929, along with
a certain amount of prosperity and good luck. But if his secret wish,
censored by scoring out the word, was for an affair of the heart
then it did not happen, then or ever.

Sometimes no-one is at all anxious to hide sexual misdemean-
ours, but there can still be other problems. Another important class
of material which often tends to vanish is information about
money – above all, details about tax evasion or evidence for sheer
mismanagement and incompetence, which is not uncommon
among people with more interesting things to think about. The
story of Burra's American money is precisely the kind of tale which
gets tidied away in case of retribution from the tax authorities: it
would certainly not be possible to work it out from the papers
deposited in the Tate. But fortunately, if the subject of a biography
is fairly famous or well-connected, it is often possible to triangulate
on information from other archival deposits relating to famous
friends, ex-lovers or relatives.

This particular sorry saga unwinds itself in Burra's letters to
Conrad Aiken, held in the Huntington Library in California.
Conrad Aiken's widow, who deposited these letters, may have
weeded on her own or her husband's account but had no reason
to bother herself about Burra's financial peccadilloes. The
background information which is needed to make sense of this is
that it was then difficult to move money between England and
America, so Burra's dollar earnings for paintings sold in America
were deposited in the Scudder, Stevens & Clark Fund Inc.,
administered by the Second National Bank of Boston: the earliest
evidence for this is 1944. This paid him dividends and so the bank
sent him dollar cheques at intervals, which he was supposed to send
back to America to be paid into his Boston account.[9] Conrad
Aiken, his principal American friend, seems to have tried to keep
Burra au fait with his own financial position.[10] But in 1958, Burra
comments: "I got several Scudder cheques which Ive shut in a
drawer & never send when I ought to & dont worry about drawing
out the money for the Income Tax". In 1962, he again says, "I have
dozens of Scudders checks [sic] here and have never sent them to
the bank out of sheer laziness and inaction."[11] But, because he did

9 TGA 939.2.4, Second
   National Bank of
   Boston to EB, 9
   March 1944
10 Huntington Library,
   AIK 2392, EB to MA
   and CA ?April 1954:
   "Thank you for the
   Bank slips. There was
   a Scudder check
   which I promptly lost
   and now they swear
   must have been
   burned – so that's
   that – however I have
   no doubt Scudder in
   about 6 months time
   will begin screaming
   about their bks not
   being made up so
   they may send
   another one if I say
   that one was lost."
11 From AIK 3940–
   3942, EB to CA, 28
   December 1958; AIK
   3940–3942 (?) EB to
   CA, 14 June 1962

not pay tax in America, tax was due on these earnings in Britain, and eventually "the Inland Revenue have unearthed my Scudders S[tevens] & Clerk & are threatening to charge me Income Tax for the last 30 years! ... They can go fuck themselves − I don't realy care, things have reached such a pitch − the chartered accountant says they rarely go back further than 10 years − ! if they dont hurry it will be too late HA HA and they can go back to the burning of Atlanta!" (a reference to *Gone with the Wind*).[12]

The somewhat random archival material on Burra's financial affairs in the Tate, though obviously incomplete, is quite illuminating in other respects. If one looks at the surviving information about Burra's finances during the forties, it is clear that design work represented a very significant aspect of his overall earnings. Though Burra was born into a very wealthy family (they had made their money in banking), the Burra's were living on unearned income: their capital survived World War I, only to fall victim to the war against their social class which began after World War II. Consequently Burra was not, at least in his own mind, free of financial worry in the forties. Though he had two exhibitions at the Leicester in 1947 and 1949, his actual earnings during the War and for a decade afterwards were almost entirely from design work of one kind or another, and he probably thought of himself as primarily a designer, professionally speaking. In 1942, he notes "... 'm supposed to be doing a book cover for Collins... I only hope I may get 15£ I need it." He did a great deal of design work in 1948, including a suite of drawings for an edition of *Huckleberry Finn* commissioned by Paul Elek, and costumes and a set for the Royal Ballet:

[Gerald Corcoran has] gone on at Elek bloody Huckleberry F. you know ... gone to such lengths that he seems to think we shall get a first payment of 75£ & another 75 later. 100£ for a second edition if any & half the drawings returned ... Im now supposed to be doing a ballet for Fred Ashton based on *Don Juan* − based I say its all they have in common I hope it comes off well.

A surviving invoice shows that the eventual fee for Don Juan was £315.

The Tate archive also reveals that eventually Burra and the Lefevre came to an arrangement which suited them both and brought an end to his anxiety. Burra undertook to produce enough paintings for an exhibition every other year and they paid him a salary in six-monthly instalments.[13] The crucial evidence is a letter from Gerald Corcoran, dated 30 October 1957.

12 From AIK 2197–
   2380, EB to CA, 4
   September 1962
13 TGA 939.2.4, Gerald
   Corcoran to EB, 30
   Oct 1957

What a bore about missing you in Paris… I don't thing you missed anything not seeing the show in Paris. I was very against the whole thing, and it is an appalling gallery… Here is the first cheque for £500 & we will send you another every six months.

It is also possible to see that the Lefevre managed Burra's money conscientiously, but the painter himself took no further interest in the matter.[14] A somewhat startling letter from Gerald Corcoran in 1974 reveals that he had sent £12,791.41p to the Inland Revenue on Burra's behalf, which left £39,025.52p in the care of the Lefevre Gallery. Corcoran also reports that he had invested about three thousand in Krugerrands and sovereigns on Burra's behalf, leaving £36,150.52p in the deposit account. At this time Burra was living, by his own choice, on £3,600 a year, which he received as £1,800 in cash twice yearly.

Archives can also reveal aspects of an artist's work which have simply been forgotten. In the account of Burra's life and work which was put together for the Hayward exhibition in 1985, and has been drawn on ever since by students of his life and work, there is no mention of Burra's ever having been involved with the world of film. The first intimation I had that he had done any such thing came from a letter to Conrad Aiken written in 1948.

Well dearie here lies a mere hulk of poor Edward Burra the darling of our crew. As what with designing the death trap & spies parlor in the cellars of Doomesday Grange for Highbury Studios a hacking cough with phlegm on the side & an attack of my old complaint which commenced with a quartern ague lasting half an hour I couldnt keep still for a minute & chattered all the time, I realy am half crazy. I keep getting telegrams from Highbury and go trailing off with a paper bag containing a very dirty cigarette tin containing some frowsy mumbled old tubes of mud & one or two cleaned up brushes & pencils & proceed to put in & take out spiders webs, chandeliers put in archs all in five minutes & straight off, only somebody with no scruples & completely insensitive could ever do it. however I enjoy it very much.

In a subsequent letter, he explained that "The film I was doing was a blood curdling 2nd feature called 'a piece of cake'". This, naturally, sent me off on a frenzied search for evidence and, luckily, the British Film Institute was able to find me a copy of *A Piece of Cake*, which was terrible beyond description. The reason why it was quite so bad is that the Rank Organization had contracted Cyril Fletcher

14 TGA 939.2.4, Gerald Corcoran to EB, 31 July 1974

and his wife Betty Astell, established music-hall troupers, to star in a film called *The Venus Touch*, only to discover that Mary Pickford held the rights to the story and refused to release it. Fletcher and Astell were contracted to work for six weeks but, having lost their script, were compelled to devise, write and shoot an alternative film within that time period. They mostly used the sets which had been built for *The Venus Touch* but the new plot required Astell to be kidnapped by a demon and carried off into his lair: at this point, a set needed to be created and the producer, John Croydon, thought of Burra, whose work he had presumably seen. Burra seems to have rather enjoyed it, from what he says, but had immense difficulty in getting paid, which put him off further film work.

The Burra archive also reveals a great deal about his reading, which often impacts on his art, and also illuminates his response to contemporary writers. Because of Burra's delicate health, much of the time when he was not actually painting was spent reading. One author he seized on with enthusiasm in the twenties was Ronald Firbank. It took him some time to get hold of a copy of *The Eccentricities of Cardinal Pirelli*. "I am having such a set too over Cardinal Pirelli, after about a week and me thinking the assistant had snaffled the money and said nothing about it I receives from Selfridges a letters saying Pirelli was out of print but they would advertise for a new or second hand copy free of charge & it would take about 10 days or thereabouts. I see he has written quite a lot of Books."[15] When he finally did get hold of it, it clearly made a great impression on him, while bemusing his father: "Pa commenced to read it and said Realy Ronald Firbank doesn't seem to make his meaning clear at all oh ses I clear enough to some I assure you engendering a mistle thrush through the nostril was what got the wind up him I believe".[16] One piece of evidence for his reaction to Firbank is a drawing; another is a poem which he sent to Barbara Ker-Seymer:

> Copulation is vexation
> cry the choir boys as they stand
> washing their rose pink hands
> In the bishops enamel frying pan
> the cardinals upon the rocks
> gather whelks in ivory pots
> theres nothing so strengthening after a tussle
> the sinister superior sleeps with a thistle
> > concealed in her bustle
> > of ivory ninon
> > Sits THE POPES MIGNON

15 TGA 974.2.2.39, EB to Barbara Ker-Seymer [BKS], 20 December 1927
16 TGA 2.2.48, EB to BKS, 3 Feb 1928

The rococo Catholicism and sexual innuendo is a direct reflection of the world created in *Cardinal Pirelli*, but the other influence on this bizarre composition is Edith Sitwell: *Façade*, with its associative, sound-based verses, was first performed in the summer of 1922 and Burra's poem is very much in a Sitwellian manner. Burra read a great deal of poetry throughout his life and, though he makes no direct reference to Edith Sitwell, it is evident from this that he read her verse.

Another obvious way in which archives are an invaluable resource is in providing photographs of the subject and his friends and context. This can pose difficulties of its own. In Burra's case, very usefully, his friend Barbara Ker-Seymer was a professional photographer for part of her career, and tidy-minded. The photographs in her personal albums, which are also at the Tate, are captioned, making it possible to put names to faces. They are consequently invaluable as a reference. (One of the most useful positive things someone considering donating an archive can possibly do is to identify people and places in photographs.) By contrast, Billy Chappell's archival material in the Lefevre includes many photographs, all of which are unlabelled. Those of Billy himself, and of Burra, are easy to identify, as are famous faces like Frederick Ashton, but there are also any number of mystery figures, dateless and contextless. He thought these images worth keeping, but without a word of identification on the back, it is now impossible to say why.

Archival material can also help with dating an artist's pictures, especially if he himself does not date his work. On the fourth of September 1963, Clover Pertinez wrote to Conrad Aiken:[17]

At last I have met your daughter Jane and family, delightful people, Jane and younger girl so like you. We all sat down to supper at the Chapel House and got hilarious as the bottles went round but Oh Dear Me, the next morning poor Ed had such a hangover he was unable to go to the Ypres to meet them… I took them up to his studio and showed them the latest paintings which are better and better we all agreed. There is a black and red two-faced portrait of PURE RAGE…

This can only refer to one painting, which Andrew Causey lists as a work of 1970–1, a date presumably based on its inclusion in a 1971 show at the Lefevre; here conclusively redated to 1963.

Dating can be quite important. For example, a painting now in Edinburgh's National Gallery of Modern Art called *Izzy Ort's* is

17 Clover Pertinez to CA, 4 Sept [1963]

Letter to Barbara
Ker-Seymer dated
10 October 1928

dated 1955 by Andrew Causey, who draws a major conclusion from it: "while living with the Aikens in Boston [in 1955] he painted scenes derived from visits to nightspots which gave pictures such as Izzy Ort's and Silver Dollar Bar, reminiscent of pre-war work, though not mere pastiches, these pictures show the liberating effect on Burra of a long period away from Rye".[18] But Burra's pocket diary for 1937 reveals the following:[19]

18 February Lunch Harvard Club Conrad [Aiken] dinner [Gordon] Bassett
22 February Dinner at Greeks [a restaurant, the Athens Olympia] with Walter [Piston] & wife
24 February May Sarton dinner
25 February drove to Concord
27 February Oneills [a bar]

18 Andrew Causey,
*Edward Burra:
Complete Catalogue*,
London: Phaidon,
1985, pp.73–4
19 TGA 939.1.3

28 February ONeills
1 March Silver Dollar [a bar]
2 March ONeills
3 March Recuperating
5 March ONeills
7 March Finished Silver $

This diary evidence of Boston bar-hopping is confirmed by an interview with M.J. Rosenau published in the *Boston Herald* in March 1937: "The only work he has completed since coming to Boston six weeks ago, for example, is a somewhat painfully exact reproduction of a night spent in one of the Hub's most garish honky-tonks. No imagination is needed to identify the buxom hostess, the Negroid orchestra and entertainers, the barkeeps, the waiters, or the customers. 'Well, I went there four times', Burra said. 'I ought to remember them'."[20] The hostess, orchestra, and barkeeps feature in *Izzy Ort's* and not in the picture now called *Silver Dollar Bar*, which, again on archival evidence (there is a photograph of him working on it), was painted in 1955. *Izzy Ort's* is demonstrably a picture of the Silver Dollar Bar, painted in 1937: therefore it reveals nothing about his state of mind in 1955.

But perhaps the most important thing a good archive does is to remind its users that life is not lived in retrospect. Once a painter is famous — and there has been a string of one-man shows, a catalogue, a retrospective, a centenary exhibition, documentaries and critical works — it is only too easy to believe that he was marked for stardom from the beginning and critical comment in catalogue essays will tend, if anything, to enhance that impression. Early letters, by contrast, will show the struggle as it actually was: the excitement of meeting established artists, the first encounters with the galleries. For example, Burra wrote in 1927:

> a strange old person called Mrs Dew Smith who knows dear Dotty Warren said to me not long ago you know I realy think you ought to have a show at Miss Warrens Galleries she is so interested in young artistes so I ses there are young artistes and young artistes and I am one of the other artistes, my dear it seems Dew S saw Dot the other day and said I know such a clever young artiste named Edward Burra do you know anything of him. "Ive heard a <u>great deal</u> about Edward Burra" says Dot & what she has heard I should very much like to know.[21]

Nothing came of this, but things looked up a couple of years later: "My dear <u>what</u> do you think arrived on Saterday a great

20 Reproduced in its entirety in the Hayward Gallery's Edward Burra exhibition catalogue (London, Hayward Gallery, 1985), pp.64–6.

21 TGA 974.2.2.37, EB to BKS, 9 December 1927

typewritten letter from the Leicester Galleries saying 'Paul Nash tells me you have some more interesting drawings, I should like to see them soon, as we <u>might</u> be able to show them in the course of a <u>few months</u>".[22] They did. However, Burra was not free of anxiety about selling his work until after the Lefevre took him on in 1952: through his thirties and most of his forties he was still far from certain he could make a living as a painter.

In short, archives are far more than the history of gossip. The realities of a person's life can only be revealed by knowing what they were bad at as well as their great achievements: letters and other papers reveal stories of struggle and sacrifice, generosity, dumb luck and feuding which, between them, tell so much of why an oeuvre took the shape it did. Archival records may help with dating and, at the very least, they shed floods of light on the artist's social and intellectual context. Burra himself professed to despise this: "& what may I enquire has all that crap to do with Painting?" he demanded indignantly, à propos of being interviewed.[23] But the answer is, a great deal.

22 TGA 974.2.2.61, EB to BKS, 10 Oct 1928
23 TGA 779.1.106, EB to JB [end of November 1971]

Editors:

Victoria Lane

Victoria is Collections Manager for the Black Cultural Archives and was formerly the archivist for Richard Deacon, the Barry Flanagan Estate, the Henry Moore Institute and Tate Archive. Her publications include: 'New Model Arkives' in *Arkive City* and 'Situating the Archive and Archivists', with Jennie Hill, in *The Future of Archives and Recordkeeping*. She is currently a member of the Art+Design Archives Committee, ARLIS.

Karyn Stuckey

Karyn manages the archive and special collections of Foster+Partners. She is Chair of the Art+Design Archives Committee, ARLIS and Secretary of Architectural Records Section, International Council for Archives. Previously, Karyn was project archivist on the 'Man and Cameraman' project at LSE which culminated in an exhibit with the National Trust. Prior to this, Karyn was archivist for the University of the Arts, London, working mainly on the archives of Stanley Kubrick, Jocelyn Herbert, Edward Bawden and Tom Eckersley, and consultant for the John Latham Archive. Other posts held include: Royal Botanic Gardens, Kew and the Britten–Pears Archive. Karyn has contributed to a number of conferences and publications.

Judy Vaknin

Judy is an archivist and was formerly responsible for the management of the archives and special collections at Middlesex University. Her publications include: *Smoke Signals: 100 years of tobacco advertising* and *Driving it Home: 100 years of car advertising*. She was Chair of the Art+Design Archives Committee, ARLIS when two study days on artists and their archives were held at Tate.

Contributors:

Frederico Câmara

Frederico has lived and worked in London for the last ten years. He graduated in Printmaking from Escola de Belas Artes (UFMG, Belo Horizonte) and obtained an MA in Fine Art from Chelsea College of Art (University of the Arts, London). Frederico is both a researcher and an artist. His research intersects with natural sciences and visual anthropology, looking at human perceptions and representations of the environment, migration, photography and travelling both as research tools and as items to collect and archive. His output is usually in the form of photographic and video installations, books and text. Frederico has taken part in both group and solo exhibitions and won a number of awards including Darwin Now (British Council, London).

Penelope Curtis

As a student, Penelope worked in the archives of E. A. Bourdelle and Auguste Rodin, having been deprived of access to that of Barbara Hepworth. She later helped to develop the archive of sculptors' papers as a key aspect of the Henry Moore Institute in Leeds, from its transformation in 1999 through to her departure a decade later. Her aim was to develop an archive representing the kind of sculpture that could not be represented in galleries, and to return the sponsor, Henry Moore, to the context which helped explain why he was different or significant. Since 2010 she has been Director of Tate Britain.

Meirian Jump

Meirian is an archivist specialising in artists' archives. She graduated from UCL with an MA in Archives and Records Management having previously completed an MA in Twentieth Century British History at Queen Mary, University of London and a BA in Modern History at the University of Oxford, where she pursued her research interests in twentieth-century British and Spanish history. She was Archivist and Catalogue Manager at the Estate of Barry Flanagan from 2010 to 2012. Meirian currently works as Archives and Drawings Coordinator at the Antony Gormley Studio, London.

Ruth Maclennan

Ruth first became interested in conceptual and performance art whilst studying in Russia, 1989–90. In 2000, she completed a Masters in Fine Art at Goldsmiths College. Ruth's work includes video installations, photographs, bookworks, drawings, live events and curatorial projects such as the Archway Polytechnical Institute for artists' interventions in the city. Landscape and the traces of past actions, including those in and of the archive, lie at the heart of her recent works. Ruth's 2010 film and accompanying body of work, *Anarcadia*, deepens this examination. Her current project investigates changing perceptions of the Arctic and the North Sea. Solo exhibitions include: John Hansard Gallery, Southampton; ffotogallery, Wales; Stills, Edinburgh; and Castlefield Gallery, Manchester.

Sas Mays

Sas is Senior Lecturer in Cultural and Critical Theory in the Department of English, Linguistics and Cultural Studies at the University of Westminster, London, where he leads the online and offline research events and the publications project 'Archiving Cultures'. His major area of research is in the gender politics of the archive in historical and contemporary culture. Publications include: co-editor, *Literature and Photography in the Twentieth Century*; 'Between the Codex and the Net', for a special issue of *New Formations*; *The Machine and the Ghost*; editor, *Literatures, Libraries, Archives*; and 'Consigning Badiou to the Past', for *Cultural Politics* 5:1.

Bruce McLean

Bruce McLean is a sculptor. For the last 40 years he has been trying to make the new sculpture, and is still working on it. When offered an exhibition at Tate in 1972, he opted to hold a one-day 'retrospective', an image of which appears as the cover of this book.

Anna McNally

Anna qualified as an archivist in 2004 completing an MA in Archive Administration at UCL, having initially studied Philosophy there. Since then she has worked for the Tate, Lloyds Banking Group and the University of Westminster. Whilst at the Tate Archive, she catalogued several major art-related collections including the Institute of Contemporary Arts, Charles Harrison, Ithell Colquhoun and Naum Gabo. Formerly a member of the Art+Design Archives Committee, ARLIS, Anna helped to organise ARLIS's 'Archiving the Artist' study day, Tate Britain, 2009.

Jo Melvin

Jo is an art historian with particular interest in archive curation and display. She teaches Fine Art Theory at Chelsea College of Art (University of the Arts, London). Exhibition projects include 'Barry Flanagan – Silâns' at Dublin City Art Gallery, 2012. Jo's 2007 piece 'Tangential and Awry Archive Stories', in *The Archive, the Event and Its Architecture*, came out of the final 'event' of artist Lucy Gunning's residency at the Wordsworth Trust. It is both a documentation and a component of an interrelated body of work seeking to provide a point of triangulation between the archive, the event and its architecture, exploring whether any of these can exist as the other: can an event be a building? a building an archive?

Gustav Metzger

Gustav was born in Germany but came to England as a refugee in 1939. He studied with the painter David Bomberg, but renounced painting in 1959 when he published his manifesto on Auto-Destructive Art. He was a founder of the anti-nuclear Committee of 100, was one of the initiators of the International Destruction in Art Symposium in 1966, called for an Art Strike from 1977 to '80 and commenced his Historic Photographs series of obscured photoworks in 1995. The book of his 2005 Vienna retrospective exhibition, *Gustav Metzger: History History*, is the principal source of information on his life and work.

Uriel Orlow

Uriel is a senior research fellow in art at the University of Westminster, London. He studied Fine Art at Central Saint Martins College (University of the Arts, London) and the Slade School of Art, graduating with a PhD in Fine Art in 2002. Uriel is an artist, educator and sometime writer. Uriel's work explores the spatial and imaginary conditions of history and memory, focusing on blind spots of representation and forms of haunting. His work has been presented at Manifesta 9, Limburg, the 54th Venice Bienniale and 8th Mercosul Biennial, Brazil. He has held exhibitions and screenings, including: Tate Modern; Kunsthalle, Budapest; Oberhausen Short Film Festival; South African National Gallery; and Whitechapel Gallery, London.

Clive Phillpot

Clive is a writer, curator and former librarian. He was Director of the Library of the Museum of Modern Art, New York, having previously been Librarian of the Chelsea School of Art (University of the Arts, London). Clive was President of ARLIS North America and has been a member of ARLIS UK since its founding in 1969, for whom he was formerly a member of the Art+Design Archives Committee, ARLIS. His publications include: *Booktrek: Selected Essays on Artists' Books Since 1972*; and *Ray Johnson on Flop Art*. He also co-edited and co-curated a number catalogues and shows, including: Voids: a Retrospective, Paris; Live in Your Head, London; Artist/Author: Contemporary Artists' Books, US tour.

Donald Smith

Donald studied at Camberwell College of Arts (University of the Arts, London), the University of Ife, Nigeria, and Chelsea College of Art (University of the Arts, London) where he founded, and now is Director of Exhibitions for, CHELSEA space. From 1992 to 2002 he was the photographer and editor of the Contemporary Art Slide Scheme, a visual archive of exhibiting activity in London. Donald has gained a reputation for experimental interdisciplinary shows crossing art, design and popular culture, often incorporating archives. He has exhibited widely since the 1980s across Europe, America and Japan. He was included in the recent survey exhibition Same as it Ever Was... Painting at Chelsea 1990–2007.

Barbara Steveni

Barbara conceived and founded the Artist Placement Group (APG) in London in 1966 with a group of artists, including John Latham and Ian Breakwell, all of whom were working in the emerging fields of multi-media and conceptual art. The organisation sought to reposition the role of the artist within a wider social context. Active as artist, archivist and lecturer, Barbara is currently engaged in a personal work entitled I AM AN ARCHIVE tracing, through a series of walks and interviews, her life and role within APG. A recent exhibition at Raven Row Gallery, London explored APG's methodology and legacy and Barbara's role within it.

Jane Stevenson

Jane published *Edward Burra: Twentieth Century Eye* (Jonathan Cape) in 2007. Since then she has contributed to *Inculps and Aspershums: Burra's Life and Letters*, edited by Simon Martin. Jane has given talks on Silver Dollar Bar and Edward Burra and Spain for the National Gallery of Scotland. She was a contributing editor for the recent film presented by Andrew Graham-Dixon, *I Never Tell Anyone Anything*. As well as works on Burra, Stevenson has written two books of novellas, a trilogy of historical novels and a detective story. In addition, she has contributed articles and chapters to publications as part of her activity as Regius Chair of Humanity at the School of Divinity, History and Philosophy, University of Aberdeen.

Athanasios Velios

Athanasios is a Research Fellow at the University of the Arts, London. He graduated from the Technological Educational Institute, Athens with a degree in Archaeological Conservation and also has qualifications in 3D Modeling and Animation. His PhD work at the Royal College of Arts and Imperial College looked at computer applications for conservation and particularly at conservation documentation. His current research focuses on conservation documentation and archiving, working in the field of artists' archives. He has proposed a 'Creative Archiving' methodology, a way to interpret artists' ideas through their own papers, specifically John Latham's Archive. Anthanasios is also Deputy Director of Ligatus.

Neal White

Neal is currently Associate Professor of Art and Media Practice at the Media School, Bournemouth University. He is an artist, researcher and a founding member of Soda, a collective of artists and programmers that became acclaimed for online projects and computer-mediated installation. Group shows include: Museum of Modern Art, Stockholm; Austin Museum of Digital Art; and InterCommunication Center, Tokyo. From 2002 to 2005, Neal worked as independent artist until collaborating with the Office of Experiments and the social architecture group N55 (DK). The Office of Experiments is a loose structure that, according to project, consists of artists, academics, scientists, curators, amateur enthusiasts and activists.

Index of Names: